Intelligent Business

Coursebook

Advanced
Business English

| Tonya Trappe | Graham Tullis |

Pearson Education Limited
Edinburgh Gate
Harlow
Essex CM20 2JE
England
and Associated Companies throughout the world.

www.pearsonlongman.com

© Pearson Education Limited 2011

First published 2011

Intelligent Business Advanced Coursebook/CD Pack 9781408255971
Intelligent Business Advanced Coursebook 9781408217733

Set in Economist Roman 10.5 / 12.5

Printed in Slovakia by Neografia

Acknowledgements
The authors would like to thank the following people and institutions for their assistance in the research and writing of this project: students and colleagues at the IAE Gustave Eiffel – University of Paris Est Creteil; students and teachers at ESIEA Paris; the director of Théâtre Atelier Montreuil.

With particular thanks to the following people for permission to use material provided by them: Diederik Van Goor; Harrie Barron; Cyril Rollinde; Bruno Guattari; Abdoulaye Sy.

And also to the following people for their support and advice: Gilles Béguin; Laurence Beierlein; André Boutleroff; Jeremy Cocks; Nicolas Dufeu; Magdalena Fijałkowska; Jean Philippe Girod; Jane Jacquemet; Elise Lamare; Mia Leahy; Martin Leiby; Gillain Orr; Susan Power; Dorota Swiecka; Charles Talcott; Peter Wilson.

The publishers would like to thank the following people for their helpful comments on the manuscript for this book: Lut Baten (prof. dr.), ILT KULeuven, Belgium; Louise Bulloch, Intercom Language Services, Hamburg; Stephen Bush; Fiona Mackie, China; Elzbieta Jendrych, Ph.D., Kozminski University, Warsaw, Poland; Sarah Quiger, France.

The publishers would like to thank the following people and institutions for their help in piloting and developing this course: Richard Booker and Karen Ngeow, University of Hong Kong; Adolfo Escuder, EU Estudios Empresariales, University of Zaragoza; Wendy Farrar, Università Cattolica del Sacro Cuore, Piacenza; Andrew Hopgood, Linguarama, Hamburg; Ann-Marie Hadzima, Dept of Foreign Languages, National Taiwan, University, Taiwan; Samuel C. M. Hsieh, English Department, Chinese Culture University, Taipei; Laura Lewis, ABS International, Buenos Aires; Maite Padrós, Universitat de Barcelona; Giuliete Aymard Ramos Siquiera, São Paulo; Richmond Stroupe, World Lanaguage Center, Soka Univeristy, Tokyo; Michael Thompson, Centro Linguistico Università Commerciale L. Bocconi, Milan; Krisztina Tüll, Európai Nyelvek Stúdiója, Budapest.

The publishers are grateful to The Economist for permission to adapt copyright material on pp 9 (© 2007), 13 (© 2007), 19 (© 2007), 21 (© 2004), 29 (© 2007), 32 (© 2008), 41 (© 2008), 51 (© 2007), 54 (© 2008), 61 (© 2008), 73 (© 2008), 75 (© 2008), 83 (© 2008), 87 (© 2006), 93 (© 2007), 105 (© 2007), 115 (© 2008), 119 (© 2007), 125 (© 2008), 128 (© 2008). All articles copyright of The Economist Newspaper Limited. All rights reserved.

We are also grateful to the following for permission to reproduce copyright material:

Figures: Figure in Unit 3 from 'A Framework for change', Managing Change, 4/ed, Pearson Education Ltd (Bernard Burnes 2004) pp.326-327, 2004, copyright © Pearson Education Limited.

Tables: Table in Unit 8 adapted from 'Leadership that gets results', Harvard Business Review, Vol 78. No. 2, pp.78-90 (Daniel Goleman 2000), copyright © Harvard Business Review.

Text: Interview in Unit 1 adapted from 'Talent Management' by Sharon Fraser, Granted by kind permission of Sharon Fraser and Deloitte & Touche LLP; Extract in Unit 3 adapted from 'Oticon – the disorganised organisation' Managing Change, 4/ed, Pearson Education (Bernard Burnes 2004) pp.347-355, copyright © Pearson Education Limited; Extract in Unit 4 from 'What is Greenwashing? It's Whitewashing, But with a Green Brush', http://www.greenwashingindex.com/what.php, reprinted with permission from EnviroMedia Social Marketing and the University of Oregon School of Journalism and Communication; Extract in Unit 5 adapted extract and company logo, Nokia, http://www.nokia.com, copyright © Nokia UK Limited; Extract in Unit 5 from Microsoft, www.microsoft.com, copyright © Microsoft®; Extract in Unit 5 from Pfizer 'Charter PDF' www.pfizer.com, copyright © Pfizer, Inc.; Extract in Unit 6 adapted from Entrepreneurship: Successfully Launching New Ventures, 2nd Edition (Barringer, B., and Ireland, D) pp.109-110, copyright © 2008. Reprinted by permission of Pearson Education, Inc., Upper Saddle River, NJ.; Extract in Unit 6 adapted from 'Discount seating on empty private jet flights', 2008, https://www.lunajets.com/en/press/index/sideways03102008/, copyright © Lunajets SA; Extract in Unit 6 from 'More custom energy bars', 14/08/08, http://www.springwise.com/food_beverage/more_custom_energy_bars/, copyright © ElementBars.com, Inc; Extract in Unit 6 from 'Pop-up nightclubs launch in Singapore', 03/10/08, http://www.springwise.com/food_beverage/more_custom_energy_bars/, copyright © ElementBars.com, Inc; Extract in Unit 9 adapted advertising slogan 'I think therefore I BM (IBM)', IBM, copyright © IBM, reproduced by kind permission. IBM® is a registered trademark of International Business Machines Corporation; Extract in Unit 9 adapted advertising slogan 'Taste not waist (Weight Watchers frozen meals)', Weight Watchers, copyright © H.J. Heinz Company Ltd; Extract in Unit 9 adapted advertising slogan 'It 'asda be Asda! (Asda)', Asda, copyright © ASDA Stores Limited 2009; Extract in Unit 9 adapted advertising slogan 'Burton's menswear is everywear (Burton's menswear)', Burton's, copyright © Burton; Extract in Unit 9 adapted advertising slogan 'Farley's baby food – So Farley's so good', Heinz, copyright © H.J. Heinz Company Ltd; Extract in Unit 9 adapted advertising slogan 'Cell phones cost when in Roam', Roam Simple, copyright © Roam Simple; Extract in Unit 9 advertising slogan 'Michelin tyres – When it pours it reigns', reproduced by kind permission of Michelin; Extract in Unit 9 adapted advertising slogan 'Mumm's champagne – one word capture's the moment. Mumm's the word', Mumm's Champagne, copyright © G.H. Mumm & Cie; Interview in Unit 6 about 'Comptoir Atlantique' with Bruno Guattari, reproduced with permission; Extract in Unit 9 adapted from 'The Second Life of Second Life', Second Life Issue 129, Fast Company, Inc., 01/10/2008 (Cohen, A.), http://www.fastcompany.com/magazine/129/the-second-life-of-second-life.html copyright © Mansueto Ventures LLC, permission conveyed through Copyright Clearance Center; Extract in Unit 9 adapted from Creative Showcase: 'From London to Geneva. In one take, on one tank'; 'Fill the Indigo'; 'The X Factor challenge', 2008, http://www.creativeshowcase.net/; Interview in Unit 10 about risk management with Diederik Van Goor, reproduced with permission; Extract in Unit 10 adapted from 'Scientists find secret ingredient for making (and losing) lots of money – testosterone', The Guardian, 15/04/2008 (James Randerson), copyright © Guardian News & Media Ltd 2008.

In some instances we have been unable to trace the owners of copyright material, and we would appreciate any information that would enable us to do so.

Photograph acknowledgements
The publishers are grateful to the following for their permission to reproduce copyright photographs:

(Key: b-bottom; c-centre; l-left; r-right; t-top)

Alamy Images: Archimage 23, Bob Johns / expresspictures.co.uk 30, Dave Bowman 127c, david hancock 95, directphoto.bz 125, Dunca Daniel Mihai 100, image100 17, INSADCO Photography 91, Johann Helgason 52, Ken Welsh 92l, Marvin Dembinsky Photo Associates 122, MBI 132, Mode Images Limited 11, Nik Taylor 25t, Payless Images, Inc. 51, PHOTOMAX 100l, Photos 12 25b, Roberto Herrett 127b, Simon Reddy 100tr, Somos Images 115, Team 25c, Transtock Inc. 92t; Bridgeman Art Library Ltd: The Money Lenders (oil on oak panel), Massys or Metsys, Quentin (c.1465-1530) (attr. to) / Museo de Bellas Artes, Bilbao, Spain / Index 9; Carpigiani Gelato University: 29; Comptoir Atlantique: Bruno Guattari 63t, 63b; Corbis: Bettmann 117b, Digital Art 33, H. Armstrong Roberts 27, Image Source 83, image100 36, John Lund / Drew Kelly / Blend Images 80, Matthias Kulka 1r, 81, Matthias Tunger 86, Natalie Fobes / Science Faction 40l, Paul Burns 26, VERNIER JEAN BERNARD / CORBIS SYGMA 127t; David Simonds: The Economist 93, The Economst 54; Diederik Van Goor: 107; Mary Evans Picture Library: AISA Media 85; Getty Images: ANDREW YATES / AFP 112, James Lauritz 119, JGI 128, John Labbe 61, Stephen Chernin 117t; iStockphoto: sweetym 87; Kobal Collection Ltd: CHAPLIN / UNITED ARTISTS 53, COLUMBIA / DANJAQ / EON 92r; Linden Lab: 97; Marks and Spencer plc (company): 3bl, 41; Panos Pictures: G.M.B. Akash 39; Pearson Education Ltd: Digital Vision 45, MindStudio 64; Pearson Education Ltd: 6; Photolibrary.com: Dev Carr 1l, 123, Franco Vogt 113; Prakti Design: 62; Reuters: BP 40cr, Chip East 114b, Darren Staples 40tr, Kimberly White 18, Larry Downing 126tl, Mario Anzuoni 126bl, Paulo Whitaker 109, Phil McCarten 13, Ray Stubblebine 126tr, Robert Galbraith 32, Robert Galraith 126br; Rex Features: OLYCOM SPA 22, Photoreporters Inc. 114t; Science Photo Library Ltd: ANTHONY COOPER 76c, J.M. PETIT, PUBLIPHOTO DIFFUSION 1c, 71, ROGER HARRIS 108, SAM OGDEN 65, VICTOR DE SCHWANBERG 72; Sharon Fraser, partner at Deloitte: 12; The Economist: 43; Thinkstock: Comstock Images 3br, 59, 60t, 67, 73, Digital Vision 55, iStockphoto 48, 60tc, 60c, 60b, 75, 76b, 90, 105, Jack Hollingsworth 8l, 8c, John Foxx 76t, Jupiterimages 16, 57, 77, Ryan McVay 8r, 58, 60bc, Stockbyte 19

Cover images: Front: Corbis: Matthias Kulka r; Photolibrary.com: Dev Carr l; Science Photo Library Ltd: J.M. PETIT, PUBLIPHOTO DIFFUSION c

All other images © Pearson Education

Picture Research by: Charlotte Lippmann, Kay Altwegg

Every effort has been made to trace the copyright holders and we apologise in advance for any unintentional omissions. We would be pleased to insert the appropriate acknowledgement in any subsequent edition of this publication.

Illustration acknowledgements
Kevin Kallaugher (KAL) pp 3t, 5, 7, 49, 103
John Bradley pp 14, 24, 34, 46, 56, 66, 78, 88, 98, 110, 120, 130

Designed by Wooden Ark

Contents

Talent management

Winning the war for talent

As knowledge becomes a more and more valuable component in the economy, employers are doing all they can to retain their top performers and to develop the talents of the new generation. However, finders of talent are not always keepers of talent.
page 9

Business principles

Just good business

In the new age of globalised business, companies are having to be more forthright about their activities and more attentive to the impacts that they are having on ecosystems, on the environment and on society in general. Corporate Social Responsibility has become the modern corporate mantra and the focus has switched from how well a corporation is performing in financial terms to how much good it is doing as a corporate citizen. **page 41**

Water and business

Running dry

Accessing and securing resources is becoming a major strategic concern for businesses all over the world. But the impact of how such increasingly valuable resources are used has wider implications that go far beyond the business community or the boardroom, affecting society as a whole. **page 73**

Intelligent Business Style guide

Advanced Business English

| Tanya Trappe | Graham Tullis | The Economist

Learning to write well in a foreign language is one of the most difficult challenges facing the language learner. This pocket-sized style guide will help you find the right words, use an appropriate style and write effectively.

See inside the back cover.

Bookmap

Uncertainty
The perils of prediction

The crisis on the world's financial markets has just shown how potentially dangerous the modern business world has become. So it comes as no surprise to see that risk management is moving up the corporate agenda. Identifying risk and planning to deal with the unexpected are now part and parcel of developing a coherent strategy for troubled times. **page 105**

From the authors

We are both very proud to be the authors of the new advanced level of *Intelligent Business*. As experienced teachers ourselves we have witnessed spectacular changes, not only in the teaching of business English but also fundamental shifts in the business world that provides the foundation of business English. Globalisation and the spectacular rise of the Internet have swept away the comfortable business models of the past and brought us all into a new, faster-paced business environment where reactivity and flexibility are the hallmarks of success.

As the use of English has spread throughout the international business community there is an increasing demand for preparation materials and coursebooks that accurately reflect the complexities of a global, wired economy. *The Economist*, our partner on *Intelligent Business*, has its finger on exactly that pulse and provides weekly analyses of the financial, political and economic activities that directly impact the corporate world. Indeed the resources of *The Economist* newspaper and of the Economist Group have been invaluable to the research and design of this advanced level of *Intelligent Business*.

Although the basic structure of the course follows that of the previous levels, this advanced level introduces a number of new features specially developed for students who need to deal with more challenging language content and more complex topics. These include a greater focus on vocabulary with a special section which focuses on idiomatic usage, and an enlarged skills section which introduces truly advanced language, communication and life skills such as making ethical decisions, debating and influencing people.

In addition to providing students with a stimulating range of new topics, we believe that *Intelligent Business Advanced* bridges the gap between the upper intermediate and advanced level coursebooks. We are confident that after completing the course, students will have acquired the high level of skills necessary for a truly international career. Moreover, they will also have gained awareness of some of the complex issues that face the business community, and indeed society as a whole, in the coming years.

We hope that you will enjoy using *Intelligent Business Advanced* as much as we have enjoyed researching, writing and piloting this new material.

Tonya Trappe
Graham Tullis

Unit 1
HR

www.longman-elt.com   www.economist.com

People power

Keynotes

The primary role of the Human Resources **(HR)** department is to ensure that an organisation gains maximum strategic benefit from its staff and from its personnel management systems. HR managers supervise the administration of the employees of an organisation and also plan and manage its **manpower** requirements in order to ensure that it has the right number of employees with the appropriate **skills**. To do this successfully, HR managers are also in charge of setting up **performance evaluation schemes** which provide **appraisals** of employee efficiency and potential. Other critical responsibilities of an HR department include **payroll management**, **recruitment**, **training and development**, **career management** and **conflict resolution**. In many businesses today, HR also plays a key role in ensuring **workforce diversity** and the **well-being** of all members of staff.

Choosing who to work for

Which of the following criteria do you think are the most important when deciding what sort of organisation to work for? Rank them in order of importance.

- ___3___ Career opportunities: chances of mobility, promotion and development
- ___4___ Career breaks: the possibility to take extended leave
- ___6___ Ethics: a socially responsible business culture
- ___8___ Alumni programme: the company keeps in touch with ex-employees
- ___2___ Perks and privileges: workplace sports facilities, child care, free canteen, health care, etc.
- ___1___ Performance related pay: bonuses and pay rises based on results
- ___7___ International assignments: opportunities to work abroad
- ___5___ Training and development: the chance to acquire new skills

Listen to three recently recruited graduates talking about what attracted them to the companies they work for and say which of the above they refer to.

1 Brad Johnson	2 Jane Ford Hadden	3 Klaus Beckhaus
Finance Solutions	Martin, Peters and Jackson	Farnham Global Business Solutions

How do you think HR managers decide which employees have the most potential?

Talent management

Read the text on the opposite page and use the information in the text to give short explanations of the following statements.

1 Finding and keeping the most talented people is more important for the Big Four than it is for most other companies.
2 Employees should not be rewarded only for their financial performance.
3 Recent legislation has made it harder for the Big Four to find and keep talented employees. *sox act*
4 The Big Four have introduced changes in the way that they recruit staff. *experience professi*
5 The relationship that the Big Four have with ex-employees is evolving. *boomerangs*
6 Fewer women than men reach the top positions in the Big Four companies.
7 Today's recruits have different expectations from their predecessors. *decent ethical reputation*

Talent management
Winning the war for talent

Surprising as it might seem, the Big Four accountancy firms have lots to teach other companies about managing talented people

¹ It is not just that they collectively employ some 500,000 people around the world. Many companies are as big. Unlike most, however, the Big Four titans of accountancy – Deloitte Touche Tohmatsu, Ernst & Young, KPMG and PricewaterhouseCoopers (PwC) – really mean it when they say that people are their biggest assets. Their product is their employees' knowledge and their distribution channels are the relationships between their staff and clients. More than most they must worry about how to attract and retain the brightest workers.

² Time is regularly set aside at the highest levels to decide how best to do this. Detailed goals are set: Deloitte's business plan includes targets for staff turnover, the scores it seeks in its annual staff survey and the proportion of female partners it would like to have. Partners are increasingly measured and rewarded as managers of people, not just for the amount of money they bring in. People-related items account for one-third of the scorecard used to evaluate partners at PwC. KPMG's British firm has introduced time codes so that employees can account for how long they spend dealing with staff matters. The idea is that those who devote lots of time to people-related matters are not disadvantaged as a result in pay rises and promotion.

³ Job cuts earlier in the decade created a shortfall of people now. Regulatory changes, such as America's Sarbanes-Oxley Act, have boosted demand from clients not just for accountants' services but also for their staff. There were never enough skilled people and now as competition to get the best is increasing, the pool of available talent is changing and in the US baby boomers are flooding into retirement. To add to their difficulties the Big Four are now aggressively re-entering the field of advisory services, necessitating a new burst of hiring.

⁴ Much of this recruitment is aimed at hard-to-find experienced professionals, especially important in the advisory businesses where corporate knowledge is highly valued. Robust selection procedures are used to ensure that they fit in. Programmes that help keep the firm in touch with former employees are also being strengthened so that people who leave can more easily find their way back (these "boomerangs" account for up to a quarter of those hired by the Big Four in America).

⁵ Former employees can also act as useful recruiting agents and help to drum up new business. For these alumni programmes to work "a massive cultural switch" is needed, says Keith Dugdale, who looks after global recruitment for KPMG. Few employers are used to helping people leave on good terms. But in an era of job-hopping and a scarcity of skills, loyalty increasingly means having a sense of emotional allegiance to an employer, whether or not that person is still physically on the payroll.

⁶ A similar change in attitude is needed to manage the careers of female employees. Each of the Big Four wants to promote more women, who account for about half of their recruits but around a quarter, at best, of their partners. Many women drop off the career ladder at some point, usually to have children or to care for an elderly relative and find it difficult to get back on again. Options such as career breaks and part-time working are part of the accountants' response.

⁷ Retaining good people is the biggest challenge. Mobility is seen as a useful way to retain and help employees develop. International assignments can also be critical in attracting new graduates. According to Pierre Hurstel, Ernst & Young's global managing partner for people, new entrants want to work abroad. High-minded young people also want to work for companies with a decent ethical reputation. As well as tying reward schemes to the better management of people, Deloitte's British firm asks partners to spend a minute with their staff immediately after client meetings to provide feedback so that they fulfill more of a training role.

⁸ As the "war for talent" is joined across industries and countries, it could be worth keeping an eye on how the Big Four are quietly leading the charge. ∎

Which foreign country would you most like to work in if you had to work abroad? Why?

1 Find the words or expressions in the text that correspond to the following definitions.

1 The rate at which employees leave a company or organisation (para 2)
staff turnover

2 A sheet or table that shows quantitative results (para 2) _scorecard_

3 A result or outcome that is lower than expected (para 3) _shortfall of people_

4 The different methods used to recruit employees (para 4) _boomerangs_

5 Moving frequently between positions in different companies (para 5)
job-hopping

6 A list of all the employees who are paid by the company (para 5)
payroll

7 Programmes to remunerate employees (para 7) _International assignments_

2 All of the statements below illustrate vocabulary items that appear in the text. Write the words in the spaces.

1 Every year we conduct a full review of all our employees. (para 2)
Scorecard

2 Well, of course, knowing that you will earn more if you reach your performance goals is very motivating for all employees. (para 2)

_____

3 It's more or less inevitable that when turnover is down, companies will reduce their headcount. (para 3)
job cuts

4 The government is planning to introduce new legislation which will directly affect the way that we do our business. (para 3)
Sarbenes-Oxley act   _2002_

5 When our staff reach the age of sixty-five most of them decide to give up work. (para 3)
retirement

6 Without doubt one of the most important assets that we have in our organisation is our shared expertise and experience. (para 4)
experienced professionals

7 Being able to keep in touch with many of my former colleagues really gives me the feeling of belonging to a community. (para 5)
alumni programes

8 How far people move up the company hierarchy depends on both their aptitudes and their motivation. (para 6)

_____

9 I think that taking a year off after the birth of my daughter was exactly the right thing to do. (para 6)
career brake

10 For the next twelve months I will be managing a project for one of our foreign subsidiaries. (para 7)
International assignment

Collocations with *set*

The article includes the verb–noun collocation 'Detailed *goals* are *set*'.

Other nouns can be used in collocations with *set*. Replace the underlined phrases in the following sentences with an appropriate collocation using *set* and a word from the box, with the article *a(n)* or *the* if necessary.

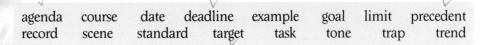
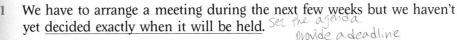

agenda	course	date	deadline	example	goal	limit	precedent
record	scene	standard	target	task	tone	trap	trend

1 We have to arrange a meeting during the next few weeks but we haven't yet <u>decided exactly when it will be held</u>. *Set the agenda.*

2 If supervisors don't <u>tell their staff exactly when they expect work to be completed by</u>, the productivity of their departments will suffer. *provide a deadline*

3 The HR director has <u>fixed the objective</u> for this year: reduce recruitment costs by at least 10%. *Set up a target*

4 It will be impossible to introduce all of the government's new employment guidelines simultaneously, so what we need to do is to <u>decide which ones we will introduce and in what order</u>. *Set a course*

5 An Australian firm has recently banned the use of mobile phones outside break periods and it seems this could well <u>mean that other companies will follow suit</u>. *Serve as a procedure*

6 As a result of the new stress reduction initiative, we've <u>put in our best ever performance</u> with absenteeism at just 5%. *updated record*

7 Candidates were put into teams that were <u>given the job</u> of designing a new training programme for manual workers. *charged with a task*

Contrast and similarity

When we want to point to contrasts or similarities that exist between things, we can do so in a number of different ways. The words and expressions that we use will depend on whether they are included in a simple sentence or in a connected piece of written or spoken discourse.

For more information, see page 154.

Single sentences

In single sentences we can use words and expressions like these.

Contrast	**Similarity**
unlike (prep)	*like/as* (prep)
in contrast to (noun)	*similar* (adj), *similarly* (adv)
unalike (adj)	*alike* (adj/adv)
while, although, whereas (conj)	*as ... as* (adv)
on the one hand ... on the other hand (noun phrase)	

Like *the vast majority of companies, the Big Four accounting firms pay close attention to their recruitment procedures and policies.*

Connected sentences

The following words and expressions are used when contrasts or similarities are presented in consecutive or connected sentences.

Contrast
nevertheless (adv)
however (adv)
conversely (adv)
on the contrary (noun phrase)

Similarity
similarly (adv)
likewise (adv)

*Enhanced human resource practices tend to increase satisfaction and productivity. **Conversely**, poorly prepared policies lead to lower output and employee resentment.*

Practice | **Complete the following passage using appropriate words or expressions. In some cases there may be more than one correct answer.**

Workforce diversity

The term 'workplace diversity' refers to the extent to which an organisation's employees are drawn from diverse socio-economic, cultural and educational backgrounds. Not all members of society are ¹_____ , the argument goes, and workplaces should reflect such differences. ² _Although_ not everyone agrees on the precise definition of the term itself, workplace diversity has already become an accepted practice in HR management in many countries. ³ _However_ , implementing a successful diversity programme still remains a major challenge. Take the whole question of gender, for example. If gender diversity is being achieved, then surely we should expect to see more female managers appointed to senior management positions? ⁴_____ , we should also see an increase in female intake at all levels. Now ⁵_____ it may be true that women are entering the workforce in greater numbers but ⁶ _whereas_ it is also quite clear that they are still not reaching the upper levels of management. Some traditionalists suggest that diversity actually results in higher costs to employers. Needless to say, supporters of diversity strongly disagree. ⁷_____ , they claim that diversity not only enhances productivity but also provides a sense of shared values to employees and managers ⁸_____ .

Listening 2 ◉ | ## High-potential staff

Sharon Fraser

Sharon Fraser of Deloitte Touche Tohmatsu talks about how her company manages talented employees. Listen to the interview and answer the questions.

1 What is the official title of Sharon's position in the organisation?
2 What exactly is she in charge of?
3 Sharon lists several things that are involved in her job, including recruitment and resourcing. What are the others?
4 What is the strategic objective of the company and how does Sharon suggest that talent management could contribute to achieving this?
5 How successful has Deloitte been in its talent management policy?
6 Sharon refers to hiring as the first aspect of the company's 'talent agenda'. What is the second aspect that she mentions?
7 Summarise what Sharon has to say about each of the following things:
   a high-performance culture
   b complex transactions
   c individuals

Read the text below about how Jim Goodnight successfully retains and motivates talented people. Make a list of the policies that have made this possible.

The Economist

Face value
Managing creative talent

Hard work and work-life balance go hand in hand

1   The ritual of handing out sweets to employees every Wednesday morning at SAS, probably the world's biggest software maker, has come to symbolise the famously employee-friendly culture that Jim Goodnight, the CEO, has cultivated at his firm. Every aspect of life on the large, leafy SAS campus in Cary, North Carolina, is designed to bring the best out of employees by treating them well. Most SAS employees have their own offices, for example, with the exception of one sales team which wanted to be open-plan.

2   Since its foundation in 1976, the company has provided free snacks and subsidised cafés. The SAS campus also offers magnificent sports facilities, subsidised child-care and early schooling, and the jewel in the crown, its own health-care centre, free to staff. SAS estimates that this has reduced its health bills by around $2.5m a year. It also has a long-term "wellness" programme, supported by two nutritionists and a "lifestyle education" scheme, which is expected to yield further cost savings. Already, the average SAS worker is off sick for only 2.5 days a year.

3   The only popular employee benefit that SAS does not offer is a stock-option package, usually mandatory in the software industry. That is because it is a privately owned company. "We don't have

to deal with Sarbanes-Oxley or minority shareholders suing us every time we turn around, or 25-year-old Wall Street analysts telling us how to run our business," Mr. Goodnight says enthusiastically.

4   Not surprisingly, employees tend to stick around, which means SAS has to be careful whom it recruits and severe in dealing with mistakes: a philosophy that Mr Goodnight calls "Hire hard, manage open, fire hard". The average rate of staff turnover at SAS is around 4% a year, compared with around 20% in the software industry as a whole. A few years ago a business-school professor calculated that this alone saved SAS $85m a year in recruitment and training costs.

5   Mr Goodnight points out that it is not just the benefits that keep people at SAS – "it's the challenge of the work." SAS is a leader in the field of "business intelligence", which helps companies use data to understand their own businesses. As other software has become increasingly commoditised, business intelligence has become a hot field. His goal is to remain in the more interesting, higher value-added parts of the software business – not least, presumably, to prevent his employees from getting bored. ■

The Economist

Speaking   **Do you agree with what Mr Goodnight says in the quotation below? Why/Why not? What problems might result from this policy?**

'Creative people can be trusted to manage their own workloads. To support the creative process and meet the demands of family life, flexible work day guidelines encourage people to start each day at whatever time is best for them.'

@   An Internet search using the question 'How creative are you?' will list websites that include creativity tests. Select a site and take a test to see how creative you are.

Career skills

Managing appraisals

Most businesses evaluate the performance and potential of their staff by using appraisals. Appraisals are normally organised in different stages (see chart below). As part of the process, the *appraisee* (the person who is being evaluated) and *appraiser* (his/her supervisor) both agree on the specific objectives that the employee should achieve. The supervisor provides ongoing feedback before conducting a final evaluation during an appraisal interview.

The interview is a key moment of the appraisal process. A well-conducted interview should provide an employee with the motivation to improve his/her performance. The appraiser must set the right tone during the interview and ask the right questions in order to encourage exchange and dialogue. Asking the wrong questions may have the opposite effect.

Self-appraisal is a method that is often used before the appraisal interview takes place. Staff are given a questionnaire or asked to access one online which they complete. The document is then used to prepare for the interview.

1 Set Objectives **2** Provide Feedback **3** Evaluate performance

Look at the following guidelines for formulating appraisal questions.

a Use open questions to get the appraisee to talk about different aspects of his/her work experience: *What's your view of this?*

b Try not to use too many closed questions: *Have you changed your opinion about that?*

c Avoid leading questions: *You didn't manage that aspect of the project very well, did you?*

---

1 Here is a selection of questions from appraisal interviews. Decide which question in each pair is the most appropriate to use in an appraisal interview.

1 Frankly your performance was quite disappointing, wasn't it?
   Shall we discuss how you could go about improving your performance?

2 Why have you sometimes found it difficult to meet your deadlines?
   How come you never manage to complete your work on time?

3 I have heard that you are not getting on very well with your new colleague. Can you confirm that?
   Is there anything that you'd like to mention about your working relationship with your colleagues?

4 How could we help you to manage your life outside work?
   You are planning to do something about your attendance record, aren't you?

5 Would you agree that you are clearly out of your depth when it comes to analysing accounts?
   Are there any areas where you could use some extra training or support?

6 It is true that you have been losing your temper quite a lot recently, isn't it?
   Would you like to receive some training to help you to manage your stress more effectively?

2 Give some examples of other questions that you think could be used in an appraisal interview.

Listen to two extracts from appraisal interviews and answer the questions.

1 How would you describe the atmosphere?
2 What sort of relationship do the two people have?
3 What have they achieved?

1 Read the following short descriptions of situations at work. Form pairs; Student A is the appraiser and Student B is the appraisee. Choose one situation and conduct a short appraisal interview. Compare the outcome of your interview with another pair.

Appraisee 1
This employee has had a long history of absenteeism. The last time he/she was appraised it was agreed that he/she would make a special effort to improve in this area. Unfortunately the attendance record shows that only minor progress has been made.

Appraisee 2
This employee has always made a major contribution to the company and has consistently met performance targets. This is still the case. However, there have been a number of incidents with fellow employees where tempers have become frayed and the atmosphere in the department has deteriorated to a point where it is starting to affect performance.

Appraisee 3
This employee was originally tipped to become one of the young stars of the division and last year it was agreed that if he/she continued to produce above average results then he/she would be allowed to join the prestigious internal group of 'fast track' high-potential staff. However, his/her performance has been erratic of late and he/she can no longer be considered for the programme.

2 Look at the four sample questions from a self-appraisal questionnaire and decide how you would answer them. Then compare your answers with a partner.

- How successful have you been in achieving your objectives over the last year?
- In what ways could you develop your existing skills or learn new ones?
- Are there any areas of your work where you would welcome guidance?
- What specific objectives would you like to fix for the coming period?

Assessing colleagues

Attitudes to performance appraisal can depend on culture. In some cultures, for example, subordinates are encouraged to give constructive criticism of the hierarchy and managers adopt a 'hands on' approach which gives employees the confidence to discuss problems openly. In this 'egalitarian work culture', feedback is given freely across the hierarchical divides. In other cultures the appraisal procedure is perceived as a 'command and control' tool for management. Which is closest to your culture? How might this difference cause misunderstanding in multinational teams?

Dilemma & Decision

Dilemma: Getting back on track

Brief

Computer Solutions Corporation (CSC) produces problem solving software for data intensive industries such as insurance and banking. When John Curry took over as CEO five years ago it was an expanding, profitable business with a strong focus on customer relations. Highly motivated teams of software engineers worked closely with clients to produce quality, tailor-made solutions. His vision was to double growth in ten years. His newly appointed team of finance experts set about introducing aggressive cost-cutting strategies. Pressure to produce products for new customers within tighter deadlines meant that staff worked longer hours. Curry closed the expensive on-site child care facilities which forced many of the female staff to go part-time, making team work complicated. In the short term, however, financial results did improve and Curry seemed well on the way to achieving his goal. He generously rewarded senior management with exclusive privileges, bonuses and promotions.

This isolated the staff and made them resentful. They saw it as unfair and felt that the boss arbitrarily rewarded his friends accusing him of 'cronyism'. Sales began to fall and the best software designers, looking for more flexible working hours, started to leave the company to work freelance. This caused several high-profile clients to take their business elsewhere. Curry was forced to resign. In a company where the product is dependent on staff creativity and knowledge he had failed to motivate and reward the right people. The new CEO Patricia Donohue hired an interim HR specialist to recruit, retain and nurture new talent. He advised the introduction of a fair and transparent performance appraisal system designed to improve employee motivation and commitment.

Task 1

Divide into groups of three. You are members of CSC's HR department. You know that all appraisal systems are designed to avoid the problems CSC has experienced. Your job is to choose the best one for the company's present situation. Student A, turn to page 135, Student B to page 137 and Student C to page 138. Read the profiles of performance appraisals carefully and prepare to present your profile to the others.

Task 2

Meet to discuss the benefits and drawbacks of each type of appraisal system.

Task 3

Choose the appraisal scheme you like best and present your arguments to the class.

Write it up

Write a memo to Patricia Donohue explaining which system you have chosen and why.

For more information, see *Style guide*, page 18.

Decision:

Listen to the HR expert giving his opinion on which system should have been chosen. Which other appraisal system does he refer to?

Unit 2
Organisations

www.longman-elt.com   www.economist.com

More like orchestras than armies

Keynotes

The **organisational structure** of a company defines how tasks are formally distributed, coordinated and harmonised. In today's world of constant change and technological advancements it is increasingly important to be **flexible**. Companies are therefore becoming less **centralised** and more **organic**, with **cross-hierarchical teams** participating in the **decision-making process** and coordinating work activites. Workers, therefore, have more **autonomy**, and **authority** is more evenly distributed, allowing them the freedom to carry out their jobs without **supervison**. In today's modern **decentralised** structures, **work space** is also being redesigned. Colleagues can work together **virtually**, using the latest technological tools. **When they do** meet physically, it is in new environments rather than in the **traditional office**. Often they **hot desk** rather than have a designated personal office. This new **organisational model** presents leaders with demanding **challenges** for the 21st century.

The deskless CEO

Work in pairs. Discuss whether you would rather have your own office, or whether you prefer the flexibility that hot desking offers. Why/ Why not?

1 Listen to Jonathan Schwartz, former CEO of Sun Microsystems, talking about life at a major computer company and indicate the order in which he refers to the following topics.

a ☐ personal identification and access to networks

b ☐ what he does after work

c ☐ employee workspaces

d ☐ interactions between staff

e ☐ his role as CEO of Sun

f ☐ the advantages of communicating by SMS

g ☐ using videoconferencing

2 Listen again and take notes to answer the following questions.

1 What two items does he carry with him wherever he goes?

2 Why does he prefer to use SMS messaging rather than the phone?

3 What can he do with a SunRay device?

4 How does his own desk compare to the desk of the CFO?

5 How did Sun employees react to the option of working from home?

6 What can staff do at the company's cafés?

7 Why is Sun investing in videoconferencing facilities?

8 How does he describe his role as CEO of SUN?

Jonathan Schwartz

Would you like to lead the same sort of lifestyle as Johnathan Schwartz? Discuss your reactions with a partner.

The business model for the 21st century

Read the text on the opposite page and answer the questions.

1 According to a recent book by Stanford graduates, what will the model for 21st century organisations be?

2 What does Clayton Christensen think will be the biggest challenge for these companies?

3 What other challenges will they face?

4 Why are fewer people willing to become leaders nowadays?

Glossary

neural network a biological term to describe neurons that are connected or functionally related to the central nervous system

score a musical composition in printed form

sufficed was enough

The business model for the 21st century

Making music

Companies need to be more like orchestras than armies

1 JEFFREY Joerres, the chief executive of Manpower, one of the world's biggest temporary employment agencies, says that today's "business organisations are like theatre troupes". What he means is that a number of players from the troupe (i.e. the business organisation) come together for a performance, complete it to a high standard, disband and reassemble with other players for a different sort of performance, and so on.

2 A recent book by two Stanford MBAs, "The Starfish and the Spider", claims that the modern organisation is like a starfish. Organisations of the past, say the authors, used to be like spiders. Cut off their heads and they're dead. Starfish, on the other hand, are decentralised structures. They don't have heads as such. Cut certain types of starfish into pieces and "each one will generate into a whole new starfish". This sort of "neural network", say the authors, is the model for the 21st century organisation. It has no central point of control, no brain. Every bit of it can communicate with every other bit.

3 No metaphor for modern corporate life has stuck with quite the same tenacity as the late great Peter Drucker's long-ago suggestion that the "institution that most closely resembles a knowledge-based business is the symphony orchestra, in which some 30 different instruments play the same score together as a team."

4 Clayton Christensen, a management guru, started a recent article in the *Harvard Business Review* with just such an image. "The primary task of management," he wrote, "is to get people to work together in a systematic way. Like orchestra conductors, managers direct the talents and actions of various players to produce a desired result."

5 Drucker, the man who first coined the expression "knowledge worker", recognised that workforce productivity was coming to depend less and less on organisational systems and more and more on individual skills. Such a dramatic shift requires a change in the way we talk about corporate life. For sure, the military imagery that has sufficed for a century is no longer adequate.

6 What businesses do today is more like making music than it is like making war. That is not to say that it is less competitive than it was. Companies still want to play the best music possible and gain the biggest audiences. But their primary focus is not on destroying the opposition, on wiping out other orchestras' ability to perform. It is more inward-looking, focused on themselves playing ever better music as an ensemble.

7 Viewed through this lens, the workplace looks very different. The challenge for companies is not to find the most talented people on the planet – by definition there are never enough of them to go round. Rather, it is to find enough adequate people and give them the equipment, the environment and the motivation to make them produce at their peak.

8 That does not mean that every player needs a Stradivarius, or its equivalent. But for sure they need an instrument that meets certain minimum standards, and they need one musical score that they all can follow. To some extent, they also need to get on well with their fellow players in the orchestra.

9 One feature of the orchestra that is echoed strongly in the modern workplace is the requirement that its musicians work alone on occasions, practising in solitude, whilst coming together at regular intervals in order to play as a team. Today's knowledge workers increasingly work at remote locations, be it in their own homes, in the back of their cars, at airports or in their clients' offices – anywhere other than on premises owned by their employer.

10 Knowledge workers spend far more time than did previous generations "in meetings", getting together with colleagues, physically or virtually, to discuss and measure progress. At the same time, the amount of office space available to workers has shrunk. With the ability to work in remote locations, employees are prepared to put up with a smaller space at head office or, indeed, to 'hot desk'.

11 Another key element in the metaphor of the orchestra is the role of the conductor. Today's organisations demand different skills and a different style of leadership to that which was appropriate when organizations were run in military fashion. What it takes to motivate and lead today's loose associations of individual specialists is very different from what was required to drive regimented departments.

12 The big challenge for the future may be to persuade enough people to take up the leadership baton at all. More and more of them, it seems, may be content to remain mere players in the orchestra. The Families and Work Institute (FWI), a New York-based research organisation, has found that a remarkable number of senior executives in large corporations have recently "reduced their career aspirations". Their reason, says the FWI, is "not that they couldn't do the work, but that the sacrifices they would have to make in their personal lives were too great." ∎

In pairs, discuss the advantages and disadvantages of working from home and only meeting colleagues occasionally at the office.

反意语

Find antonyms in the text for the following terms.

1 permanent (para 1) _Temporary_
2 flexibility (para 3) _stuck_
3 disorganised (para 4) _systematic_
4 insufficient (para 5) _sufficed_

5 lowest potential (para 7) _adequate / most wanted_
6 expanded (para 10) _Shrink_
7 unsuitable (para 11) _appropriate_
8 undisciplined (para 11) _regimented_

Coined expressions

In the text we read that Peter Drucker 'coined' 造出生词 the expression 'knowledge worker'. The business world regularly 'coins' or invents new words and expressions to describe new ideas or activities.

A	B
team	overload
best	line
core	speak
social	crunch
information	networking
net	practice
bottom	competency
credit	player

Match words from each column to form common coined expressions. Which of these refers to the following?

1 Internet language _____
2 the state of having too much information to make a decision or remain informed about a topic _____
3 a period when there is a sharp reduction in the availability of finance from banks and other financial institutions _____
4 a particular specialty or expertise _____
5 an activity or procedure that produces superior results _____
6 a person who participates and works well with others _____
7 the most important information, originates from the last line in an audit; the line that shows profit or loss _____
8 a phenomenon defined by linking people to each other online, e.g. Facebook, MySpace _SNS_

Metaphors and similes

Metaphors and similes allow us to make descriptions more interesting by associating things from very different contexts: a simile by saying one thing is *like* another and a metaphor by referring to it as if it *is* the other.

1 Which metaphors and similes from music are used in the text to illustrate the following?

1 business organisations x 2 (para 1) _____
2 a business project (para 1) _performance_
3 employees or colleagues x 2 (paras 4 and 9) _Players, musician_
4 leaders or managers (para 4) _____
5 customers and consumers (para 6) _audiences_
6 a team (para 6) _ensemble, orchestra_
7 improved performance (para 6) _better music_
8 equipment (para 8) _instrument,_
9 company directives/policies (para 8) _musical Score_

2 Which three metaphors from biology are also used to describe today's businesses? What differences do they illustrate?

Keeping it in the family

Read the text and answer the following.

1 What makes it difficult to calculate the age of big complex companies?
2 Which sectors of industry do the oldest companies come from?
3 At what stage in their development do most businesses fail?
4 What has helped family businesses to survive, according to William O Hara?
5 Which other factors affecting longevity does John Davis identify?

The Economist

The world's oldest companies
The business of survival

What is the secret of corporate longevity?

1 According to *Centuries of Success*, published by William O'Hara, the oldest company in the world is Japanese. Kongo Gumi, founded in Japan in 578, is a builder of Buddhist temples, Shinto shrines and castles – and now also offices, apartment buildings and private houses. It is a family business.

2 Calculating the age of big complex companies – many of which are public, not family owned – is tricky, for many of these firms have grown through multiple acquisitions. That makes it hard to know to what extent they are truly descended from their oldest part. Harsco, for instance, a big American engineering and industrial-services company, can proudly trace parts of its operations to 1742, when a firm called Taylor-Wharton began life as a colonial iron forge. But Taylor-Wharton was not absorbed into what is now called Harsco until 1953.

3 Today's biggest, best-known companies are mostly spotty youths by comparison with the ancient firms listed above. Microsoft was not born until 1975; even General Electric cannot trace its roots further back than 1876. Most of the world's corporate elderly are in very old-economy industries, such as agriculture, hospitality and building.

4 What is clear is that corporate longevity is highly unusual. One-third of the firms in the *Fortune* 500 in 1970 no longer existed in 1983, killed by merger, acquisition, bankruptcy or break-up. Corporate infant mortality is particularly high; the first year is the hardest.

5 How, then, have a few elderly firms succeeded in defying the corporate life-cycle? For most of them, luck has played a part, says Mr O'Hara. But he also identifies several other factors that have helped family firms in particular. Primogeniture has often ensured that a firm did not get torn apart by feuding heirs during generational succession – a common problem now that the eldest son no longer automatically inherits the lot in most countries. In general, unity and trust within the family have been vital. Long-lived firms have also been progressive about taking women into management – albeit usually out of necessity. And they have often been willing to take on new managers through legal adoption when the older generation's seed has fallen on fallow ground.

6 John Davis, of the Harvard Business School says that three factors lie behind longevity: "By the end of every generation, family firms need to have built a reservoir of trust, pride and money so that the next generation has enough of them to maintain the momentum of the business and the spirit of the family." Surviving succession is often a huge test.

But most older firms have also had to evolve in order to keep pace with the times. Kikkoman, for example, founded in 1630 and now the world's leading maker of soy sauce, has expanded into food flavouring and, latterly, into biotech. This, says Mr Davis, requires a boldness that may be possible only with plenty of trust, pride and money. It also needs a good grasp of the firm's core competence: in this instance, knowing lots about yeast, a common factor in all of Kikkoman's activities.

7 This point is echoed by Jim Collins, a co-author of the enduring *Built to Last – Successful Habits of Visionary Companies*. Survivors, he says, are very good at, on the one hand, following a set of unchanging principles and, on the other, separating what they do and how they do it from "who they are". Over hundreds of years, the firm must hold its fundamentals dear, yet constantly change, he says. Surely the point of being in business is to do something remarkable, not merely to survive? A lot of mediocre companies endure for many decades, but, he says, "what's the point?" ■

Glossary

primogeniture the right of the eldest son to inherit

fallow ground land left unplanted during a growing season

longevity length or duration of life

The Economist

Speaking **Jim Collins thinks the point of business is not survival but doing 'something remarkable'. What other reasons can you think of for staying in business? Can you think of any examples of companies which have achieved something remarkable?**

*Gianni Agnelli and
John Elkann*

Listening 2 **The text argues that many family businesses have succeeded in 'defying the corporate life-cycle'. Listen to Barry Cosgrave, an expert on family business, being interviewed by a journalist, talking about that and other aspects of family business, and answer the questions.**

1 What statistics does he give in order to illustrate the importance of family businesses in the global economy?

2 Which successful family businesses does he mention?

3 Why can these firms be difficult to run and what are the main pitfalls?

4 What does he say about the importance of documentation?

5 What is the 'waiver agreement' he refers to and why is this important in family business arrangements?

6 What does he say about the importance of communication?

7 According to him, how should succession planning be organised?

8 What percentage of family businesses continue beyond the third generation?

Speaking

Some people believe that while the founder of a family business may be driven by the need to succeed, the next in line may take that success for granted and not be the best qualified to run the business.

What, in your opinion, is the best way to prepare a member of the younger generation for running the family firm?

– Business studies and then an MBA

– Work in the family company from the bottom up

– Work in a similar company to the family's with no privileges

– Work in a difficult and physical job with poor pay and bad conditions

@ An Internet search using the keywords 'succession planning' will list websites that deal with different aspects of this subject. Find a website that gives advice about how to prepare for the replacement of key staff.

Language check

Determiners

When we use nouns, we usually precede them with one or more 'determiners'. These include different categories of words such as the articles (*a, an, the*), possessive adjectives (*their, your*, etc.), demonstrative adjectives (*this, those*, etc.), numbers and quantifiers (*any, each, either, every, some*, etc.) and the negative determiners (*no, neither*). Other determiners include the *wh*-determiners *whatever, whichever* and the relatives *which* and *whose*. By using determiners we can form noun phrases which give key information about what the noun is referring to. Some determiners can be combined together but must follow a particular order.

 For more information, see page 154.

1 Place each underlined determiner under the correct category heading.

Articles	Possessive adjectives	Demonstrative adjectives	Quantifiers	Wh-determiners	Negative determiners
2. the 3. the 5 the 6. an	4. our 7. Its	3. those 4. this 4. last 8. each	4. more 5. all 5 three 6. some 7. half	2. whatever 3. whose	1. few 2. Neither 4. No. 6 no

1   New investment in machinery has been postponed for the <u>next</u> <u>six</u> months because we have so <u>few</u> orders.

2   <u>Whatever</u> the outcome of the merger, the contract stipulates that <u>neither</u> party may use <u>the</u> other's proprietary information. 規定 82

3   Only <u>those</u> workers <u>whose</u> contracts are up for renewal will be affected by <u>the</u> layoffs.

4   <u>Our</u> safety record shows that there have been <u>no</u> <u>more</u> accidents <u>this</u> year than <u>last</u>.

5   <u>All</u> <u>the</u> employees are entitled to <u>three</u> weeks of vacation leave.

6   <u>Some</u> people would argue that there is <u>no</u> such thing as <u>an</u> Internet business model.

7   Obitek's main advantage is that it can develop applications in <u>half</u> the time it takes <u>its</u> competitors.

8   <u>Each</u> business unit has a specific operational focus.

2 How many other determiners can you find in the sentences?

Practice

Complete the text by adding the appropriate determiners from the box.

any	whose	neither	the	one	its	no	whatever	few	a

IKEA: Flatpack accounting

IKEA, [1] ~~the~~ its founder Ingmar Kamprad is currently rated as possessing one of Sweden's biggest fortunes, has always followed a business model that has been [2] The envy of its competitors. [3] whatever the economic climate, IKEA has always been able to maintain its popularity among consumers and to continue its successful expansion into new markets around the globe. [4] Neither other mass market retailer has managed to do that quite so well. Innovative design and clever marketing are part of the winning formula but [5] no factor is sufficient to explain the IKEA phenomenon. However, if you add organisational efficiency, cost-cutting and an obsession with competitive pricing then you have an unbeatable combination. IKEA is one of the [6] few major retailers that is still privately owned and understanding its unique structure is a bit like assembling one of [7] The famous flatpacks! IKEA is a family company which has organised itself so that it is immune to [8] _____ attempt at a takeover. The company also set up [9] a charity that is [10] one of the world's richest foundations.

Career skills

Team building

Team leaders in global organisations are often faced with the task of forming a team whose members may be based in multiple locations, with different cultures and backgrounds. Selecting the right people for a job or business project therefore requires careful planning and skill. There is a lot more involved than simply mixing complementary skills. The list of team building practices below can help build teams that operate efficiently.

1 Set clear objectives
Start by doing this because once the team agrees and understands the goals and targets they are better able to work together to achieve the required results.
This is important because _____ *b* _____

2 Match tasks to skills and motivation
Recognise people's fields of expertise. People will be more motivated doing things they are good at.
This is important because _____ *e* _____

3 Think about interpersonal dynamics
Putting people with complementary skills on the same team isn't enough. Personality types are also important. If personality clashes arise, the team leader needs to help resolve the issues quickly.
This is important because _____ *a* _____

4 Develop a good team leadership style
When leading a team it is generally better to be a 'coach' rather than a 'star player'. Good leaders allow members to save face when they fail and praise and acknowledge achievements.
This is important because _____ *d* _____

5 Communicate constantly and review performance
Keep the team informed of any developments or changes that will impact on their performance or completion of tasks. Give regular feedback on performance and negotiate ways to move forward after these sessions.
This is important because _____ *c* _____

Read the list above and then complete the second paragraph of each point above with one of the following.

a   ... unbalanced teams with incompatible personalities may result in time wasting arguments which often lead to long term divisions in working relationships if not dealt with promptly.

b   ... it helps the team form a shared vision of what is expected of them, right from the start.

c   ... keeping everyone objective and focused on the project is the most important role of the team leader. Regular, open and productive meetings about progress are therefore paramount to success.

d   ... if you indulge in fault finding and fail to accept your part of the blame when things go wrong the team will become resentful and unproductive.

e   ... if you allow your team members to progress in the areas where they excel and have most interest, you will effectively keep them engaged and avoid having unhappy and frustrated team members.

Speaking

Look at the pictures of some corporate team-building activities and answer the questions.

- Have you ever done any of these activities?
- Which activity, if any, appeals to you?
- Would you refuse to participate in any of them? Why/Why not?
- Do you think that these kinds of activities can help promote 'team spirit' among colleagues? If so, how?
- What other team building activities can you think of?

Listening 3 ⊙

Listen to the team leader and take notes summarising what she says about each team-building activitiy.

Food and refreshments for meetings	
Evening drinks and meals	
Clubs, dancing, theatre	
Away days	
Challenging sports pursuits	
Games and 'fun' activities	
Charity events	
Training courses	

Speaking

Which of the above requires cultural awareness and sensitivity? Why?

Culture at work

Working across cultures

In order to develop effective international teams it is necessary to create an environment which both acknowledges and values cultural differences. Cultural diversity can cause problems but can also be beneficial. For example, in cultures where individuals are viewed more as independent selves, individual achievement and recognition will be important; in cultures where individuals are viewed more as interdependent, interactive and connecting members of the group – or team – to which they belong, collective goals will be more important.

Recognising the nature and implications of cultural differences will lead a team to a shared vision about how best to achieve common goals. On the whole, a cultural mix will benefit an organisation, especially where its customers are also from a range of different cultures. What special qualities and positive characteristics could someone from your culture bring to an international team?

Dilemma & Decision

Dilemma: Bullies on the team

Brief

Arcadia Outdoor Advertising Inc. is a successful advertising agency which specialises in creative outdoor advertising poster campaigns. The company organisational structure is decentralised and works on the basis of collaboration between all the creative and logistic teams in the company. Recruitment practices are rigorous and every effort is made to include only people with complementary skills and compatible personalities.

However, the bullying of a new recruit by more senior members of one of the teams has recently come to light. The new employee mixes well with most of the staff but is being bullied by three female team members. They continually harass her by being rude, criticising her performance and blaming her for their mistakes. One woman, who appears to be the instigator of the bullying, has been with the company for three years and is a key team member, while the other two have two years of service and a good performance record. The nature of the organisational structure means that the bullying situation is putting a strain on all the teams, who collaborate on a daily basis. Therefore the situation is detrimental to the whole department's effectiveness.

The head of the department, Anna Kidder, needs to find a solution. She has tried talking to the 'bullies' but without success. The victim seems to be under a great deal of stress, the department's work is suffering and it reflects badly on Ms Kidder's own promotion chances if the situation continues. There are four options open to her at this time:

- Issue written warnings to the three bullies and then arrange to meet them to discuss the problem.
- Build a case, with the help of HR and the legal experts, which will allow her to dismiss the instigator in the hope that the other two will not continue.
- Arrange for the victim to attend a self-help course to deal with bullying.
- Transfer those responsible for the bullying to another department.

Task 1

In pairs or small groups, evaluate the advantages and limitations of each of the four options. Consider long term as well as short term solutions.

Task 2

Decide which of the options or combinations of the options you think Anna Kidder should take and prepare to present your arguments to the other pairs or groups.

Task 3

Present your decision to the class.

Write it up

You are Anna Kidder. Write a memo to your senior director informing her of the decision you've taken.

 For more information, see *Style guide*, page 18.

Decision:

⊙ Listen to Naomie Dreiblatt, who runs a consulting firm that deals with bullying, talking about the problem.

1 What is the true cost of bullying in an organisation?

2 What does she say about each option open to Ms Kidder?

3 What advice does she give about meeting with the bullies?

4 What advice does she give about establishing a policy to avoid bullying?

Unit 3
Change

www.longman-elt.com   www.economist.com

Meeting the change challenge

Keynotes

Companies that refuse to adapt their **business models** when there is a **shift** or dramatic change in **market forces** can stagnate or fail in the highly competitive fast-paced business environment of today. Effective leaders who are willing to **initiate** change are referred to as **change agents** or **change champions**. Some changes involve making small and gradual improvements to business but sometimes a complete **overhaul** or turnaround, which involves **restructuring** and **redesigning** the organisation as well as changing the cultural **mindset**, is needed to keep a business afloat. One of the biggest challenges facing managers today is how to **implement** change successfully and how to keep **resistance** to a mimimum.

How do you react to change?

1 Implementing and adapting to change have become a major part of daily working life. In pairs, do the questionnaire below to determine how open or averse you are to change. Answer 'yes' or 'no' to each question.

How do you cope with change?

1 Do you tend to have a low tolerance for situations which are not clear? Yes

2 Do you creatively maximise your resources? No

3 Do you feel uncomfortable managing situations which involve uncertainty? No

4 Do you ever take unnecessary risks? Yes

5 Do you think the world is unpredictable and contradictory? yes

6 Do you feel that your skills and competences are limited? no

7 Do you find it difficult to break from the established ways of doing things? yes

8 Do you ask for help when you don't understand something? yes

9 Do you have a problem with resolving conflicts? no

10 Do you feel comfortable with stress? No

11 Do you have a hard time changing priorities? No

12 Do you challenge your own assumptions about how things should be done? Yes

13 Do you prefer to concentate carefully on doing one thing at a time? Yes

14 Do you find it easy to ask for help when you don't understand a task? Yes

2 Turn to page 135 to discover your scores.

1 Harrie Barron, a management consultant, is talking about change. Listen to part 1 and answer the questions. In his opinion:

1 What does 'change management' mean?
2 How do people normally react to change in a work environment?
3 What are the three stages of change management?

2 Now listen to part 2 and answer the questions.

1 What can be done to persaude people to accept change?
2 What are some of the mistakes managers make when introducing change?

Italian change champions

The following questions refer to information given in paragraphs 1–6 on the opposite page. Which paragraph(s) are referred to in each question?

1 How did Gino Cocchi turn the company around? 3,4
2 What led to Carpigiani increasing its market share in the US? 5
3 Which factors caused Carpigiani's decline? 2
4 What are the positive and negative impacts of globalisation on the company? 6
5 What do we know about the company's current situation? 1
6 What does Gino Cocchi say the company had forgotten? 3

Glossary

gelato a type of ice cream

emblem a symbol or mark which identifies an organisation or person

sweltering very hot

stringent very strict

propagate spread

posh expensive and luxurious

fend off defend oneself against something

Italian champions

A sweet success

Ice-cream equipment manufacturer takes a rocky road to world domination

1 WHETHER cone or cup, soft-serve or gelato, the odds are good that the ice-creams bought by sweltering sight-seers and beach-goers across the northern hemisphere this summer came from machines made by Carpigiani, a private Italian firm. In more than 100 countries, the firm's distinctive blue and white emblem has come to stand for the very Italian art of making ice-cream. Several large franchise chains such as Cold Stone, which has over 1,400 stores in America and East Asia and expects a further 70 to open this year, depend on Carpigiani's machines. So do fast-food chains like Pizza Hut and McDonald's. The firm has won around half of the global market for ice-cream makers, according to Gino Cocchi, its managing director. No wonder, then, that Carpigiani is making money by the scoopful.

2 But Carpigiani's success has not always been assured. It stagnated for much of the decade after the death in 1982 of Poerio Carpigiani, a smart marketing man and one of two brothers behind the firm. (The other, Bruto, who designed their first machine, died in 1945, one year before the company was founded.) Complacency had set in. Quality fell, complaints rose and Carpigiani's share of world sales slipped from 25% in 1980 to 15% in 1990.

3 Mr Cocchi, who was brought in from a sister firm that year, resorted to the sort of overhaul that many struggling Italian companies now face. "We had to relearn the importance of customer service, of quality and of being ahead of competitors with new products," he says. He cut costs and simplified the Carpigiani's structure by cutting its 1,000-strong workforce by half. He scrapped television advertising, always an extravagance for a machinery manufacturer. Carpigiani also resorted to outsourcing. Its four factories (two in Italy, one in Spain and one in America), which produced about 40,000 machines last year, are essentially assembly lines, as few parts are made in-house any more.

4 The introduction of a system for quality control also helped get Carpigiani back on track. It was the first firm in the business to win a major industry accreditation. A renewed emphasis on research and development was especially important, since poor materials caused many of the firm's problems. Carpigiani's technical department had 10 employees in 1990 when the payroll at its factory and headquarters in Anzola Emilia was 300; it now has 50 out of a payroll of 250. Its Gelato University teaches the nuances of ice-cream making, and collaboration with traditional universities reinforces its internal research. The university in nearby Bologna, for example, is helping it to develop special steels, composites and plastics.

5 All this helps Carpigiani meet stringent regulations for machines that make food in countries such as America. The firm generates about one-third of its income there, with its 85% share of the American market for machines that make posh Italian ice-cream and 30% for machines that make soft ice-cream. Hygiene is fundamental. Machines that minimise intervention by human hands by cleaning themselves, for example, are more expensive, but help to ensure that the ice-cream they produce is safe to eat.

6 Cost-cutting, quality control and technical innovation, in turn, have helped Carpigiani fend off cheaper Chinese rivals, many of which have copied its designs. It is even building a new factory in China, to make machines for the local market. Globalisation may have subjected Carpigiani to stiffer competition, but it is also helping to propagate a taste for genuine Italian ice-cream among China's swelling middle class. ■

While globalisation increased competition for Carpigiani it also created opportunities. What are the other drawbacks and benefits of operating in a global market?

@ An Internet search using the keywords 'organisational change' will list websites dealing with change management. Find an example of a business organisation that has recently introduced significant changes.

Vocabulary 1

Identify the words below with the problems which provoked the changes made by Carpigiani (A) or with the change process itself (B).

Problems: extravagance, stiffer competition, stagnated, complacency, complaints

Change process: simplified, reinforce, overhaul, cost-cutting, scrapped,

simplified   reinforce   extravagance   overhaul   stiffer competition
cost-cutting   stagnated   complacency   complaints   scrapped

Vocabulary 2

Prefixes with verbs

The vocabulary of change includes many words with the prefix re which introduces the idea of doing something again, e.g. relearn, renew, reinforce in the text. Other prefixes include counter, out, over, under, de, co, mis and sub.

In pairs, form as many new verbs as you can by combining these prefixes with the words below.

act   come   consider   contract   date   design   divide
estimate   grade   locate   manage   operate   perform   value

counteract overcome? reconsider subcontract outdate redesign subdivide
react overact
underestimate degrade relocate undermanage cooperate underperform overvalue
overestimate degrade   mismanage   outperform undervalue
*   devalue*

Practice

Complete the text below with words from Vocabulary 1 and words you have formed in Vocabulary 2.

Banks in England plan major branch overhaul

In an effort to ¹*counteract* a growing number of ²*complaints* from their customers who say that banks are out of touch with changing needs. As well as ³*stiffer competition* from Internet banking, many major English banks are bringing in make-over experts to help them to upgrade their image by ⁴*redesigning* the interiors of branches as well as ⁵*relocating* many of them to more popular areas of towns and cities. Some branches will include trendy coffee areas, Internet access and meeting rooms, proving that banks are finally ⁶*reconsidering* long-held beliefs that they need to be very serious and sober environments.

An analyst said banks completely ⁷*underestimated* the impact that Internet banking would have on new business. That's what happens when ⁸*complacency* sets in and you start to take the fact that there will be new customers for granted. However, they did ⁹*react* quickly to the new situation and the changes being introduced are designed to appeal to young people, who might otherwise have been attracted to online alternatives.

Speaking

Do banks need an attractive interior design, a café and Internet access to attract you? If your bank was about to embark on a complete overhaul in order to improve customer satisfaction, what would you advise them to do?

Usage

Idioms with *track*

1 In the text we read 'The introduction of a system for quality control also helped get Carpigiani back on track'. There are many idioms using *track*. Match these *track* idioms with their definitions.

1	to track something or someone down *d*	a	to be informed about
2	to backtrack *f* (backpedal)	b	to conceal one's actions and/or intentions
3	to be on the right track *c*	c	to find the correct procedure, person or course of action
4	to keep track of *a*		
5	to lose track of *h*	d	to search till you find
6	to fast track *e*	e	to accelerate the pace of the normal process of something
7	to cover one's tracks *b*	f	to revert to a previous opinion or position
8	a proven track record *g*	g	impressive professional achievements
		h	to lose touch with, to forget and/or be unable to find

2 Replace the underlined words with the appropriate form of an idiom from above.

1 It's impossible to know the truth about what's going on, they are so good at hiding what they're up to! *Covering their tracks.*
2 I still haven't been able to get hold of him for you but I'll keep trying. *To track him down*
3 Sorry I'm late – I was so engrossed at work that I completely forgot about the time! *lose track of*
4 I've checked her CV and she has had a varied and sucessful career. *a proven track record*
5 They got off to a bad start but I think they know what they are doing now! *are on the right track*
6 We promised to deliver within two days – we can't change our minds now! *back track*
7 I need the results right away – can you speed up the analysis phase? *fast track*
8 The new software will make it much easier for us to follow all our unpaid invoices. *keep track*

Listening 2

A framework for change

There are many different approaches to developing and implementing change and each company tries to adopt the most appropriate model for their needs and requirements. The diagram on page 140 represents four such models. A and B represent situations where organisations operating in an unstable environment need to make large-scale, organisation-wide changes to either their culture or structure. C and D represent situations where organisations operating in stable environments need to make small, gradual adjustments to attitudes and procedures.

1 Listen to Ewa Baczynska, a change consultant, talking about the different models for change. Listen and identify which approach (A–D) she is referring to in each part of her talk (1–4).

2 Listen again. What does she say about resistance to change for each of the change models?

Read the text and answer the questions.

1 What made Dell computers so successful when they first arrived on the computer market?

2 What factors led to Dell's falling market share?

3 What changes have been put in place in order to regain that market share?

4 Which of the change models referred to correspond best to the change framework at Dell?

The Economist

Glossary

tenacity determination 粘り強さ, 根

delve explore 探研する, 誰精する

hitherto until now 今まで0こ=3川(期)

Take two

Getting back on top

Michael Dell pioneered a new business model at the firm that bears his name. Now he wants to overhaul it.

1 So why, after three years of relative distance as chairman of the board, did Michael Dell take charge again at Dell, the company he had founded in his dorm room at the University of Texas at the age of 19? "When you start a company, it's a very personal thing," answers Dell. "I will care about what happens to the company even after I'm dead. I just can't let it go."

2 Mr Dell's tenacity seems to be paying off. His firm, which used to be the world's biggest maker of personal computers, but had lost its crown to Hewlett-Packard, is beginning to regain market share.

3 Ever since Mr Dell started selling computers, he has focused on a different sort of innovation from the rest of the industry. In contrast to Apple, for instance, Dell has never worried about designing sexy devices or building a global network of fancy shops. Instead, the firm tried to make a commodity of customisation, allowing clients to choose the features they wanted online, using cheaper generic parts and maintaining an impossibly lean supply chain. This model went down well with corporate customers, particularly in America, where Dell remains number one.

4 Turning customisation into a commodity served Dell exceptionally well, and not just in the PC market: it successfully used the same approach with server computers, printers and storage devices. Yet just when the firm seemed unstoppable, its world began to change. Growth migrated from corporate markets to consumers and from rich countries to emerging markets, where people are warier of shopping online. As PCs became more powerful, buyers could no longer be persuaded to add extra processing power or a bigger hard drive when they bought them – one of the firm's specialities. Profits began to erode. Add deteriorating customer service and accounting problems to the mix, and it is easy to see why Mr Dell felt he needed to come back.

5 Back in the driver's seat, he is now trying out new approaches and diversifying Dell's business model both geographically and commercially. One of Mr Dell's first decisions was a push into what Internet types call "social media". He set up a corporate blog and a website called IdeaStorm that lets customers make suggestions on how Dell can improve its products. This has earned Mr Dell a reputation in the blogosphere for "getting it".

6 A much more momentous move was the decision to start selling in shops again. This is a cultural revolution for Dell. It no longer wants to sell dull black boxes, but must aim for products that build "brand lust", as Mr Dell calls it. So Dell will have to foster a whole new mindset among its engineers and designers. It will need to set up a bulk supply chain alongside the customised one. And it will have to delve into hitherto unknown realms, such as managing relationships with retailers. ■

The Economist

Continuous forms

Continuous forms of all verb tenses consist of a form of *be* followed by the present participle of a verb. They refer to actions, events or situations that are viewed as ongoing, even if this is projected into the future or recalled from the past. The main categories of continuous forms are present, future, past, perfect and modal, and they can be either active or passive.

 For more information, see page 155.

Match the sentences 1–6 with the explanations a–f.

1 We were doing research for a new system when our main competitor suddenly launched something very similar. *b*	**a** an action of a relatively short duration that is taking place at or around the moment when we are speaking
2 Most people had been expecting the boss to retire but instead she decided to remain at the helm. *e*	**b** an ongoing situation that existed for some time but that was interrupted by another action or event
3 They are considering changing all their software to Open Source. *a*	**c** an ongoing situation that began before the moment when we are speaking and that has continued uninterrupted until now
4 The two sides will be meeting to discuss the proposals later in the week. *f*	**d** an ongoing situation that will still be under way at a specific time in the future
5 Telecinco has been leading the market in terms of both audience and revenues. *c*	**e** an ongoing situation that had existed for some time before at a specific moment in the past
6 By the time she retires next year she will have been managing the subsidiary for more than fifteen years. *d*	**f** a pre-arranged plan

Practice

Complete the text with a suitable continuous form of a verb from the box in each gap. Sometimes a simple form is possible.

begin	operate	work	emerge	become
live	pour	soar	come	reinvent	look

nanotechnology

Of all the new technologies that ¹ *have emerged* during the last few years there is one in particular that ² *is beginning* to revolutionise the way that business and industry ³ *will operate* in the future: nanotechnology. This radical approach to building new materials by assembling them from atomic particles has its origins in 1976. At that time Richard Feynman, an American scientist, ⁴ *had been working* on a new concept for molecular engineering. He published his thoughts in an article and within two years his new theory ⁵ *had become* a reality.

Since then technology companies all around the globe ⁶ *have been pouring* money into nano laboratories, with the result that new patent applications ⁷ *have been soaring.* It's no longer a question of whether or not the nano boom ⁸ *is coming* – it's about how big a boom it will eventually be. At Hewlett-Packard scientists claim that they ⁹ *are reinventing* the computer. Others ¹⁰ *are looking* even further into the future. By the end of the decade some say that we ¹¹ *will be living* inside a nanotechnology world.

Speaking

In pairs, ask the following questions and discuss.

- What do you think you will be doing at this time next year? And in five years from now?
- What were you doing at this time last year?
- What have you been doing recently?

Career skills

psychological contracts

Managing resistance to change

Studies show that people have a natural tendency to resist change. Resistance to changing from a stable, comfortable state to something unknown, even if it will bring benefits, is therefore natural and almost inevitable. People may fight against change because they:

- fear they will lose something they value
- don't understand the change and its implications
- don't think that the change makes sense
- find it difficult to cope with either the level or pace of the change.

Resistance may be based on a genuine understanding of the nature and consequences of the change or indeed on a partial or total miscomprehension. Managers who are planning to implement changes should be wary of the near inevitablity of meeting objections and they should be armed with an effective policy for introducing change from the outset.

Below is a checklist of some of the things managers can do to minimise resistance to change.

a Do some research.

b Involve staff in the planning and implementation process.

c Ensure that objectives are clearly defined and communicated.

d Hold employee feedback meetings.

e Renegotiate 'psychological contracts'.

f Provide training and recognise extra work.

Match the following headings to each of the points a–f above.

1 People are more likely to resist change if it comes as a surprise. They may also feel manipulated if changes have been kept secret during the planning stages. ___b___

2 Carry out a stakeholder analysis to identify which groups will be most affected by the change and try to predict their reactions. ___a___

3 Managers should encourage people to express their thoughts and feelings about the change openly, and staff concerns should be taken seriously. ___d___

4 People sometimes resist change because they lack confidence in their ability to adapt, particularly if the new situation demands new skills. Change is nearly always associated with extra work. The manager should be careful not to overlook this aspect and should reward people's efforts. ___f___

5 People need to understand exactly what is involved and what is expected of them if they are to buy into the proposed change. ___c___

6 Very often staff and managers establish unwritten 'contracts', in other words a set of beliefs and expectations about their respective roles, even though these may not be stated in their actual contracts. Employees should be encouraged to challenge and renegotiate these 'contracts'. ___e___

Listening 3

1 **You are in charge of implementing the changes described in Scenarios 1 and 2 opposite. Read them and answer the questions.**

- What level of resistance do you think you will meet? Why?

- What do you think the people who need to change will say?

- What measures and incentives could be put in place to reduce the potential resistance?

Scenario 1

Your company makes office equipment. The leading product is photocopiers, which are sold by a team of door-to-door salespeople. Area managers head teams of ten who call on companies without prior appointments, check the existing photocopier and sell new ones if they are old or unreliable. It is a comfortable routine that has worked reasonably well for ten years with steady but small increases in sales every year. However, from now on the sales force will be required to reach new, much higher targets by selling other products such as printers and scanners. In order to do this, they will have to engage with customers to assess their needs.

Scenario 2

You are the new office manager of a leading building supplies company. Your predecessor was an authoritarian and strict boss who had developed a step-by-step plan for all accounting and admistrative procedures that staff were required to follow to the letter. In your previous job, you had always encouraged staff to think for themselves and to take the initiatives whenever they spotted potential for improvement. You have decided to introduce the way you worked in your previous job as a model for this new job in an effort to improve the staff's working conditions.

2 **Listen to two extracts where change managers discuss the above scenarios and answer the questions.**

1   Why didn't the change go smoothly?
2   What could have been done to improve the situation?

Culture at work

Attitudes to change

It seems that it is human nature to resist change and this goes across cultures. However, some cultures are more adverse to change than others. 'Uncertainty avoidance' in culture refers to the level of tolerance of ambiguity. Cultures with a low level of tolerance of ambiguity, and therefore risk, will be more rule-orientated and will be more likely to have law-making institutions and regulators to minimise the possibility of unclear situations occurring in business transactions. They will often be monocultural societies with long histories. Change in these cultures will generally proceed slowly and in a step-by-step manner. Cultures with a higher tolerance for ambiguity will be more likely to accept change. Does your culture have a high or low level of tolerance for ambiguity and therefore change?

Dilemma: The disorganised organisation

Brief

Oticon, a Danish hearing instrument company, was founded in 1904. In the 1970s it was the market leader but its fortunes plummeted in the 1980s and 1990s. The market became dominated by leading electronics companies such as Siemens, Phillips, Sony, 3M and Panasonic. In 1988 Lars Kolind, the president of the company, cut staff, increased efficiency and reduced prices by 20%. By 1990 Oticon was making a profit of some £16 million on a turnover of £400 million with sales growing 2% per annum. However, the market was growing at 6%. Lars Kolind decided that if the company was to have a future, big changes were going to have to be made. He thought that they couldn't compete with the competitors on technology, so he decided they would move from a technology-based manufacturing company to a knowledge-based organisation. He wanted to establish a 'spaghetti organisation' – a chaotic tangle of relationships that would force the abandonment of perceived ideas which he saw as barriers to innovation and competitiveness. At head office he decided to abandon the concept of a formal organisation. Formal structures, job descriptions and policies were seen by him as barriers to cooperation and teamwork. This new 'disorganised organisation' was founded on four principles:

hard → soft
doire

- Departments and job titles would disappear.
- Jobs would be redesigned to each employee's needs and capacities.
- Offices would be replaced by work stations that anyone could use.
- Informal face to face dialogue would replace memos.

Task 1

Work in pairs. Discuss what you think about Lars Kolind's vision for the company. What kind of resistance do you think this kind of change could meet?

Task 2

Work in pairs. Student A, you believe that Mr Kolind's vision for change will lead to disaster. Use the information on page 136 to build arguments to support your case. Student B, you believe that the new model for change is the company's only chance of survival. Use the information on page 138 to build arguments to support your case.

Task 3

Decide what you think the fate of Oticon will be if these changes are introduced.

Write it up

Write a formal email to Lars Kolind stating your case.

For more information, see *Style guide*, page 16.

Decision:

Listen to Duncan Hobbes, a change consultant talking about what actually happened to Oticon.

1 What did most people think of Lars Kolind?

2 What would a less inspired leader have done?

3 What was offered to staff after the first negotiations had taken place?

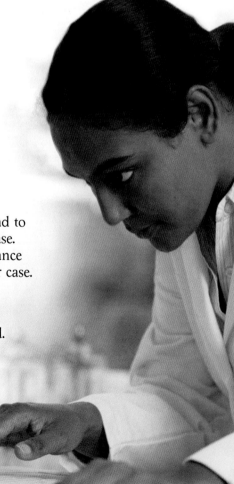

Review 1

Language check

Contrast and similarity

Choose the best form of the words in italics.

PERFORMANCE MANAGEMENT

The creators of a new web based appraisal system, Rypple, say employees can use it to ask questions ¹ *like/as* 'What did you think of my presentation today?' to peers and mentors. ² *Like/As* a spokesperson for the company says, ³ '*Unlike/Conversely* traditional appraisal systems, Rypple encourages employees to build their own coaching network, taking pressure off managers.' ⁴ *However/Although*, by making it easier to solicit assessment, managers may spend even more time giving feedback with this method. ⁵ *Conversely/Nonetheless*, companies using Rypple have expressed satisfaction with the product.

Determiners

Complete the article by adding an appropriate determiner from the box in each space.

others	a	her	this
past	some	few	where

A NEW LOOK

¹_____ fashion season, many designers chose to abandon the expensive catwalk. ²_____ designers opted for thrifty presentations where models were hired to stand on podiums like mannequins for a ³_____ hours. ⁴_____ are pursuing digital means to reach a broader audience. Catherine Malandrino, ⁵_____ French designer, spent the ⁶_____ three months reworking her website. She wants to promote ⁷_____ brand widely and cheaply through the Internet.

Continuous forms

Complete the dialogue with the continuous form of the verbs. Sometimes a simple form is also possible.

A: What (¹you/do) _____ over the past few months?

B: Well, as you know, all last year I (²change) _____ our software system, so recently I (³check) _____ with all departments to see if it (⁴function) _____ properly. There are still some problems I'm afraid.

A: We (⁵meet) _____ to discuss that in more detail next month.

B: Yes, I heard that. I must say I was surprised about that. I (⁶expect) _____ a little more time before the meeting to get it right.

A: More time? By the time we have the meeting you (⁷work on) _____ that project for over a year and a half!

Consolidation

Chose the correct form of the words in italics.

Our company ¹ *has been going through/ has gone through* a major change process for the last six months. ² *Similarly/Unlike* many companies struggling to survive, we merged with ³ *the/our* biggest competitor, giving us ⁴ *the/some* edge we needed. ⁵ *However/ Conversely* the process hasn't been ⁶ *that/half* easy. Managers ⁷ *have been getting/will be getting* the timing ⁸ *plenty/all* wrong. ⁹ *Whereas/In contrast to* experts say not to tell staff too early because they panic, ¹⁰ *their/ our* management told us months before the actual signing of ¹¹ *the/a* deal. ¹² *Conversely/ Nonetheless*, in recent weeks things ¹³ *have been getting better/were getting better* and we seem to be getting back on the right track now.

Vocabulary check

1 Complete the text with the correct form of the following words.

resist	close	layoff	restructure
underperform	cut		

Hawkesland Inc. has announced a major overhaul. It expects to save $50 million a year by [1] _____ 1,000 jobs in the US and [2] _____ down three overseas factories. There has been strong [3] _____ to the changes from the labour unions. The issue of [4] _____ is sensitive at the moment with unemployment levels reaching their highest levels for many years. However, a company spokesman said that shedding [5] _____ businesses was a necessary step in the company's [6] _____ process.

2 Combine the prefixes in A with the verbs in B, the second column, then complete the sentences with the correct form of those words.

A	B
mis	operate
counter	value
under	perform
sub	act
out	grade
up	manage
co	contract

1 Their problems stem from the _____ of funds by the incompetent finance team.

2 He resigned because he felt _____ by his peers and managers.

3 There was a communications breakdown and both departments refused to consider any form of _____ .

4 We have made considerable savings by _____ part of our production to a factory in South East Asia.

5 We are currently _____ the competition by 20%.

6 We reduced our prices by 5% so they _____ by reducing theirs by 7%.

7 If we want to charge top prices we may have to _____ our product range.

Usage

Coined expressions

Complete the sentences with the correct expression from the box.

team players	core competency
bottom line	big four

1 They decided to stop expansion and concentrate instead on their _____ .

2 We've considered this proposal carefully but the _____ is that we simply can't afford it.

3 The _____ accountancy firms are careful to recruit only top performers.

4 We need not only team leaders but _____ too.

Career skills

Managing appraisals

Match questions 1–5 with responses a–e.

1 Why have you been missing deadlines? _____

2 Are you sure you used everything at your disposal? _____

3 Are there any areas where you could use some support? _____

4 How have things been going with colleagues? _____

5 Do you feel you have a work–life balance? _____

a Actually there has been a little friction.

b Things didn't turn out quite as I'd expected.

c I don't feel stressed and I manage my time well.

d I must admit I had problems with some of the systems.

e I'd appreciate some training in certain areas.

Team building

Match the terms a–e with the strategies 1–5.

a compatibility and flexibility

b feedback and pointers

c observing and delegating

d empowering and encouraging

e sharing a vision

1 Set clear objectives _____

2 Match tasks to skills _____

3 Consider interpersonal dynamics _____

4 Develop team leadership style _____

5 Review performance _____

Unit 4
Responsibility

www.longman-elt.com   www.economist.com

Better business

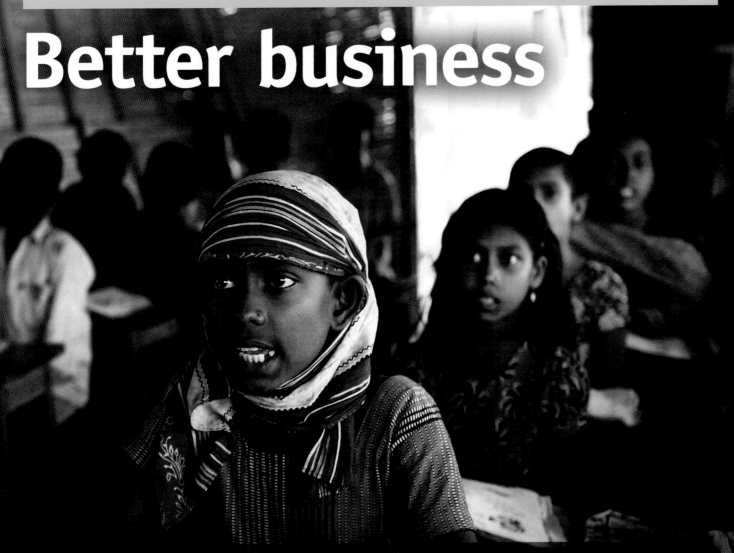

Keynotes

Corporate Social Responsibility, or **CSR**, is a concept that is changing the way that companies conduct their business operations at home and abroad. Otherwise known as **Corporate Citizenship** or **Corporate Responsibility**, CSR encourages firms to adopt practices that are based on principles of **good conduct** in relation to issues such as **sustainable development**, **climate change**, **human rights** and **ethical business**. In addition to this, CSR provides public relations opportunities for companies to promote themselves in new and existing markets and to develop innovative products and services which are more **environmentally friendly**. CSR also motivates companies to put in place **risk management** strategies that eliminate business practices which could expose them to negative publicity in the media.

Business and the community

Look at the pictures which show a variety of problems that businesses have had to face. What messages do they convey about the companies or industries involved? What do you know about the stories or issues behind the photos?

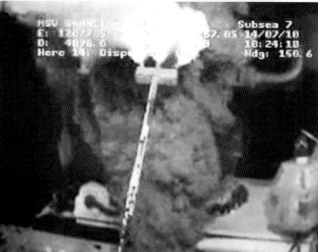

Listening 1 🎧

Listen to David Du Cane, a business journalist, talking about how businesses are increasingly having to accept responsibility for the impacts that result from their activities. Answer the following questions.

1 How has the relationship between business and the media evolved?
2 The speaker refers to two critical events. What happened in each?
3 How were the victims compensated?
4 What lessons has the business community learnt from these two events?

Speaking

How important is it to know how responsible a company is when you are buying one of its products or services? How do you know whether the products that you buy are environmentally-friendly or not?

Reading 1

Business principles

Read the text on the opposite page and answer the questions that follow.

Business principles

Just good business

Corporate social responsibility, once a do-gooding sideshow, is now seen as mainstream

1 IN the lobby of Marks & Spencer the words scroll across a giant electronic ticker. They describe progress against "Plan A", a set of 100 worthy targets. The company will help give 15,000 children in Uganda a better education; it is saving 55,000 tonnes of CO2; it is tripling sales of organic food.

2 The M&S ticker says a lot about the current state of what is commonly known as corporate social responsibility (CSR). First, nobody much likes the CSR label. Some companies prefer to describe it as "corporate citizenship", or "building a sustainable business". One Nordic executive glories in the title of Director, Accountability and Triple-bottom-line Leadership. All this is convoluted code for something simple: companies meaning (or seeming) to be good.

3 Second, the list shows what a vast range of activities now comes under the doing-good umbrella. It spans everything from volunteering in the local community to saving the planet. With such a wide-ranging subject, many companies find it hard to know what to focus on.

4 Third, the M&S ticker demonstrates that CSR is booming. Big companies want to tell the world about their good citizenship. Their chief executives queue up to speak at conferences to explain their passion for the community or their commitment to making their company carbon neutral.

5 Why the boom? For a number of reasons, companies are having to work harder to protect their reputation. Scandals at Enron, WorldCom and elsewhere undermined trust in big business. An army of non-governmental organisations (NGOs) stands ready to do battle with multinational companies at the slightest sign of misbehaviour. Myriad rankings put pressure on companies to report on their non-financial performance as well as on their financial results. And, more than ever, companies are being watched. Embarrassing news anywhere in the world – a child working on a piece of clothing with your company's brand on it, say – can be captured on camera and published everywhere in an instant, thanks to the Internet.

6 Now comes concern over climate change, probably the biggest driver of growth in the CSR industry of late. The great green awakening is making company after company take a serious look at its own impact on the environment. As well as these external pressures, firms are also facing strong demand for CSR from their employees. Ask almost any large company about the rationale for its CSR efforts and you will be told that they help to motivate, attract and retain staff.

7 Too much of a good thing? Since there is so much CSR about, you might think big companies would by now be getting rather good at it. A few are, but most are struggling. CSR is now made up of three broad layers. The most basic is traditional corporate philanthropy. Companies typically allocate about 1% of pre-tax profits to worthy causes. But many feel that simply writing cheques to charities is no longer enough. Shareholders want to know that their money is being put to good use, and employees want to be actively involved in good works.

8 Money alone is not the answer when companies come under attack for their behaviour. Hence the second layer of CSR, which is a branch of risk management. Starting in the 1980s, with environmental disasters such as the explosion at Bhopal and the *Exxon Valdez* oil spill, industry after industry has suffered blows to its reputation.

9 So, often belatedly, companies responded by trying to manage the risks. They talk to NGOs and to governments, create codes of conduct and commit themselves to more transparency in their operations. Increasingly, too, they get together with their competitors in the same industry to set common rules, spread the risk and shape opinion.

10 All this is largely defensive, but there are also opportunities for those that get ahead of the game. The emphasis on opportunity is the third and trendiest layer of CSR: the idea that it can help to create value. If approached in a strategic way, CSR could become part of a company's competitive advantage. That is just the sort of thing chief executives like to hear. "Doing well by doing good" has become a fashionable mantra.

11 Nonetheless, the business of trying to be good is confronting executives with difficult questions. Can you measure CSR performance? Should you be co-operating with NGOs and with your competitors? Is there really competitive advantage to be had from a green strategy?

12 Done badly, CSR is often just window-dressing and can be positively harmful. Done well, though, it is not some separate activity that companies do on the side, a corner of corporate life reserved for virtue: it is just good business. ∎

1 Look at the four sets of possible paragraph headings. In each set, the headings appear in the wrong order. Scan the article and rearrange the headings in the correct order.

☐ The name of the game; Setting objectives; *(1)* A little bit of everything *(2) The name of the game;* (paragraphs 1–3)

☐ Growth sector; Getting greener; Keeping watch (paragraphs 4–6) *(1)* *(2)* *(3): Getting greener*

☐ Getting together; Dealing with danger; Giving it away (paragraphs 7–9) *(3)* *(2)* *(1)*

☐ Unanswered questions; Opportunity knocks; Making business sense (paragraphs 10–12) *(2)* *(1)* *(3) Unanswered questions;*

2 Read the text again and answer the following questions.

1 Paragraphs 2–4 list three things that can be inferred about CSR. Summarise what is said about each.

2 Paragraphs 7–10 describe various components of CSR. How many components are mentioned and what does each consist of?

Speaking

Do you think that CSR is an important consideration for all businesses? Should companies focus more on making a profit and less on doing good?

@ An Internet search using the keywords 'CSR companies' will list companies that have adopted CSR. Choose one of the examples. How are they using CSR? What initiatives have they taken?

Vocabulary 1

Read the definitions of six key words from the text. Which words are defined?

1 avoiding the depletion of natural resources (para 2) ___~~Sustainabt~~ sustainable___
2 the quality of being held responsible for something (para 2) _accountability_
3 an accounting approach which includes financial performance as well as environmental and social performance (para 2) _triple-bottom-line_
4 belonging to a community (para 4) _citizenship_
5 producing as little CO$_2$ as possible and paying compensation for all gases emitted (para 4) _carbon-neutral_
6 the condition of having fair, honest and visible business practices (para 9) _~~transparency~~_

Vocabulary 2

Compound nouns

In the text there are several examples of compound nouns that are formed with an adjective followed by a noun.

organic food   *big business*   *financial results*

What other compound nouns can be made with the following adjectives?

environmental	financial	corporate	competitive
activist, group, issue, safety, policy, pollution, protection	advisor, aid, analysis, crisis, highlight, institution, performance, service, year	culture, earnings, finance, governance, hospitality, identity, life, office, officers, planning, strategy	advantage, edge, field, position, price, sport, market, strategy

diferem   (carbon tax)

Usage	**Synonyms**

Synonyms allow you to avoid repetition and are an excellent way to build vocabulary and to develop speaking and writing skills. Find the expressions in the text that correspond to the underlined sections in the sentences below.

1   The time and energy that firms are devoting to their role in the community says a lot about what is <u>often called</u> corporate social responsibility. (para 2) _commonly known as_

2   There is a huge assortment of different things that <u>can be included as part of</u> CSR. (para 3) _comes under_

3   Many non-profit groups are ready to <u>confront</u> businesses that transgress. (para 5) ~~to battle with~~ _do battle with_

4   Businesses are having to <u>examine in detail</u> how their activities affect the environment. (para 6) _take a serious look at_

5   Currently CSR is <u>composed of</u> three main components. (para 7) _made up of_

6   Investors want to be reassured that their investments are being <u>managed effectively.</u> (para 7) _put to good use_

7   Businesses are trying to <u>influence the public's attitude.</u> (para 9) _shape opinion_

8   Some companies consider that CSR gives them the chance to <u>take a leading position.</u> (para 10) _get ahead of the game._

Listening 2 ⊙	**Making the commitment**

Daniel Franklin

Daniel Franklin is the *Economist* editor who wrote the article on page 41. Before you listen to an interview with him, prepare a short list of questions about CSR.

1 Now listen to the complete interview. Are any of the questions similar to the ones that you prepared?

2 Listen again to parts 1–4 and answer the questions below.

Part 1
Daniel Franklin refers to two 'sets of issues' which have affected the way that companies conduct their activities. What are these and what does he say about them?

Part 2
1   Why is it not necessarily a good idea for a company to deal with CSR via its corporate communications department?

2   List the three examples of activities that can be included in CSR.

3   What is the danger of having a 'scatter-gun' approach to CSR?

Part 3
1   How could CSR have a harmful effect on some businesses?

2   What should companies do to protect the interests of workers in poorer countries?

Part 4
What two reasons does Daniel Franklin give to explain why some companies are ignoring CSR?

Paired structures

Paired structures are pairs of words or phrases which appear in different parts of a sentence. They are used to present options or alternatives, introduce similarities and refer to the timing of events.

not only ... (but) also	*both ... and*	*neither ... nor*
either ... or	*whether ... or*	*some ... other*
one ... the other/another	*as ... so ...*	*once ... then*
on the one hand ... on the other hand ...		

Which of these paired structures could be used to do the following?

1 Present two different views (or two sides of an argument). *on the one hand / on the other hand*
2 List two things (or sets of things) that are similar. *not only, also both, and . one, another .*
3 Show two alternative options. *either, or, whether, or*
4 Show a chronological sequence for two events. *once / then*
5 Point to two things that occur simultaneously. *as / so*
6 Present two examples in the negative. *neither / nor .*

 For more information, see page 155.

Complete the following sentences with a paired structure.

1 People often have different attitudes to CSR; _either_ they consider it to be a cynical effort by companies to cover up unethical activities _or_ they see it as a genuine effort to integrate core values.
2 _Once_ businesses have determined which areas of their operations they need to improve, they can _then_ start to implement procedures.
3 _As_ employees' values and attitudes change over time, _so_ do their work styles and their career aspirations.
4 It is now increasingly being accepted that _neither_ society _nor_ the economy can continue to operate successfully unless the environment around them remains healthy.
5 Participants in the survey were asked _whether_ they were in favour of the government's proposal to subsidise alternative energy development _or_ against it.

Paired comparatives

Another common form of paired structure uses two comparatives preceded by *the*. The second clause expresses the consequence of the first clause.

The more *money that is spent on energy research,* **the greater** *the chance of one day finding a new, clean fuel.*

Rewrite the following sentences using the comparative adjectives in brackets. Make any changes necessary.

1 There are more and more cars on the roads so the impact of pollution is increasing. *(more, great)* *The more cars there are on the road, the greater the impact of pollution.*
2 With fuel becoming more costly, people are using their cars less frequently. *(expensive, less)* *The more expensive fuel becomes, the less people use their cars.*
3 Companies that are 'responsible' will attract more job applicants. *(responsible, attractive)* *The more responsible companies are, the more attractive they are to job applicants.*
4 A lightweight vehicle uses less energy. *(light, less)* *The lighter a vehicle is, the less energy it uses.*
5 In countries where people have low per capita incomes, it is more difficult to implement sustainable policies. *(low, hard)* *The lower the per capita income, the harder it is to implement sustainable policies.*

Greenwashing

Read the extract from the Greenwashing Index and answer the following questions.

1 What is the main purpose of this document? Who do you think might have prepared it and why?

2 How might this type of document influence business organisations?

● GREENWASHING INDEX

Promoted by EnviroMedia Social Marketing & the University of Oregon

Email [　　　　　　　]
Password [　　　　　　　]
Login   Register

Post and Aid   View/Rate Ads   About Green washing   In the News   Commentary   [　　　] Search Ads

Green claims

以こ及び の 数まん的な 環境派水

Greenwashing

What is Greenwashing? It's Whitewashing, but with a Green Brush

Everyone's heard the expression 'whitewashing' – it's defined as 'a coordinated attempt to hide unpleasant facts, especially in a political context'. 'Greenwashing' is the same, but in an environmental context.

It's greenwashing when a company or organisation spends more time and money claiming to be 'green' through advertising and marketing than actually implementing business practices that minimise environmental impact. It's whitewashing, but with a green brush.

A classic example might be an energy company that runs an advertising campaign touting a 'green' technology they're working on – but that 'green' technology represents only a sliver of the company's otherwise not-so-green business, or may be marketed on the heels of an oil spill or plant explosion.

Or a hotel chain that calls itself 'green' because it allows guests to choose to sleep on the same sheets and reuse towels, but actually does very little to save water and energy where it counts – on its grounds, with its appliances and lighting, in its kitchens and with its vehicle fleet.

Or a bank that's suddenly 'green' because you can conduct your finances online, or a grocery store that's 'green' because they'll take back your plastic grocery bags, or ...

You get the picture!

Speaking

Look at the following examples of environmental claims that have been made by businesses. Would you say that these are examples of greenwashing or do they demonstrate genuine environmental commitment?

1 A US deodorant manufacturer has placed bright labels on spray canisters which guarantee that they contain no CFC gases.

2 The president of a British group which includes several airline companies has announced plans to open the Caribbean's first eco-friendly resort on a private island that he owns in the West Indies.

3 A major petroleum company is running an ad which shows one of its factories with flowers growing out of the chimneys. The slogan says: 'We use our waste CO_2 to grow flowers'.

4 A car manufacturer has produced an advertising campaign which shows one of its cars on a deserted road in a beautiful wild landscape. The text of the advertisement mentions that future buyers need not feel guilty as the car is 'carbon neutral'.

@ An Internet search using the keyword 'greenwashing' will list companies and products that have been accused of greenwashing. Choose one example to discuss.

Career skills

Taking responsibility

Part of a manager's or team leader's task is to take responsibility when things go wrong. This can cover a wide range of problems from admitting that a deadline can't be met to dealing with a major crisis which involves negative media cover. It is important to have an effective crisis management plan in place in order to restore confidence quickly and limit damage as much as possible when problems occur.

The following are some strategies for effectively taking responsibility in a crisis.

1 Acknowledge there is a crisis

The quicker you accept that there is a problem, the quicker a solution can be found. Say that you recognise the consequences and that steps are being taken to limit any further damage. In the case of bad publicity, always contact the press to say that you are aware of the problem and that something is being done.

2 Address the issues

Accept responsibility for you and/or your team's part in the application of weak or ineffective strategies and decisions. In the case of damage to the reputation of the company, apologise publicly for any distress caused by the company's actions.

3 Describe the positive action that is being taken by the company

Explain what steps are being taken to right any wrong doings and to avoid similar problems in the future.

4 Challenge information you know to be wrong

In a time of crisis, people panic and rumours spread quickly. Gently deny any false information. Unchallenged rumours are as damaging as facts.

5 Divert the attention to something positive

It is important to restore confidence and raise staff morale in a crisis. You can do this by talking about past and present successes in other areas. You can talk about the fundamental values of the company and refer to any CSR policies that the company has.

Look at the following examples of useful language.

a We have set up a quality control department which will help avoid any recurrences.

b It's not true that our department was warned about a possible ...

c I'm afraid that, this time, our usual formula didn't make the grade.

d These are serious allegations and we are not taking them lightly.

e Our company has always been deeply committed to ...

f We are shocked and saddened to hear that conditions in our suppliers' factories are substandard.

g We have always subscribed to fair trade practices in the past and will continue to do so.

h We have changed suppliers and should meet delivery deadlines from now on.

i It is simply misleading to imply that ...

j I'm fully aware of the current situation and our department is on to it.

Now match phrases a–j with the five strategies outlined above.

1 ___J___   2 ___f,c___   3 ___h, a___   4 ___b, i___   5 ___e, g___

A major pharmaceutical company sells a drug that has been producing serious side effects in patients using it. A 'whistleblower' has said that the pharmaceutical company launched the drug onto the market even though clinical trials revealed that it had negative side effects.

Listen to a journalist interviewing a spokesman from the company.

1   Which of the strategies opposite did the spokesman use when accepting responsibility?

2   Do you think he handled the situation well?

Speaking   **Choose one of the following scenarios and, working with a partner, prepare a short interview. Student A should play the role of the journalist and Student B that of the company spokesperson.**

1 Fruitolito is a company which produces natural fruit juices using only organic fruit. The company has expanded rapidly. However, because it seeks to provide genuine natural-tasting juices it does not pasteurise its products. The communication department has just received news that the government health agency has detected bacterial agents in a recent batch of Fruitolito apple juice and is recommending that all stocks be withdrawn immediately from all stores. The press are now asking to speak to a company representative.

2 The Paminoco Corporation is specialised in providing entertainment solutions for young people and especially children. The company produces films, toys and also runs entertainment parks in several countries. Recently Paminoco has launched a series of spectacular websites where young children can interact with other children in a virtual online environment where they can also see a selection of the goods and accessories that the company has for sale. Recently, a parental association has openly criticised the company, claiming that it is deliberately targeting young people and children in an effort to influence them to buy the company's products. A television journalist has asked to speak to a Paminoco representative.

Culture at work   ## Variations in values

What is perceived as ethical or unethical behaviour can vary from culture to culture. The actions of a company are judged according to a culture's core values. Some cultures, for example, see giving incentives as a natural part of bargaining, whereas it is considered unethical in other cultures. The role of business in society at large is also perceived differently in different cultures. Is business expected to have socially responsible policies in your culture or is the role of business simply to provide jobs and make a profit?

Dilemma & Decision

Dilemma: Called to account

Brief

The Progenerra Corporation is an international utilities company which owns and operates a variety of different types of power generating facilities in different countries around the globe. In the United Kingdom Progenerra possesses several power stations, most of which are now reaching the end of their working lives. All of the company's UK operations use either imported or domestic coal which they burn to produce electricity that is then sold to both industrial and private consumers. One of the company's oldest installations is the Marsdale power station, which is located near the south coast, not far from the coastal environmental reserve which is home to several unique bird and animal species. The technology at the Marsdale plant is rapidly becoming obsolete and last month the company's directors reached a decision on the future of the plant. It will be closed within the next five years but will be replaced by a much larger new generation coal-burning power station which will be able to supply enough electricity for 1.5 million homes. The company has submitted its plans for the new facility to the government and to the local planning authority and is now expecting to begin construction within the next six months.

Alicia Fry, the company's communications director, has just received an email from the director of the Marsdale plant, and what he has to say is not to her liking at all. Apparently as part of a nationwide campaign, a large group of environmental activists has set up a protest camp just outside the plant. They have announced that they will do everything that they can to prevent Progenerra from building a new power station and instead they are asking the company to cease all coal-fuelled power generation. The email also says that there have been unconfirmed reports that the protesters may attempt to enter the Marsdale facility by breaching the perimeter fence in order to force the company to close the plant down.

Task 1

Divide into small groups. You are all members of Alicia Fry's communications team. Using the information provided on page 136, you should decide on the best communications strategy to adopt during the crisis.

Task 2

Alicia Fry has already arranged for her team to give a press conference tomorrow. Prepare a short five-minute statement to be delivered by the spokesperson for your group.

Write it up

Write a short press release explaining Progenerra's position in relation to the Marsdale protest.

For more information, see *Style guide*, page 24.

Decision:

Listen to Daniel James, a public relations consultant, commenting on this dilemma.

1   How had Eon prepared to face the same sort of protest that occured at Marsdale?

2   What argument did the company use to support its plans to build a new power station?

3   Why did the company decide not to negotiate with the protestors?

4   What qualities does Daniel James say are important when dealing with a crisis like this?

Unit 5
Governance

www.longman-elt.com   www.economist.com

Taking charge

Keynotes

Corporate governance is about how public companies are directed and controlled. It is concerned with how company **stakeholders** (shareholders, **regulatory agencies**, as well as customers, suppliers and the community in general) can use tools like **legislation** and **incentives** to ensure that the **board of directors** runs the company in their interests. **Shareholder activism** refers to investors who attempt to alter company behaviour when they are unhappy about the way a company is run. **Independent auditors** such as the **SEC** (Securities and Exchange Commission in the US) and the **FSA** (Financial Services Authority in Britain) put controls in place which hold mangers **accountable** for irregularities. The **Sarbanes-Oxley Act** (SOX) was introduced to ensure honest accountancy and practices in the US.

The role of committees

The boards of most major companies appoint committees to analyse and report back on specific corporate governance issues. The number and titles of committees vary from company to company. However, many major companies will have the following three:

– audit committee
– compensation committee
– nomination committee.

1 Read the extracts from the websites of Pfizer, Microsoft® and Nokia and decide which committee they each refer to.

1 ... establishing annual and long-term performance goals and objectives for the CEO and reviewing the goals approved by the CEO for the members of the Executive Leadership Team.

2 ... must annually evaluate and report to the board on the performance and effectiveness of the board to facilitate the directors fulfilling their responsibilities in a manner that serves the interests of the shareholders.

3 ... established by the Board primarily for the purpose of overseeing the accounting and financial reporting processes of the company and audits of the financial statements of the company.

@ Look at the company websites and read about the other governance committees each company has. Look at what other companies' websites say about governance.

2 Read the headlines from business publications about shareholder activism and say which aspect of corporate governance each one refers to: auditing, compensation or nomination.

1
Investors call for a new chairman

2
SHAREHOLDERS DEMAND 'SAY ON PAY' VOTES

3
ROGUE TRADER TRANSFORMED BANK INTO CASINO!

4
MAJOR SHAREHOLDER CAMPAIGNS TO GET ELECTED TO BOARD

Investors demand explanation for irregularities
5

6
Shareholders say 'no' to severance deals

Corporate governance in Japan

Listen to Tom Standage, business editor at *The Economist*, talking about Japan's attitude to American-style governance, and answer the questions.

1 In what way are the Japanese adopting the American model?
2 Why have they accepted this in spite of their attitude towards American business culture?
3 What kinds of questions are foreign investors asking Japanese companies?
4 What did the Japanese say about the boss of Steel Partners?

Read the text on the opposite page and answer the questions.

1 What was Steel Partners' biggest mistake?
2 How did the Japanese board stop the transaction?
3 What evidence is there of changing attitudes to corporate governance in Japan?

Glossary

storm in a teacup when people get angry or worried about something that is not important

cast into sharp relief brought attention to

villain of the piece the negative or bad person in the situation

hefty big, heavy

thwarted defeated

litmus test something which is regarded as a simple and accurate test of a particular thing

baubles worthless jewels

Corporate governance in Japan

Message in a bottle of sauce

Japan's corporate governance is changing, but it's risky to rush things

1 IT was not a storm in a teacup but a battle over a bottle of sauce. The fight for Bull-Dog Sauce, a Japanese condiment-maker with 27% of the sauce market, cast into sharp relief the conflict between no-holds-barred Anglo-Saxon capitalism and the traditional Japanese approach to corporate governance.

2 The supposed villain of the piece was Steel Partners, an American investment fund that since 2000 has invested more than $3 billion in some 30 Japanese companies. Having built up a 10% stake in Bull-Dog, Steel launched a takeover bid offering to buy all outstanding shares in the company for around $260m, a 20% premium over the share price at the time. Bull-Dog's management opposed the bid. Steel was accused of being a "greenmailer" – a predator that buys a large share in a company, threatens to take it over and then agrees to drop its bid and sell its stake back to the company at a hefty premium. Warren Lichtenstein, Steel's boss, insisted that Steel had a long-term commitment to Bull-Dog. But on a visit to Tokyo to meet Bull-Dog's management, he made matters worse by saying he planned to "educate" and "enlighten" Japanese managers about American-style capitalism.

3 At its shareholder meeting in June, Bull-Dog proposed to enact a "poison pill" defence that involved issuing three new shares for every existing share to all shareholders – except Steel, which would instead receive cash, diluting its original stake. Mr Lichtenstein gave Bull-Dog a warning saying that the poison pill could set a dangerous precedent and deter investment in other Japanese companies. But that, of course, was the whole idea. The poison-pill motion was passed, and although Steel mounted a legal challenge, Bull-Dog's right to use the device was upheld by the courts. So the foreign investors were thwarted, but at great cost to Bull-Dog.

4 The Bull-Dog saga was a litmus test for attitudes to shareholder capitalism. Those who believe that companies should be run to maximise the returns to shareholders thought that shareholders should have accepted Steel's generous offer; but those who hold the traditional Japanese view that companies are social communities, not baubles to be bought and sold, disapproved of Steel's treatment of a venerated 105-year-old company. Gerald Curtis, a Japan-watcher at New York's Columbia University, says Steel's "heavy-handed, flat-footed approach" has made it more difficult for others to argue that companies should pay more attention to their shareholders."

5 However, a Japanese investment fund, Ichigo Asset Management, did manage to successfully persuade shareholders in Tokyo Kohtetsu, a steel company, to reject a merger plan with Osaka Steel. Ichigo, which held a 13% stake in Tokyo Kohtetsu, approved of the logic of the deal but felt that the proposed share-swap, which is a financial arrangement by which shares of one company are exchanged for another, short-changed Tokyo Kohtetsu's shareholders. It was the first time that shareholders in a Japanese company had ever rejected a merger plan. This shows the changing attitudes to shareholder value.

6 Other aspects of Japanese corporate governance are also being slowly transformed. Recently the Japanese government gave Japanese companies a choice of two models of corporate governance: the traditional Japanese system with statutory auditors and an alternative committee-based system, modelled on the American approach, which involves separate audit, remuneration and nomination committees with a majority of outside directors. This was the most explicit example of the government's efforts to encourage Japanese companies to adopt a more American style of corporate governance. ■

1 Do you think that 'companies should be run to maximise the returns to shareholders' as some people connected with the Bull-Dog saga did, or do you believe, like traditionalists in Japan, that 'companies are social communities, not baubles to be bought and sold'?

2 Give examples of how you think the approach of 'Anglo-Saxon capitalism' to business would be manifested. Think about as many different aspects of business as you can, for example attitudes to time, money, people and negotiations.

Vocabulary 1

1 Find words in the text that correspond to the following definitions.

1 A person who purchases enough shares in a firm to threaten a takeover and thereby force the owners to buy those shares back at a premium in order to stay in business. _____

2 A measure undertaken by a corporation to discourage unwanted takeover attempts by diluting the acquirer's share value. _____

3 A corporate alliance in which the acquiring company uses its own stock to pay for the acquired company. _____

2 The meaning of the following expressions is evident from the words used to form them. Write definitions for them and check your answers in a business dictionary.

1 merger plan   _____

2 shareholder value   _____

3 shareholder capitalism _____

3 We read in the text: 'Having built up a 10% stake in Bull-Dog, Steel *launched a takeover bid*'. There are other examples of verb–noun collocations in the text. Find the verbs used with the following nouns.

1 _____ a warning   4 _____ a challenge
2 _____ an offer   5 _____ a right
3 _____ a motion   6 _____ a view

4 Other verbs may be used with the same nouns and this can sometimes create different meanings. Which of the verbs below can we use with the same nouns? Some may be used more than once. Write sentences using the collocations you have formed.

claim	face	have	issue	table	establish

Vocabulary 2

Adjective + past participle

We sometimes use adjective/past participle compounds to create adjectives. Look at this example from the text.

Steel's '*heavy-handed, flat-footed* approach' has made it more difficult for others to argue that companies should pay more attention to their shareholders.

1 Combine the adjectives in column A with the past participle of the infinitives in column B to form compound adjectives.

A	B
close	fetch
deep	forget
far	hit
fast	pace
hard	root
long	run

2 Complete the sentences with the most appropriate compound adjective from exercise 1.

1 _____ by the economic downturn, some companies are seeking government assistance.

2 The _____ traditions in Japanese business culture make introducing reforms difficult.

3 An intense battle is waging between shareholders and the board members and the result will be a _____ thing.

4 Nobody believed the incredible and _____ arguments made by the angry and unreasonable protestors.

5 Cultures which have a flexible attitude to time find it difficult to adapt to the _____ world of American business.

6 Some nostalgic US business gurus are preaching the _____ values and principles of putting people and not profit first.

Usage # Idioms

We use idioms to make our language more colourful and to communicate meaning more efficiently. An example from the text is *a storm in a teacup*. Read the idioms below and see if you can discover their meaning by thinking about the images they create.

1 to drive a hard bargain

2 to put someone on the spot

3 to throw the baby out with the bath water

4 to fight a losing battle

5 to be in the firing line

6 to put a spanner in the works

Match these definitions with the idioms above.

a to try hard to do something when there is no chance of success

b to be in the leading or most vulnerable position in an activity

c to cause problems and prevent something from happening as planned

d to demand a lot or refuse to give much when making an agreement with someone

e to lose the good parts when you get rid of the bad parts of something

f to cause someone difficulty or make them embarrassed by forcing them to make a difficult decision

Listening 2 ⊙ # The great pay debate

1 Listen to part 1 of an interview with business journalist Carl Underwood about his report 'The great pay debate' and answer the questions.

1 Why are people so angry about CEOs' pay?

2 What do shareholders hope to achieve by gaining some control over pay?

2 Now listen to part 2. How does the speaker justify high salaries?

Speaking **Do you think that CEOs should be paid extremely high salaries?**

Read the text below which gives a journalist's opinion on the same subject. Does he/she think that ...

1 pay is too high?
2 bad governance is the reason for high pay? Why/Why not?
3 legislation placing restrictions on levels of pay would be a good idea? Why/Why not?

The Economist

Glossary

under the thumb under the influence or power of someone

bonanza boom

crack the whip show who's in charge

cronies close friends

Corporate governance and pay
Let the fight begin

Give shareholders a vote on pay; but don't let regulators interfere too much

1 "OBSCENE", "bizarre", "a scourge": Europe's politicians are in no doubt that bosses' high pay is a scandal. If they are right, the continent's companies are in grave danger. Executive pay is not only a measure of what society judges as fair; it is also a test of whether a business is run for its shareholders. If a board can motivate managers, it will get the best out of them. If it cannot stand up to the chief executive and his cronies over their pay, then it will struggle to control them when they want to buy this dud rival or diversify into that dead-end business.

2 But are the politicians right? They have certainly caught the mood in equality-conscious Europe, where the millions earned by some are stirring up resentment. Politicians in the Netherlands, France and Germany are squaring up to bosses over pay and America is joining in. But while it is easy to find executives who look undeserving it is far harder to show that managers in general are overpaid. At companies owned by private equity, for

example, the board and the shareholders are one and the same: their directors are hardly under the thumb of managers. But they still believe managers make enough difference in a company to spend money on hiring the best ones. Indeed, they are willing to pay successful bosses several times more than listed firms do.

3 Managers' pay has grown faster than workers' pay, but the reasons for this are not sinister. Whereas workers' pay depends on the labour market (and has been kept down by the huge numbers of people joining the global economy), managers' bonuses are chiefly tied to returns on capital. Boards introduced stock options and hurdles because investors wanted executives to worry about profits. Profits have recently been good, so pay has been high. Similarly, as the assets inside companies grow, you would expect them to pay more in the market for talent.

4 Governance in Europe is not perfect but European boards have generally

done more than American boards to link pay to performance. And pay, though lower, has broadly tracked the increases in America over the past few decades even as monitoring by shareholders has improved. That is not what you would expect if poor governance were behind the bonanza. So politicians should reject laws about pay, which are too sweeping to be useful. Legislation and demagoguery will only drive managers away from listed companies and make pay packages even more complex – and so harder to monitor.

5 At the same time, boards will sometimes fall victim to overmighty bosses. Hence politicians need to insist that shareholders can hold the board to account through a vote on pay – as, indeed, they can in many countries. That will not lead to peace over pay. But how could it do so when shareholders sometimes need to crack the whip? ∎

Discourse markers

Discourse markers are words or expressions that we use to mark transitions between different segments of our speech and writing. They help to convey our attitudes to what we are communicating and send signals to our readers or listeners to help them to follow what we are saying or writing. Here are some common discourse markers.

actually	anyway	by and large	by the way	finally
first of all	for instance	furthermore	luckily	on the whole
so	such as	then	to sum up	unfortunately

1 Which of these discourse markers are used mainly in the following forms of communication?

1   informal or spoken discourse
2   formal or written discourse
3   both spoken and written discourse

2 Discourse markers can serve a number of different purposes. Decide which of the words and expressions above could be used for each purpose.

1   to summarise or generalise   _____
2   to present examples   _____
3   to indicate an attitude   _____
4   to sequence or to list   _____
5   to signal a change of topic   _____

 For more information see page 156.

Choose the most appropriate discourse markers in italics to complete the text below.

GETTING INTERNATIONAL DIRECTORS ON BOARD

Some of Canada's largest companies are increasingly seeking to appoint international directors to their boards, often preferring those with global experience over directors who have never worked abroad. ¹*Generally speaking/Luckily/By the way*, the boards of Canada's biggest companies tend to be staffed by regional directors with only 4% of directors from outside. While some major companies, ²*say/such as/otherwise* Canada's big banks ³*for instance/then/futhermore*, have focused on achieving national representation on their boards, executive search consultants say that recruiting non-Canadians is now rapidly becoming a priority for many organisations. ⁴*In fact/Of course/Then*, it would appear that companies are now seeking insights and experience from outside Canada's borders rather than from within. This is in sharp contrast to US board recruitment where, ⁵*moreover/anyway/surprisingly*, the number of non-national directors is quite low. As Dwight Jefferson says, '⁶*Quite/Frankly/Absolutely* I don't understand why US boards are not hiring directors who have had international exposure. For me it just doesn't make

sense, ⁷*obviously/naturally/especially* at a time like this when almost all businesses have some exposure to international markets.' ⁸*As a matter of fact/In general/By and large*, even some Canadian companies which do not operate outside Canada are also interested in hiring non-nationals. CaltechMining, ⁹*such as/nonetheless/for example*, has recently appointed Romano Skodi to its board. As Piet Svenson, the

company's president, says: 'It's just a question of time because ¹⁰*subsequently/initially/ultimately* all companies will have to face the fact that the market is getting tougher and more global ¹¹*actually/so/generally* bringing in people who have experience outside Canada is the best way to prepare for that.'

Career skills

Presenting arguments

When you present an argument for/against something or a particular course of action, it is important to be convincing, firm and tactful. There are different approaches to presenting arguments and your choice may depend on the personalities and relationships involved. However, your chances of success will greatly increase, in all cases, if you build solid arguments based on persuasive and realistic points. The following are some approaches.

a Use your place in the hierarchy.
b Base your argument on reason and logic.
c Create a sense of common purpose.
d Offer a counter argument.

need fact, not opinion
politics, religion
fact can not win
(change people's mind)

Complete the headings below with points a–d above.

1 _C: create a sense of common purpose_

To get people 'on board' or to follow your line of thinking, you can first talk about something you know you agree on before putting forward your point of view.

2 _b: base your argument on reason and logic_

Show the listener that you have researched the area and draw on examples to give 'proof' or evidence to support your case. Where possible quote from reliable sources that your listeners have confidence in.

3 _d: offer a counter argument_

Addressing the claims of the opposition is an important component in building a strong argument. Conceding to some of your listeners' concerns shows respect for their opinions and makes them more likely to listen seriously to your argument.

4 _a: use your place in the hierarchy_

This is not always the most effective way to get people to adhere to or agree with your arguments; but sometimes people who hold powerful positions give ultimatums and threats which force people to adopt this position. It is often used only as a last resort.

Speaking

Read the scenarios below. Then, in pairs, discuss the approach(es) mentioned above that you would use to present your arguments in each case.

(a) use hierarchy
(b)

1 Several smokers have been smoking in the staff canteen despite the 'No smoking' signs. You are the manager and have been asked by some non smokers to enforce the no smoking rule.

(b) (c)
(d)

2 You are an assistant buyer in a department store. You want your boss to introduce a new line of hats that is selling well at your competitors' stores. She thinks they are too expensive for your price range.

(c)

3 You are a team leader. You want your team to work overtime for the next two weeks in order to reach a tight and important deadline.

Listening 3 ⊙ **Answer the following questions after listening to each of the three recordings of people presenting arguments.**

1 The speaker wants the listeners to take a particular course of action. What is it?
2 What arguments does the speaker use?
3 The speaker uses a mix of approaches to present his/her arguments. Which ones from the list opposite are used?
4 Which discourse markers does the speaker use and how effective are they?
5 Do you find the speaker convincing? Why/Why not?

Speaking **Work in pairs to debate the following controversial issues. Student A, choose and present arguments in defence of the first issue. Student B, choose and present arguments against it. Then swap roles for the second issue, and so on.**

1 More women should be appointed as board members.
2 CEOs whose companies have been involved in corporate crime should be sent to prison.
3 Board members should not be allowed to sit on the boards of more than one company.
4 Companies should be legally responsible for damage caused by their subsidiaries.

@ An Internet search using the keywords 'controversial business issues' will list further issues which you can debate in the same way.

Culture at work **Giving an opinion** *should be based on facts. = credibility*

In some hierarchy-centered cultures, junior colleagues are never expected or permitted to oppose their boss's opinions or to propose alternative ideas or solutions which they think are better. In more open cultures, brainstorming sessions are organised so that all levels of the hierarchy can present arguments and counter-arguments for the different situations and solutions being discussed. Which is closest to your culture? How might this difference cause misunderstanding in multinational teams?

Dilemma & Decision

Dilemma: When to listen to the shareholders

Brief

Joe McKenna & Sons, a chain of DIY stores, is one of the biggest retailing success stories in business today. The company has its roots in 1890 when Joe McKenna started selling tools door-to-door in rural areas. He later expanded his range of products for mail order selling, to reach more isolated areas. Eventually he opened stores to support the rapidly expanding catalogue-based business. By the 1980s the stores were operating right across America and Joe McKenna was a household name. By then, the company had gone public but with family members still running the day-to-day business. It was no longer only a retail business as Tod McKenna, his son, had diversified into the lucrative area of insurance and later Ed McKenna, his grandson, bought a real estate company.

But by the 1990s, stores were rapidly losing market share. Discount stores and big trendy competitors flooded the market. Joe McKenna & Sons' image looked dated and unappealing. However, they survived the 90s thanks to their thriving insurance and real estate subsidiaries. But shareholders started to feel restless. They insisted on a complete restructuring of the company. They called for the separation of the roles of CEO and chairman of the board. They felt it would be better to break the traditional management style of the family with a dynamic new CEO. They wanted the company to 'spin off' the profit-making subsidiaries by selling them to shareholders so as to invest in the core retail business which they felt could regain its market share. The board had to decide whether or not it was time to let the shareholders make strategic decisions for the company.

Decision:

Listen to what Jerry Adams, a business journalist, has to say about what really happened.

1 Did the board initially listen to the shareholders?

2 Why did the board's initial decision appear to be satisfactory?

3 Which prize did the company win in 2009?

4 According to Jerry Adams, what does this case demonstrate?

Task 1

The board appointed two speakers to help them make up their minds. Student A is the board representative who feels the board should do what the shareholders advise. Use the information on page 137 to build arguments to support your case. Student B feels that the best way forward is for the board to ignore shareholder demands and build their own strategy for future growth. Use the information on page 138 to build arguments to support your case.

Task 2

Meet to present your arguments.

Task 3

Try to agree on which course of action the board should take.

Write it up

Write a press release explaining the decision.

For more information, see *Style guide*, page 24.

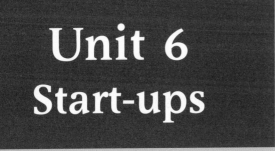

Unit 6
Start-ups

www.longman-elt.com   www.economist.com

Going into business

Keynotes

New business **ventures** originate when **entrepreneurs** set up companies either to sell innovative products or services or to compete against established businesses. Before starting a new business, entrepreneurs often conduct **market research** to determine the **validity** of their idea and the **feasibility** of their business model. All start-ups face a high degree of risk and it is estimated that only twenty per cent of new businesses are actually successful in the long term. Future entrepreneurs always have to provide a **business plan** in which they describe their concept and their business approach. They may receive assistance from outside organisations such as **incubators** and **venture capital firms** or from individual **business angels**, usually in exchange for a **stake** in the company. Start-ups can be funded either directly by the founders or by using **capital** provided by **investors** or **banks**. In some countries governments may provide low-interest loans or interest-free **grants** to entrepreneurs.

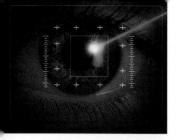

New ideas

1 How creative are you? Look at the following questions from a creativity quiz. Decide whether you agree (✓) or disagree (✗) with each of the statements, then turn to page 139 for an analysis of their significance.

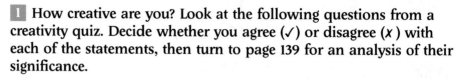

1 ☒ I don't mind if I break the rules when I am doing something.
2 ☑ I like to spend time daydreaming, even when I am working on a project.
3 ☒ I usually do things in a logical manner.
4 ☒ People sometimes object to my opinions.
5 ☒ What other people think of me is very important.
6 ☒ I prefer working in a team to working on my own.

2 Work in pairs. Compare your answers. How can your answers to these questions reveal how creative you are?

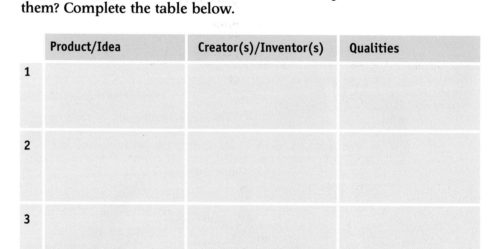

3 Look at the illustrations of some famous products that were introduced by entrepreneurs. What do you know about the people who created them? How do you think they got the ideas for their products or services?

Listening 1 ⊙ Listen to Howard Wiseman, a consultant in business start-ups, talking about how three innovators developed their ideas. What qualities did each of them possess and what can future entrepreneurs learn from them? Complete the table below.

	Product/Idea	Creator(s)/Inventor(s)	Qualities
1			
2			
3			

Reading 1 **Setting up**

Read the text on the opposite page and answer the questions that follow.

@ An Internet search using the name 'Endeavor' will list websites that mention Linda Rottenberg. Find an example of a video interview with her.

Glossary

stigmatised regarded as disgraceful

seed capital money allocated to start up a project

doggedness persistence or tenacity

Entrepreneurship
Spreading the word

An effort to promote entrepreneurship in the developing world is bearing fruit

1 EARLIER this year Mario Chady faced a crucial decision. Having built up Spoleto, his chain of casual Italian restaurants, to 150 outlets in Brazil, and opened in Mexico and Spain, the time had come for Mr Chady to choose between expanding into America or putting the idea on hold. To help make up his mind, he asked for help from an organisation called Endeavor, which had chosen him as a potential "high-impact entrepreneur".

2 Endeavor is a non-profit group dedicated to promoting entrepreneurship in emerging economies. But as he spoke to members of the Endeavor network, ranging from leading business tycoons to fellow up-and-coming entrepreneurs, he became convinced that it was the right strategy but the wrong time. Mr Chady decided to concentrate on expanding even faster in Brazil, and leave America for later. It is routine for entrepreneurs to consult their networks of mentors in Silicon Valley. But in much of the world, such networks are notable by their absence – and so, too, are examples of Silicon Valley-style successful entrepreneurship.

3 "Why can't the next Silicon Valley pop up in Cairo or São Paulo or Johannesburg?" asks Linda Rottenberg, who co-founded Endeavor with Peter Kellner, a venture capitalist. Fresh from Yale, she was working in Buenos Aires for Ashoka, an organisation that supports social entrepreneurs – people with innovative, usually non-profit ideas for solving social problems – and concluded that ordinary entrepreneurs needed a similar support system. Much of the difference between countries where entrepreneurship thrives, and those where it does not, is cultural rather than regulatory, she believes. In many emerging economies, business tends to be dominated by a closed elite hostile to new entrepreneurs – and failure is stigmatised, rather than being a badge of honour as it is in Silicon Valley.

The making of a start-up

4 Getting Endeavor started required some classic start-up doggedness of its own. At first, the philanthropic foundations Ms Rottenberg courted regarded the project as too elitist. Eventually Stephan Schmidheiny, a Swiss industrialist who has given away a large chunk of his fortune in Latin America, was persuaded to provide some seed capital, and Endeavor was up and running. Endeavor's magic works most powerfully in its selection process. Entrepreneurs are screened first by a national panel of successful businessmen, and then, if they are short-listed, by an international panel. So far over 18,000 entrepreneurs have been screened but fewer than 400 have been chosen.

5 Once the selection process is over, these business figures then become mentors to the entrepreneurs. "Endeavor's genius has been to get the establishment in these countries together, not to kill these entrepreneurial companies but to support them," says Bill Sahlman, a professor at Harvard Business School who was recruited as an adviser early on.

6 Endeavor's entrepreneurs – who collectively now control companies with combined revenues of $2.4 billion and 91,000 employees – rarely say they would not have succeeded without Endeavor. But they all believe they got bigger much sooner thanks to its endorsement and support.

7 One of Endeavor's earliest successes was Wenceslao Casares, who sold Patagon, his Argentine Internet brokerage, to Banco Santander for $705m at the peak of the dotcom bubble. He believes Endeavor has started to change cultural attitudes in the countries where it has been active for a while. "When I said I was going to start a business, it was against everyone's advice, from my family to my university," he says. "Now, go to the same university and the same professors will tell you that one of their goals is to produce good entrepreneurs."

8 Brazil is perhaps most vibrant of all. Endeavor's successes include Leila Velez, who grew up in a favela and whose beauty salon firm, Beleza Natural, now has revenues of $30m, and Bento Koike, whose wind-turbine-blade manufacturing firm, Tecsis, recently struck a $1 billion deal to supply mighty General Electric.

Going global

9 Endeavor has "created islands of hope," says Mr Casares. Now it must find ways to "change continents, not just little islands." Endeavor is confident that it now knows how to adapt its model to new countries, having learnt from early stumbles in Chile, South Africa and Turkey.

10 Funding has long been a problem for Endeavor. As a non-profit, it has to rely on donors. Would it make more sense to be a for-profit operation? Endeavor has struggled constantly with whether to pursue profits, but each time has concluded no, says Ms Rottenberg. "If Endeavor had been an investor, rather than an independent, objective, non-profit enabler, it would not have been trusted by the business elite, or the entrepreneurs," she insists. "Trust is everything." ∎

Read the summaries below, which relate to individual paragraphs in the text. Tick those that are accurate and amend the others.

1 After successfully launching his restaurant business, Mario Chady took the decision to enter the US market. (para 1) _not to enter the US market._

2 Linda Rottenberg founded Endeavor with a partner. (para 3) _correct_

3 Endeavor was launched with money collected from a group of would-be entrepreneurs. (para 4) _donated by a philanthropist._

4 New businesses that have been chosen by Endeavor can get assistance from members of the selection panels. (para 5) _correct_

5 Endeavor has revenues of several billion dollars and a staff of almost 100,000. (para 6) _Businesses that have been promoted by Endeavor have revenues_

6 Attitudes towards entrepreneurship in some countries are changing as a result of Endeavor's activities. (para 7) _correct_

7 One of the companies that Endeavor assisted has recently been taken over by General Electric. (para 8) _has signed a major contract with_

8 Endeavor has decided not to expand its activities to new countries. (para 9) _____

Speaking

What do people in your country think about entrepreneurs? Are they seen as role models? Is failure 'stigmatised' or seen as 'a badge of honour'?

Vocabulary 1

Find the words in the text that are used to describe people who ...

1 create new businesses _entrepreneur_
2 support and advise people _mentor/ advisor_
3 are wealthy and powerful business people _business tycoon/ business elite_
4 invest in new businesses _venture capitalist/ investor_
5 have interests in manufacturing _industrial_
6 create organisations for social change _social entrepreneur_

Vocabulary 2

Verbs with prepositions

Some verbs are often used with specific prepositions. Look at these examples from the text:

to concentrate on   *to learn from*   *to choose between*

1 Match the verbs in column A with the prepositions in column B. Some verbs may take more than one preposition.

2 Complete the text with the verbs and prepositions from the table.

A	B
account _for_	for
amount _to (等于)_	from
benefit _from_ ~受益	in
differ _from_	on
focus _on_	to
rely _on_	with
result _in/from_	
succeed _in/to_	
suffer _from_	

accounts for / accounted for / accounting for
focuss on / focused on / focusing on
suffers from / suffered from / suffering from
amounts to / amounted to / amounting to
relies on / relied on / relying on
benefits from / benefitted from / benefiting from
results / resulted / resulting
differs from / differed from / differing from
succeeds / succeeded / succeeding

Social entrepreneurs ¹ _differ from_ business entrepreneurs in the objectives that they set. Whereas traditional business ventures have only one priority – profit-making – social entrepreneurs create organisations whose activities will ² _result in_ more than just profits. One such example is the Prakti company in India. Prakti ³ _relies on_ investments from both private individuals and venture capitalists to design, manufacture and distribute efficient, non-polluting cooking stoves. If the company ⁴ _succeeds in_ penetrating the Indian market, millions of Indians will stand to ⁵ _benefit from_ their invention.

62 ■ Unit 6

Expressions with *and*

There are many expressions where two words are combined with *and*. However, such expressions are used in different ways depending on whether they are adjectives, adverbs, nouns or verbs. Look at this example from the text:

... fellow **up-and-coming** (adj) entrepreneurs

1 Look at a selection of other similar expressions. Choose words from the list to complete them.

~~above~~   don'ts   downs   ~~error~~   ~~far~~   ins   ~~give~~   loss   pick   pieces

1 _give_ and take adj/n
2 dos and _don'ts_ n
3 bits and _pieces_ n
4 _far_ and away adv
5 ups and _downs_ n

6 over and _above_ adv
7 profit and _loss_ n/adj
8 _pick_ and choose v
9 _ins_ and outs detail n
10 trial and _error_ adj/n

2 Complete the sentences with an appropriate expression.

1 When you start a new business you don't always have a precise business model, which means that very often you have to learn by _trial and error_.

2 The Rockliffe Foundation reviewed more than 100 applications for its entrepreneurial award, but _far and away_ the best project was Bill Sutton's Micromechanical Robot.

3 Small businesses can learn from experienced entrepreneurs who know the _ins and outs_ of obtaining finance.

4 In the start-up phase of an enterprise, unexpectedly high costs can arise. For example, inventory must be calculated _over and above_ the payments to suppliers.

5 Any new venture is bound to go through difficult moments, so being able to handle the _ups and downs_ of starting your own business is critical.

6 The Start-Up Emporium is a network of entrepreneurs which allows its members to _pick and choose_ suitable partners, advisors or investors.

3 What other expressions with *and* do you know?

The birth of a business

Listen to an interview in which Bruno Guattari talks about how he started his company Comptoir Atlantique. Then answer the questions.

1 How did Bruno's professional background help the development of his start-up?

2 What was Comptoir Atlantique's original main activity?

3 What support did Bruno receive from his family?

4 Where was the company first run from?

5 How did he go about financing his venture?

6 What problems did Bruno have during the first years of business?

7 How has the company evolved in recent times?

8 What are his plans for the future?

Third conditional

We use this to speculate about past events, actions and situations. It consists of two clauses: a conditional clause with *if* + past perfect, and a main clause with a past modal (*would/might/could/should* + *have*) + past participle.

In the conditional clause, we use a negative verb when we refer to something that actually happened and an affirmative verb to refer to something that did not happen (but could have). Third conditionals are often used to express functions such as regret, apology, accusation, excuse and relief.

Look at the following comments made by entrepreneurs. Do the conditional clauses refer to events that occurred (✓) or to things that did not (✗)? Which comment expresses (a) relief, (b) regret, (c) excuse, (d) accusation?

1 If I hadn't already had experience of working for a start-up, it would have been much harder for me to build the company. In fact I'm not even sure that I would have succeeded. __✓__ , __a__

2 It took much longer than I thought it would to get the business off the ground. But if we'd had access to more capital, we would have broken even much sooner. __✗__ , __b__

3 The main problem we had was that my partner and I didn't agree on how to position our product. I believe that if we'd followed my plan we would have generated enough sales to keep us in business. __✗__ , __d__

4 My bank manager told me to improve my financial skills. But even if I had, I don't think it would have made any difference – nothing would because the market just wasn't ready for something so different. __✗__ , __c__

Complete the following passage with appropriate conditional forms.

After working for ten years as an engineer, Andrea Sabatini was made redundant. As he says, 'At that time the job market was pretty tight in my field so even if I (¹find) _had found_ a new job, I don't think it (²pay) _would have paid_ anything like the same salary that I was getting before.'

After six months the only offer that he had received was for a position abroad: 'If I (³take) _had taken_ the job, it (⁴mean) _would have (meant)_ moving to Canada with my wife and children and even if we (⁵do) _had done_ that, the salary wasn't tempting.'

Eventually Andrea accepted a position with an engineering company and that was the first step on his path to becoming an entrepreneur. 'If I (⁶accept) _had not accepted_ that position, I don't think I (⁷end up) _would have (ended up)_ becoming an entrepreneur.'

In his new position Andrea worked in research and development, but in his spare time he had access to the company's facilities. He used that time to develop a new concept for a mini surveillance robot but when he proposed the idea to his boss, it was rejected. 'If they (⁸want to) _had wanted_ , they (⁹develop) _could have (developed)_ it because there was a real market for a product like that. But they weren't interested in robotics. So I went ahead on my own and today I'm managing a business which has a turnover of several million euros and provides work for thirty-five people. There's always an element of luck in everything. I mean it (¹⁰turn out) _might/could have turned out_ so differently.'

Think of a situation in the past when you were affected by an important event. What were the consequences of this event? What would have/could have/might have changed if this event had not happened in the way that it did? Share your thoughts with a partner.

| Reading 2 | **The business plan** |

A business plan helps a new venture to clarify its business model, solidify its goals and present itself to potential investors. The structure usually follows a conventional format with headings for all the key information that a potential investor will need to know.

a ~~The business~~   f Industry analysis
b ~~Executive summary~~ g Financial plan
c Critical risk factors   h Operations plan
d Management team   i Company structure, ownership and
e Marketing plan   intellectual property

1 Insert the appropriate heading from a–i above each section.

1 *b. Executive summary*

This section provides an overview of the business plan. Potential investors will focus on this section before asking for the complete plan. If it does not present a clear summary of what the new venture is setting out to achieve, it is unlikely that potential investors will read further. It is best written once the rest of the plan has been finalised.

2 *g Financial plan*

This is where the entrepreneur has to demonstrate the financial validity of the business by discussing the funding requirements and detailing the financial projections over a three-year period. This section should also show investors what sort of return they can expect on their investment and what provisions have been made in the event of the business being sold.

3 *d. management team*

The strength, experience and skills of the people who will manage the venture are of primary importance. Venture capitalists will want to know if they have the necessary qualifications and the right background. This section should also include the composition of the board of directors and the names of the legal, accounting and consulting firms that the venture will be working with.

4 *i Company Structure, ownership and intellectual property*

Tensions between the partners of a new venture often arise from a failure to clearly define who will be responsible for what. A business plan should always include an organisation chart showing exactly what the reporting relationships will be This section of the plan should also present the legal framework under which the company will operate and indicate what trademarks, patents and copyrights the venture owns.

5 *f Industry analysis*

This section discusses industry size and the major trends in the industry in which the new venture will be competing. It should also describe the business's target market and show how its products will be situated in relation to those of its competitors.

6 ~~b~~ *e marketing plan*

This is where a new venture must be able to show not only that it has a product which people will be interested in buying but also that it has a realistic plan for getting its product into the hands of those buyers. There should be a complete presentation of the product and a full description of how it will be priced, distributed and promoted.

7 *h Operations plan*

This section deals with the day-to-day running of the company. If the business is planning to manufacture a product, there should be a full description to show where this activity will take place and how much work will be done in-house or by subcontractors. Questions of quality control and customer support should also be addressed.

8 *a The business*

This should give a short description of the opportunity that the entrepreneur has identified – that is, the problem to be solved or the need to be filled – and then describe how the business will address these issues and what competitive advantage it will benefit from.

9 *c Critical risk factors*

No business plan is complete without a frank discussion of the potential dangers that a new venture faces. What those are depends on various factors such as pending patent applications or the recruitment of qualified specialist personnel.

2 Read the following extracts from a business plan. In which sections of the plan would they appear?

1 FlashGarb has now been registered as a limited company in the UK. *Company structure, ownership and intellectual property*

2 David Gestner will take full responsibility for the research and development of electronic systems and interfaces. *management team*

3 Prospective customers include a number of well-established brands which have already informally expressed interest in FlashGarb's original concept. *marketing plan*

4 The components for the modulator system will be imported from selected domestic and overseas suppliers and assembled in situ. *Operations plan*

5 The remaining capital will be sourced partly from a regional business development fund and partly from a national UK bank. *financial plan*

Career skills

Pitching

Pitching is the art of presenting a business idea or proposal to a decision maker, potential investor, supplier, customer, colleague or employee. The 'elevator pitch' is a brief summary of the business opportunity being presented. It comes from the image of the short period of time you spend with someone in an elevator. A 'sales pitch' focuses on the product or service only and is generally aimed at customers. Every pitch has to be adapted to the listener. However, whether it is for a formal presentation to a group, or an informal exchange with an individual, the guidelines below will make the pitch more effective.

a Remember pitching is selling.
b Make a call to action.
c Know your audience.
d Capture the interest of the listener at the start.
e Show the differences with competitors.

1 Match the guidelines a–e to each of the points below.

1 _d_

Say what the idea is at the outset. Use a slogan or catchy phrase to sum up the idea. Don't spend the first part of your pitch talking about yourself and your background. People want to hear what it is you're selling first. If you capture their interest in the first minute, the chances are that they will listen carefully all the way through the pitch.

2 _c_

Preparation is key. Do some research before meeting the target audience and try to discover their expectations. Address those expectations by telling them how the product or service will impact them. If you are talking to a future investor or a bank manager, for example, you will need to outline the business plan and talk about the financial projections.

3 _a_

Be passionate and engaging about your suggestion, proposal or product. Tell a story about how the idea came to you or how your product has already solved a customer's problem. People engage with real-life stories.

4 _e_

Outline the special features which give your product or service an edge over the competitors.

5 _b_

Set a time for a follow-up meeting. In most situations, people don't decide on the spot whether they are interested or not. Make sure you get a commitment from them to consider your project or product.

2 Using the information above, make a list of dos and don'ts for pitching.

DOs	DON'Ts
use a catchy slogan, prepare and research, tell a story, outline special features, capture people's interest in the first minutes, organize a follow-up meeting	talk about yourself and background, walk away without an appointment.

1 Listen to three pitches and answer the questions below.

1 What is being pitched in each one, a product, a service or a proposition?

2 Is the listener a potential customer, a potential investor or a colleague?

3 Which of the techniques opposite did the speaker use?

2 How successful do you think the start-up ideas mentioned in the listening will be?

Speaking

Work in pairs. Read the descriptions of recent start-ups below. Choose one and then prepare a short sales pitch that you would use to promote the product or service to potential customers. Take turns to deliver the pitch to your partner. Discuss your reactions. For example, would this pitch make you go out and buy the product or service?

2 Chicago-based ElementBars.com aims to give users a simple, step-by-step process for designing their own energy bars. Using the site's drag-and-drop interface, customers begin by selecting a 'core' that defines the bar's texture and base. They can then add nuts, fruits and sweets as well as protein, fibre, Omega-3 and vitamin boosts. Once the customer's order is complete, ElementBars will hand-make and deliver them in about a week; pricing is $3 per bar, with a minimum order of one box of 12 bars.

1 Geneva-based LunaJets takes advantage of the fact that many private jets fly empty when they return home after dropping passengers off or when they head out to pick passengers up. The company works with a select set of jet operators to maintain a database of all such 'empty leg' flights, as they are known, and allows users to browse that database to find flights that match their own needs. Travellers can book anything from a single seat to a whole cabin on flights shorter than two and a half hours; on longer flights, they must reserve the whole cabin. Booking and payment can both be handled online, and prices are fixed and open, beginning at €890 for a single seat on a flight up to one hour long.

3 Aqua by Grandstand is a mobile lifestyle and night-spot venue created from fold-out 'transformer' units. The two-storey-high mobile party platform is modelled out of shipping containers using a transforming mechanism that allows a single container to open up to three times its original size. Accordingly, Aqua's bar-lounge can cater to as many as 500 guests and can be constructed at any location in the world complete with electricity, audio-visual and hospitality equipment.

Writing

Write your sales pitch out in full. Use your feedback notes from above and improve on your original pitch.

Culture at work

Pitching styles

When pitching in a multicultural context, it is even more important than usual to learn about the listener first. Some cultures expect the focus to be on facts and figures. They may appreciate passion and enthusiasm, but value serious and factual pitches more. Others expect pitches to be first and foremost entertaining and pithy – but still expect pitches to have some substance. Where would the focus lie in your culture?

Dilemma & Decision

Dilemma: Finding the funds

Brief

The dilemma that most young entrepreneurs face is not finding a good business idea but finding the money to get it off the ground. There are different ways of finding the money to start a business.

Task 1

In groups, read the following descriptions of ideas for start-up ventures. Choose one of the ideas and then use the questions below to further develop the business opportunity.

1 You are a young fashion designer with a wonderful new collection which you want to launch under your own brand.

2 You want to set up an e-commerce site which will offer personalised gifts and educational toys for babies and young children.

3 You want to set up a retail business in exclusive lines of stationery and pens. You are considering trying to get premises at your local central railway station which is currently being developed and managed by a large private contractor.

– What will be your company/brand name?

– Who is your target market?

– What type of location/premises will you need?

– What price can you charge and what kind of profit margins do you hope to make?

– How much advertising will you need to do?

– Will you need to recruit employees? If so, how many?

Task 2

Decide which of the methods of funding outlined here would be best suited to the venture that you have chosen to develop.

Task 3

Prepare a full business pitch that you would use to obtain funding. Meet with another group who have chosen to develop a different business. Present your pitches and give feedback on how you think a potential investor would react.

Write it up

Write a formal letter to a venture capitalist, requesting an appointment to discuss the funding of the business venture that you presented in your pitch.

For more information, see *Style guide*, page 14.

Decision:

⊙ Listen to Oliver Peters, a venture capitalist, talking about the best way to fund these business ideas.

1 Which type of funding does he recommend for each of the business ideas?

2 What does he say about VC funding?

3 Which examples does he give of the other two types of funding?

Personal savings
Fund the business yourself from savings or by getting a second mortgage on your home.

Bank loan
Borrow money from a bank – you will have to provide a guarantee or 'collateral', as it is often called.

Government grants
Governments are often willing to encourage and support new enterprise. This varies enormously from country-to-country, but grants and free consultancy services can sometimes be obtained.

Venture capital
VC firms will sometimes invest large sums of money, essential for businesses with big start-up expenses or that plan to grow quickly, in return for a fast, high rate of return. A VC firm often offers more than just money. For example, it might have good industry contacts or a lot of experience it can provide to the company.

Crowdfunding
This is a financing technique where businesses invite people, via the Internet, to contribute small sums of money in return for a share in the profits and/or other advantages such as free samples of the new product. Success depends on the popularity of the product. Because contributions are small, thousands of investors are needed. Some music bands have raised enough money to make a record like this.

Commercial partnership
Existing businesses with a strategic interest in the success of the new venture may be willing to invest some capital.

Review 2

Language check

Paired structures

1 Combine words from the boxes below to form paired structures. Use each combination once only.

once	whether	neither	both	not only

and	but also	or	nor	then

2 Complete the dialogue below with appropriate paired words from above.

A: We need ^{1}_____ to listen to our share-holders ^{2}_____ to act on what they are saying.

B: Yes but they want us ^{3}_____ to sell our only profit making business ^{4}_____ to increase profits!

A: ^{5}_____ we sell our retail business ^{6}_____ not, we still need to improve the performance of the other sectors.

B: ^{7}_____ we sell off the retail sector we can ^{8}_____ concentrate on making changes to the other sectors.

A: Well, I think we should ^{9}_____ sell the stores ^{10}_____ meddle with the other businesses.

Third conditonal

Complete the sentences with the appropriate form of the verbs in brackets.

1 If disasters like Exxon and Bhopal (not happen) _____ perhaps companies (not develop) _____ CSR strategies to mimimise risks.

2 The clean up after the oil spill (go) _____ more quickly if the damages (award) _____ sooner.

3 If Bhopal (be) _____ operational at the time, more safety precautions (take) _____ .

4 If the Supreme Court in the US (not overrule) _____ the original decision, $5 billion would (be made) _____ available after Exxon.

Discourse markers

1 Which of the discourse markers in the box below can be used to do the following?

actually	unfortunately	then
by the way	so	luckily

1 indicate an attitude _____
2 sequence or to list _____
3 signal a change of topic _____

2 Complete the sales pitch for Luna Jets with discourse markers from the box above.

Ever fancied flying a private jet? ^{1}_____ , for most that usually remains a flight of fancy! ^{2}_____ for you all that's about to change! Luna jets provides affordable private jet travel for all business travellers. 'Impossible!', I hear you say. How can it be done? Well, ^{3}_____ very easily. Let me explain! You see, most private jets return from their destination empty. ^{4}_____ we make a deal with the operators, ^{5}_____ we post all available flights on our database. Oh yeah, and ^{6}_____ booking and payment can also be done online. Business travel will never be the same again!

Consolidation

Choose the correct form of the words in italics in the article on franchising below.

Franchising often seems like a good solution for people who want to start a business. ^{1} *As well as/ On the one hand* being more successful than most start-ups, franchises are ^{2} *also/on the other hand* a more attractive investment for banks. ^{3} *Furthermore/ However*, there are many pitfalls and ^{4} *consequently/ on the whole* many people fail. As Jack Browne told us, 'If ^{5} *I had known/I knew* ^{6} *initially/obviously* what I was letting myself in for I ^{7} *would have put/will put* my money in the bank! After a year I gave up.' ^{8} *So/Then* this begs the question: what went wrong and what could he ^{9} *have done/do* if he ^{10} *had wanted/ wants* to turn the business around? ^{11} *Subsequently/Actually* one year often isn't enough to make a business work. It takes ^{12} *not only/either* a considerable amount of hard work ^{13} *or/but* also determination and perseverance. ^{14} *Finally/On the whole*, people shouldn't be put off by Jack Browne's experience – a good franchise network, run by dedicated people does ^{15} *by and large/by the way* provide a strong platform for success.

Vocabulary check

1 Complete the text with the words from the box.

feasibility	stakeholders	governance
principles	accountable	business model
citizens	shareholder value	transparency
	entrepreneurship	

Our CSR policy – Reaching out

Central to our CSR policy are our [1]_____ of conducting business with [2]_____ and responsibility as well as adhering to the key practices of good corporate [3]_____ . As responsible corporate [4]_____ we aim to enhance communities by promoting commerce in rural areas by rewarding [5]_____ through our funding of start ups.

Applicants provide us with a [6] _____ to help us assess the [7]_____ of the concept. We study the ideas carefully before deciding because we are ultimately [8]_____ to our own [9]_____ and our first duty still has to be to increase their [10]_____ .

2 Form verb–noun collocations with a word from each box to complete the text.

issue	face	uphold	air	table

challenge	view	motion	rights	warning

Doing it the Japanese way

Recently Japanese companies have had to [1]_____ of investors protesting and loudly [2]_____ about their dissatisfaction with low dividends. Shareholders have [3]_____ at meetings designed to give them greater returns on investment. In most cases they have failed to be heard but some companies did [4]_____ of investors to earn more by making small increases. However these companies [5]_____ that short term gains could be detrimental to long term profits.

Usage

Idioms

1 driving a hard bargain _____
2 putting someone on the spot _____
3 throwing the baby out with the bath water _____
4 being in the firing line _____
5 putting a spanner in the works _____
6 fighting a losing battle _____

Which of the idioms 1–6 would you use when talking about the situations a–f?

a imposing difficult choices
b using tough negotiating techniques
c putting forward hopeless lines of argument
d getting priorities wrong during change
e creating obstacles to progress
f finding yourself in the most exposed position

Career skills

Taking responsibility

Label the parts of the statement to the press with headings from the box below. Then complete the statement with the correct form of the words in brackets.

Divert attention	Accept there is a crisis
Describe action	Address the issues

A _____

The Food and Drugs Administration alerted us to the problem with our new contact lens solution early yesterday. Advanced Optics Solutions would like to make a full public ([1]acknowledge) _____ of the issue here today.

B _____

Naturally, we reacted in the interest of public health by ([2]voluntary) _____ withdrawing the product from the market immediately.

C _____

I welcome this opportunity to ([3]apology) _____ to our consumers and hope that they haven't been inconvenienced.

D _____

AOP will continue its ([4]cooperate) _____ with the FDA and through superior technologies will carry on the ([5]develop) _____ of superior vision care products globally.

Unit 7
Resources

www.longman-elt.com   www.economist.com

Vital assets

Keynotes

All businesses require **access** to a limited supply of **resources**. Businesses rely on **raw materials** in the form of water, **minerals** and **energy supplies**. Businesses also require **labour** resources and **capital** – those inputs which have themselves been produced by other companies. **Energy** resources can be divided into three categories: **renewable** resources, which cannot be **depleted** (i.e. wind or water), **sustainable** resources, which can be used and renewed, such as managed forests, and **non-renewable** resources, of which there is only a finite quantity available (i.e. petroleum and minerals). Some non-renewable resources are subject to **geo-political pressures** which result from **scarcity** or from **security concerns** arising from their uneven distribution in the world. In order to limit atmospheric pollution and **global warming** some governments have introduced **cap and trade** schemes where companies must buy **carbon credits** to **offset** their **carbon emissions**.

tesla

Resources quiz

Take the quiz and test your knowledge of the planet's resources. Discuss your answers with a partner.

1 If current levels of population growth are maintained, how many billion inhabitants will the world have in 2050?
   a 7.0   **b** 9.1   **c** 15.5

2 What proportion of the total petroleum reserves of the world are held by the countries of the Middle East?
   a 35%   **b** 56%   **c** 90%

3 How much of the total water on Earth is fresh water?
   a 3%   **b** 10%   **c** 45%

4 In the past 40 years what proportion of the Amazon rainforest has been cut down? *sites*
   a 10%   **b** 20%   **c** 40%

5 The rich countries currently have 15% of the world's population and contribute _____ of total CO_2 emissions.
   a one third   **b** three quarters   **c** one half

6 Which of the following can be used to produce biofuel?
   a sugar cane   **b** maize *corn*   **c** trees   *all of them*

7 The solar energy that the Earth receives from the sun in just one hour would be enough to replace the total power used on Earth in:
   a one day   **b** one year   **c** one decade

8 What percentage of the world's recoverable petroleum resources are estimated to lie under the Arctic Sea?
   a 10%   **b** 22%   **c** 51%

9 How many new cities of more than a million inhabitants will emerge in the next 20 years?
   a 50   **b** 120   **c** more than 200

10 According to automobile industry forecasts, how many cars will be on the roads of the world in 2050?
   a 700 million   **b** 1.5 billion   **c** 3 billion

A 'carbon footprint' is a representation of the impact an individual or organisation has on the environment as a result of producing greenhouse gases.

What steps could businesses or individuals take to reduce their carbon footprint? Which ones would you personally be prepared to adopt? Which ones have you already adopted?

@ An Internet search using the keywords 'carbon footprint' will list websites allowing you to calculate your carbon footprint. What is your carbon footprint?

Water and business

Read the text on the opposite page and answer the questions.

1 What reasons are given for the increases in water consumption?

2 In what ways are companies already being affected by the increasing shortage of water?

3 Why is agriculture using more water than before?

4 What accusation was levelled against corporations concerning their efforts to conserve water?

5 What does Jeff Seabright suggest that companies need to do to make their use of water more acceptable?

6 Give an example of a government policy to impose restrictions on water use by businesses.

7 Why is the amount of water that a company uses inside its plants not always a true indication of total water usage related to its production?

Glossary

hanker for to have a strong desire for something

untrammelled without restrictions

mollify to appease

Water and business
Running dry

Everyone knows industry needs oil. Now people are worrying about water, too

1 "WATER is the oil of the 21st century," declares Andrew Liveris, the chief executive of Dow, a chemical company. Like oil, water is a critical lubricant of the global economy. And as with oil, supplies of water – at least, the clean, easily accessible sort – are coming under enormous strain because of the growing global population and an emerging middle-class in Asia that hankers for the water-intensive life enjoyed in the West.

2 Concerns about the availability of freshwater show no sign of abating. Goldman Sachs, an investment bank, estimates that global water consumption is doubling every 20 years, which it calls an "unsustainable" rate of growth. Water, unlike oil, has no substitute. Climate change is altering the patterns of freshwater availability in complex ways that can lead to more frequent droughts.

3 Untrammelled industrialisation, particularly in poor countries, is contaminating rivers and aquifers. America's generous subsidies for biofuel have increased the harvest of water-intensive crops that are now used for energy as well as food. And heavy subsidies for water in most parts of the world mean it is often grossly underpriced – and hence squandered.

4 All of this poses a problem for human welfare. But it also poses a problem for industry. "For businesses, water is not discretionary," says Dominic Waughray of the World Economic Forum, a think-tank. "Without it, industry and the global economy falter." Water is an essential ingredient in many of the products that line supermarket shelves. JP Morgan, one of the world's largest investment banks, reckons that five big food and beverage giants – Nestlé, Unilever, Coca-Cola, Anheuser-Busch and Danone – consume almost 575 billion litres of water a year, enough to satisfy the daily water needs of every person on the planet.

5 Although agriculture uses most water, many other products and services also depend on it. It takes around 13 cubic metres of freshwater to produce a single 200 mm semiconductor wafer, for example. Chipmaking is thought to account for 25% of water consumption in Silicon Valley. Energy production is also water-intensive: each year around 40% of the freshwater withdrawn from lakes and aquifers in America is used to cool power plants. And separating just one litre of oil from tar sands – a costly alternative fuel – requires up to five litres of water.

6 Not all companies are sitting still. Nestlé cut its water consumption between 1997 and 2006, even as it almost doubled the volume of food it produced. And at Coca-Cola bottling plants from Bogotá to Beijing, fish swim in water tanks filled with treated wastewater, testament to the firm's commitment to cleaning its wastewater.

7 Cynics say such programmes are mere public relations. There is some truth to this. Companies that use freshwater in areas where it is scarce are understandably unpopular. Activists have attacked both Coca-Cola and Pepsi, for instance, for allegedly depleting groundwater in India. Coca-Cola took the matter to court and was exonerated by an independent commission, which blamed a regional drought for water shortages, but activists were not mollified. Coca-Cola has responded by redoubling its attention to water – for instance, by backing a scheme in Kaladera to teach villagers how to harvest rainwater and irrigate crops more efficiently. "Regulatory licences to water are not enough," says Jeff Seabright of Coca-Cola. "We need a social licence – the OK from the community – to operate."

8 Cutting water consumption can also make business sense. Using less water reduces spending on water acquisition and treatment, and on the clean-up of wastewater. Some firms have no choice. Elion Chemical in China is working with General Electric to recycle 90% of its wastewater to comply with Beijing's strict new "zero-liquid discharge" rules, which bar companies from dumping wastewater into the environment. Of Nestlé's 481 factories worldwide, 49 are in extremely water-stressed regions where water conservation and re-use is the only option.

9 Such farsightedness is, alas, only a drop in the bucket. In a drought, even water-efficient factories can run into trouble. Moreover, the water used within a factory's walls is often only a tiny fraction of a firm's true dependence on water. José Lopez, the chief operating officer of Nestlé, notes that it takes four litres of water to make one litre of product in Nestlé's factories, but 3,000 litres of water to grow the agricultural produce that goes into it. These 3,000 litres may be outside his control, but they are very much a part of his business. ∎

What solutions would you propose to alleviate water shortages in water-stressed regions? How could you reduce your own water consumption?

Adverb–adjective collocations

In the article are several examples of adverbs combined with adjectives or past participles:

grossly underpriced   *easily accessible*   *understandably unpopular*

1 Complete the sentences with an adverb–adjective collocation from the boxes.

hardly	heavily	highly	hotly	widely

impractical	debated	accepted	subsidised	sufficient

1   In many major cities, sanitation infrastructure is *hardly sufficient* to deal with the pressures of a growing population.

2   Building desalination plants in remote areas is a possibility but it is *highly impractical* in places where there is no electrical power supply.

3   Introducing genetically engineered species is a controversial topic that is *hotly debated* by some scientists and agronomists.

4   Heightened concentrations of greenhouse gases (GHGs) in the Earth's atmosphere are now *widely accepted* as being the main cause of climate change.

5   The biofuel industry is currently *heavily subsidised* by the governments of several countries.

2 There are many other adverbs that can accompany adjectives. Give two examples of adjectives that could be used with each of the following adverbs.

1   totally   *untrue, free, unfair*   4   openly   *hostile, accessible, criticized*
2   well   *informed, meaning, established* 5   hugely   *successful, important, overrated*
3   badly   *damaged, managed, behaved*   6   seriously *ill, injured, worried*

Like and *as*

Like and *as* are sometimes considered to be interchangeable. Although this can be true, they mostly have different meanings and are used in different contexts.

Complete the sentences with either *as* or *like*.

1   The Pelamis wave generator lies on the surface of the sea *like* a giant articulated snake.

2   *As* in previous years, the Ministry of the Environment will be organising coastal cleanups during the month of July.

3   Hydropower development, *as* with most forms of energy production, has a direct impact on the environment.

4   Using an extremely rare and valuable resource in a mass market product is *like* using gold for the wiring in your home.

5   *As* some experts predicted, the new legislation on protecting indigenous species will not be introduced this year.

For more information, see page 157.

Power for the future

Read the text and answer the questions.

1 What role did energy technologies play in past economic booms?
2 What are the three major concerns about the oil industry?
3 List three developments that are taking place in the energy sector today.
4 How is the market for energy different to other markets?
5 What conditions will have to be met before alternative energies become more widespread?

The Economist

The future energy boom

The power and the glory

The next technology boom may well be based on alternative energy. But which sort to back?

1 Most booms happen on the back of technological change. The world's venture capitalists, having fed on the computing boom of the 1980s, the Internet boom of the 1990s and the biotech and nanotech boomlets of the early 2000s, are now looking for the next one. They think they have found it: energy.

2 Many past booms have been energy-fed: coal-fired steam power, oil-fired internal-combustion engines, and electricity. But the past few decades have been quiet on that front. Coal, natural gas and oil have been cheap and the one real novelty, nuclear power, has gone spectacularly off the rails.

3 Now all that has changed. There is concern that the supply of oil may soon peak as known supplies run out and new reserves become harder to find. The idea of growing what you put in the tank of your car no longer looks like economic madness. Nor does plugging your car into an electric socket instead.

4 Wind- and solar-powered alternatives no longer look so costly by comparison. The future price of these resources – zero – is known. That has economic value even if the capital cost of wind and solar power stations is, at the moment, higher than that of coal-fired ones.

5 The market for energy is huge. At present, the world's population consumes about 15 terawatts of power, a business worth $6 trillion a year – about a tenth of the world's economic output. And by 2050, power consumption is likely to have risen to 30 terawatts.

6 Scale is one of the important differences between the coming energy boom and its recent predecessors – particularly those that relied on information technology. Another difference is that new information technologies tend to be disruptive, forcing the replacement of existing equipment, whereas, say, building wind farms does not force the closure of coal-fired power stations. Any transition from an economy based on fossil fuels to one based on alternative energy is therefore likely to be slow. On the other hand, the scale of the market provides opportunities for alternatives to prove themselves.

7 Some complain that many existing forms of renewable energy rely on subsidies or other forms of special treatment for their viability. However, the whole energy sector is riddled with subsidies, so the subsidies offered to renewable sources of power such as wind turbines often just level the playing field. If the world were rational, all of these measures would be swept away and replaced by a proper tax on carbon – as is starting to happen in Europe. If that occurred, wind-based electricity would already be competitive with fossil fuels and others would be coming close.

8 But developing countries are also taking more of an interest in renewable energy sources. It is true that China is building coal-fired power stations but it also has a large wind-generation capacity and is the world's second-largest manufacturer of solar panels.

9 Brazil, meanwhile, has the world's second-largest biofuel industry, which should supply 15% of its electricity. These countries, and others like them, are prepared to look beyond fossil fuels. So if renewables and other alternatives can compete on cost, the poor and the rich world alike will adopt them.

10 That, however, requires innovation. And if the planet happens to be saved on the way, that is all to the good. ■

The Economist

What efforts are being made in your country to encourage people to use energy more efficiently? What changes to your lifestyle have you made or could you make to reduce your energy consumption?

Listening 1 ⊙

Alternative energies

Geoff Carr is the science editor on *The Economist* who wrote the article on page 75. Before you listen to an interview with him, prepare a short list of questions about the future of energy.

1 Listen to the complete interview and pay careful attention to the questions that are asked. Did Geoff Carr provide the information to answer your questions?

2 Listen again, pausing after Geoff Carr's answer to each question, and answer the questions below.

Part 1

1 Which two alternative energies does Geoff Carr refer to?
2 What three external factors does he cite as being responsible for the emergence of new companies and entrepreneurs in the energy sector?
3 What question still has to be resolved before new energy technologies become more widely used?
4 What reasons does he give for the level of interest in alternative energies?

Part 2

1 What examples does he give of a policy reason and an economic reason for the likely boom in the energy sector?

Part 3

1 What are the four different types of businesses that are involved in the alternative energy sector in the US?
2 What developments does Geoff Carr predict for the automobile industry?

Part 4

1 What are the main obstacles to using hydrogen to power vehicles?
2 Why does Geoff Carr suggest that electricity could be a better power source for vehicles?

Part 5

1 How will the next generation of biofuels be different?

Part 6

1 What does Geoff Carr say are the main differences between nuclear power and alternative energy sources?
2 What does he suggest is the best solution to deal with the problem of nuclear waste?

@ An Internet search using the keywords 'new energies' will list websites which refer to new developments in the energy field. Find an example of a new programme or discovery.

Speaking

The US company, Hyperion, has announced that it will begin mass production of mini nuclear reactors which will each be capable of producing enough electricity for 10,000 households. How would you react if a mini reactor was planned for your neighbourhood? Discuss your opinions with a partner.

Writing

Write an email to your local newspaper expressing your views about the plan to install a mini reactor.

76 ■ Unit 7

Future perfect

We use the future perfect to make projections about how ongoing events, now or in the future, are likely to evolve in relation to a specific time further in the future. Future perfect structures usually include a time reference introduced with the prepositions *by* or *when* which may be stated or only implied.

Look at the examples below.

1 By the end of this year the contractors *will have finished* laying the foundations for the new dam.

2 Do you realise that by the end of this month we *will have been working* non-stop on this project for more than a year?

3 If I discover in six months' time that we haven't made significant progress on making our operations greener, then I *won't have done* my job.

4 I sent her the conference programme last week so I'm sure she'll *have had* enough time to decide what she wants to say during the debate.

Which sentences focus on:

a a situation that may be complete at the time of speaking?

b a situation that depends on a future outcome?

c an uninterrupted action that will still be under way at a time in the future?

d an action that is expected to be complete at a time in the future?

 For more information see page 158.

Practice **Choose the most appropriate future forms to complete the introduction to a presentation.**

I'm sure some of you ¹ *will have had*/*will have* an opportunity to hear Dr Jeffares speak before on the subject of climate change and the effects it is having both on society and on business. However, I'm sure you ² *won't hear*/*won't have heard* that Dr Jeffares is planning to retire next year. If he does, then I ³ *shall have*/*shall have had* to accept some personal responsibility for that, as I ⁴ *won't have succeeded*/*won't be succeeding* in convincing him to continue as director of the Institute of Climatology. But if he does retire, then he can do so knowing that the twenty years he has spent with us have been among the most memorable in the history of our organisation. Before he takes that decision, his latest book on this subject ⁵ *will be publishing*/*will have been published* and very interesting it is too. I'd just like to mention one or two of the most striking things that he has to say. By 2030, if no concerted action is taken to control carbon emissions, the planet ⁶ *will have lost*/*will have been losing* more than 20% of its indigenous species and, needless to say, the future well-being of many of the Earth's inhabitants, both poor and rich, ⁷ *will be compromised*/*will have compromised*. Those are some of the very real challenges we all ⁸ *will have faced*/*will be facing* in the future and many of us, including Dr Jeffares, hope that by that date, science and technology ⁹ *will have provided*/*shall provide* some of the solutions we need to overcome them and that a worst case climate scenario ¹⁰ *will have been avoided*/*will avoid*. So here to talk about the future, our future and perhaps even his own future, ladies and gentlemen ... I'd like you to welcome Dr Bernard Jeffares.

Speaking **Work in pairs and discuss your plans for the next ten years. What do you think you will have achieved by then? What things will have happened to your ideas? Exchange ideas with another pair.**

Career skills

To participate in a debate you need to present forceful arguments in support of your position and you also need to counter the arguments of your opponents. To do this successfully you not only have to prepare very carefully what you will say but also listen attentively to what is said by the other participants, especially those who oppose your point of view.

The organisation of a debate

Debates are chaired by a moderator, who presents the subject to be discussed, introduces the participants and informs speakers of the time that they have been allocated to present their points of view. The moderator or 'chair' is also responsible for making sure that both sides respect their speaking times. A statement or motion presents the issue that the two sides will address. This often takes the form *This house believes that* … At the end of the debate the moderator usually invites the members of the audience to vote in favour of or against the motion.

Debating techniques

Preparation

This is one of the keys to effective debating and it is only once you have done the research that you will be able to decide on the best arguments to use in support of your case and to select the key facts and figures that you will refer to.

Anticipation

If you have anticipated the arguments your opponents will be using, you will be better able to counter and discredit what they have said.

Memorising

One of the difficulties of debating is that you will not normally be reading from prepared notes. You will be expected to talk directly to the audience and therefore need to memorise what you intend to say. However, you should take notes while other participants are speaking and use these to rebut or repudiate what they have said.

Rhetoric

How you phrase what you have to say will directly affect the impact that you have during a debate. Using rhetoric means combining the structure of the arguments that you will use with a convincing style and delivery in order to establish your credibility as a public speaker. Here are some examples of rhetorical techniques that you can use:

- Presenting a logical sequence of ideas
- Pointing out flaws in arguments
- Referring to experts and renowned figures
- Drawing parallels
- Using rhetorical questions
- Illustrating with practical examples
- Referring to hypothetical situations
- Presenting key facts and figures

- your opinion based on facts
- Not fact Tell facts but

rhetorical.

Which of the rhetorical techniques mentioned opposite are illustrated in the following extracts from debates?

1 How long will it be before people understand how urgent this really is? *using rhetorical question*
2 If maritime countries were allowed to exploit ocean resources as they see fit, this would clearly be detrimental to those nations who have no access to the sea. *hypothetical situation*
3 As Gandhi once said, raising the living standards of the inhabitants of poorer countries will inevitably put a greater strain on all of the planet's resources. *experts and renowned figures*
4 No one is disputing the fact that much of the mineral reserves of the planet lie under the oceans. However, it is not reasonable to suggest, as the previous speaker has, that the exploitation of these resources should be left in the hands of commercial businesses which operate outside any global regulatory framework. *flaws*
5 In 2008 the SpaceWatch foundation issued a report showing the potential dangers of the overuse of space for military and commercial purposes. At that time there were already more than 20 derelict nuclear-powered satellites orbiting the Earth and more than 4,000 pieces of space debris. *facts and figures*

Listening 2 ⊙

1 **Listen to three extracts from a debate. Which of the following motions do you think the participants are debating?**

– Building dams is not the best way to conserve water supplies.
– The effects of global warming on our water supply must be minimised.
– The bottled water industry is detrimental to the environment.

2 **Listen to the extracts again. Which of the rhetorical techniques mentioned opposite do they use?**

Speaking

Work in pairs. Choose one of the motions below and prepare to speak in favour of it or against it. Then present your arguments to a pair who have prepared a different motion.

– Cars should be banned from city centres.
– The nations that are using space for military and commercial purposes should pay compensation to countries that do not have space programmes.
– The Arctic should be declared a natural planetary reserve. ✗
– Businesses should not be allowed to conduct deep sea mining operations in international waters. *✗ cause conflict*
  ✗ should be replaced with renewables
– All households should be taxed on the waste that they produce.
  - any waste should be donated to people with food shortage
  government encourage this action.

Culture at work

Debating styles

Debating styles vary widely from one country to another. In some countries debates are formal and the participants follow rigid guidelines concerning the form and delivery of their arguments. The degree of emotional engagement in a debate will also vary depending on whether the participants are from a high- or low-context culture. In the former, speakers will assume that the audience will extract a maximum amount of meaning from a minimum amount of information; in the latter, speakers will tend to give detailed explanations of the ideas and arguments that they are using. How would you adapt your style if you were participating in a debate in a multi-cultural context?

Dilemma & Decision

Dilemma: The nuclear debate

Brief

The Republic of Malwinia is facing some difficult decisions concerning its energy policy. As it has no natural energy resources it relies on imported fossil fuels to generate enough electricity to supply growing domestic demand. As a result of economic development and rising demographics, demand for energy is increasing rapidly. All parties accept that meeting this demand will necessitate government and/or private sector investment in new power generation facilities. The situation is critical as the country's electricity suppliers are no longer able to supply sufficient power during peak periods, resulting in power blackouts that have affected both industry and households. Something has to be done. But what?

There are currently two conflicting views about future energy policy. On one side a group of influential politicians and policymakers advocate continuing with the current energy policy while at the same time introducing nuclear power plants to supplement the existing supply. This would be the first time that nuclear power has been used in the country; and the reactors would be built at five strategic locations and start contributing to the grid within five years. On the other side are a selection of environmental supporters from across the political spectrum and from international NGOs. They believe that the country has to make a radical break from its traditional energy policy and invest in the development of clean technologies that use renewable energy. The country's Institute for Energy Policy has organised a public debate on the future of the energy sector. This debate will be highly publicised and the ensuing vote could have a significant influence on the country's future energy policy.

The motion that has been decided for the debate is the following:

This house believes that nuclear energy is neither a viable nor a desirable option for the future of our energy supply.

Task 1

You are going to debate the motion. Divide into two teams; Team A will argue for the motion and Team B against. Each team can present no more than four speakers. Some background information has been provided on page 135 for Team A and on page 137 for Team B. If time allows, teams may wish to supplement this information by conducting their own research on the Internet.

Task 2

Select a chairperson who will manage the debate proceedings. He or she should consult the Team A and Team B information.

Task 3

Meet with the other team and hold the debate.

Write it up

Write a short newspaper article summarising the arguments that were presented during the debate and explaining what the outcome was.

For more information, see *Style guide*, page 4.

Decision:

Listen to Nicolas Scherrer from the Institute of Geopolitics and Energy commenting on the nuclear debate.

1. What problems are facing South Africa's energy sector?
2. Why was the plan to build a nuclear reactor abandoned?
3. Why is relying on imported fuel not necessarily a good thing?
4. What sort of energy solutions will most countries adopt?

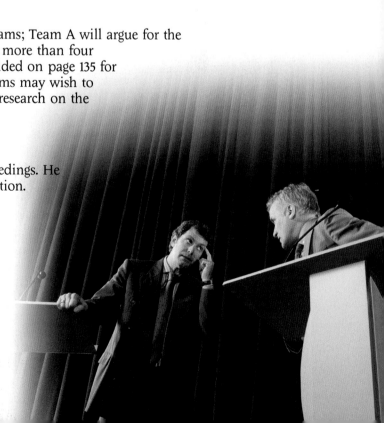

Unit 8
Power

www.longman-elt.com   www.economist.com

Keynotes

Leadership is about influencing the **behaviour** of others. **Power** provides the capacity to overcome resistance on the part of others in order to exert that influence. **Leaders** set the **business agenda** and their position of power and **status** in the **organisational hierarchy** means that people are expected to follow them. It is widely accepted that **management** and leadership are different (though some argue that leadership is simply one facet of management), because true leaders have **followers** and managers have **subordinates**. Some managers believe in employee **empowerment** and they delegate and share responsibilities with their employees, while at the other end of the spectrum some **abuse** their power by unfairly **exploiting** their employees. How managers use or abuse power will determine their leadership **style**.

Power bases

Read the descriptions of power bases. Decide which of the two categories, positional power (which comes from formal authority, defined by position in the hierarchy) or personal power (achieved through accomplishments and interpersonal skill), each one belongs to.

POWER BASES

1 Reward power: a leader has access to rewards which will be dispensed in return for compliance with instructions.

2 Referent power: a leader is likeable, charismatic and has other attractive personality traits.

3 Persuasive power: a leader has intellectual problem-solving abilities. On a list of influence tactics, 'reason' is considered to be one of the best.

4 Coercive power: a leader can administer sanctions that are considered unwelcome. *often punishment*

5 Credible power: a leader has integrity, character and competence.

6 Legitimate power: a leader has a position and title in the organisation and therefore has to be obeyed.

7 Expert power: a leader has superior knowledge relevant to the task at hand.

Speaking

1 Which combination of power bases do you think a good leader should develop and use? *2 .7*

2 The characteristics and symbols of power are often referred to as the 'trappings of power'. These may include prestigious offices and generous expense accounts, etc. What other advantages are there? Can you think of any disadvantages?

Reading 1 **The trappings of power**

1 Read the text on the opposite page. What are the main disadvantages of being a CEO, as outlined by the author?

2 Read the text again and answer the questions.

1 Why are CEOs so intensely lonely?
2 What makes a good international CEO according to Mervyn Davies?
3 What strategies for coping have CEOs come up with?
4 Why did one CEO take on an acting coach?
5 Do you think it is likely that CEOs lie about their stress levels in order to justify their salaries?

@ An Internet search using the keywords 'CEO stress' will list websites that refer to this problem. Find an example of a website that gives advice about how CEOs should deal with stress.

Glossary

tongue in cheek not to be taken seriously

wrecked very tired

introvert someone who is reserved and likes being alone

The trappings of power
Sympathy for the boss

Even chief executives are human. Really.

1 "IT'S lonely at the top. But at least there is something to read," observed a tongue-in-cheek billboard advert for *The Economist* in 1990. Little did we know how lonely. Strip away the huge salary and the executive jet, and you find much solitary misery. According to "The Secrets of CEOs", a new book based on interviews with over 150 current and former chief executives from around the world, "being a CEO should be one of the best jobs in the world. It offers the chance to make a real difference. However, real life for most CEOs is tough and many are not enjoying it."

2 Even as they cheer on aspiring chief executives, the authors – Andrew Cave, a British journalist, and Steve Tappin, an executive headhunter – have devised a "CEO Health Warning" for those who would be corporate kings: "Even if you succeed in this role, you may ultimately be forced to leave it prematurely. There is a high risk that while in the role you will have a limited life outside work and that the job will put tremendous strain on your health, happiness, and close family relationships and friendships." As the saying goes, if you want a friend, get a dog.

Life can be tough at the top

3 Around 50% of the chief executives interviewed said they found the job "intensely lonely" and did not know who to turn to for advice. A common response was, "I can't talk to the chairman because in the end he's the one who is going to fire me. I can't talk to my finance director because ultimately I'm going to fire him, and I can't tell my wife because I never see her."

4 Nor is there much time for a personal life, as they become 24/7 slaves to the job. One typical example cited by Messrs Cave and Tappin is Peter Johnson, the former boss of Inchcape, a car dealer, who admits that "My wife has put up with a lot. I was on a plane all the time, I was just never there. I once went to Australia twice in a week!"

5 Mervyn Davies, the chairman and former chief executive of Standard Chartered Bank, believes that one of the most important differentiators between good and bad international chief executives is their ability to sleep on a plane, which has a knock-on effect on their family life. "If you're a bad traveller and run an international business, it's a nightmare," he says. "You're not sleeping and you're coming home wrecked."

6 The chief executives interviewed by Messrs Cave and Tappin suggest three strategies in response to the CEO health warning: drive your own agenda, don't let the business drive you; build an active support network; always be at your best.

7 The best bosses make time to be with their family, to think in solitude and to stay healthy. Techniques range from going to the gym or fishing to turning off the Blackberry and taking that dog for a walk.

8 Around 40% of FTSE chief executives have used a personal coach. Typically, these coaches are mentors, but some bosses have sought other varieties of personal training. One FTSE chief executive said that he used an actress once a month to teach him how to act out the chief-executive role. "I am a very shy individual," he reveals. "I would not naturally engage with people. It's just a management style I have developed over the years. We all put on a show. We are all actors and I have learnt to act. The actress comes in and coaches me in body language, presentation style, and public speaking. I am an introvert and introverts get drawn in. I don't need to have a high regard for friendships or closeness. I can retain my intellectual distance with people who work for me."

9 So why do the job, given it is so lonely and miserable? And why cling to it so hard? After all, rare is the chief executive who gives up the throne without a fight. The thought occurs that, under fire for their huge salaries and other perks, chief executives have decided to talk up the misery of the job as part of a cunning public relations strategy. ■

1 Do you think you would ever become a 24/7 slave to your work?

2 In the text we read about some techniques for staying healthy. What other techniques can you think of? What do you do to relax, unwind and avoid undue stress?

Join words from each box to form word partnerships from the text. Then match the underlined phrase with the word partnerships.

personal	support	health	public	knock on

network	speaking	effect	life	warning

1 Acting coaches can help managers develop communication skills for <u>making speeches and giving presentations</u>. _public speaking_

2 He never would have managed without the help of the team of <u>competent people he organised around him</u>. _support network_

3 Due to his resignation, there will be <u>consequences</u> in terms of staff morale and efficiency. _knock on effect_

4 The HR department issued top executives with a <u>cautionary message about not staying fit</u>. _health warning_

5 CEOs complain that they have no <u>free time to relax and spend time with their families</u>. _personal life_

Phrasal verbs with *put*

1 In the text one CEO says all CEOs *put on a show*, which means 'act a role'. Complete the sentences below with the correct prepositions.

1 Working round the clock *put* a lot of strain _on_ his personal relationships.

2 The staff are finding it difficult to *put* _up_ with the team leader's mood swings.

3 The committee has refused to *put* _up_ the money for the new project.

4 He *put* the proposal _to_ the board, so now we have to wait and see what they say.

5 I've *put* _in_ for a transfer to a new department.

6 He tried to *put* the message _across_, but I don't think everyone understood.

7 She asked the manager to *put* _in_ a word for her, to help her application for promotion.

2 Match the phrasal verbs above with their meanings.

a to cause problems _1_
b to finance _3_
c to endure/to accept _2_
d to apply for _5_
e to suggest _4_
f to recommend _7_
g to communicate _6_

Proverbs

Proverbs are sayings which contain some basic truth or practical advice, and which have gained acceptance and authority through frequent use. Below are some common English proverbs.

Guess the meanings of these proverbs by thinking about the images they create. Match each proverb (1–7) to a situation in which it can be used (a–g).

1 Don't judge a book by its cover. *g*
2 Necessity is the mother of invention. *f*
3 You scratch my back and I'll scratch yours. *a*
4 Don't count your chickens before they're hatched. *e*
5 If at first you don't succeed, try again. *d*
6 Two heads are better than one. *b*
7 All work and no play makes Jack a dull boy. *c*

a negotiating and bargaining
b offering help
c talking about work–life balance
d encouraging someone not to give up
e warning someone against over-optimistic forecasts
f finding solutions in difficult situations
g advising not to place too much importance on appearance

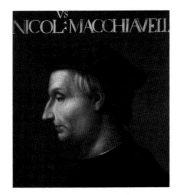

Listening 1 ⊙ ## Power politics

Listen to Raymond Townsend, an executive coach, talking about the role of politics in corporations and answer the questions.

1 What is politics really all about?
2 What matters most in the 'politics game'?
3 Which two reasons does he give for political behaviour being inevitable in large corporations?
4 Mr Townsend refers to some mangers as being 'Machiavellian'. What does the speaker say about this type of manager?
5 According to him, how do most effective managers use their power?

Language check ## Active and passive

Verb forms are either active or passive. We use active forms when we want to focus on the agent (the person or thing) responsible for an action or a situation. We use passives to focus on the effects or outcome of an action or situation without necessarily referring to the agent.

Are the underlined verbs active (A) or passive (P)?

1 Harvey <u>should have known</u> that there was a chance his contract <u>wouldn't be renewed</u>. _A_ , _P_
2 The only explanation that <u>can be found</u> for the information leak is that someone <u>must have broken</u> into the computer system. _P_ , _A_
3 You <u>could have been fired</u> for making a mistake like that, especially as it <u>could have compromised</u> the whole deal. _P_ _A_
4 We've all <u>been given</u> a copy of the conference programme but it doesn't say who <u>will be making</u> the keynote speech. _P_ _A_
5 If the current legislation <u>is changed</u>, then all our contracts will have <u>to be renegotiated</u>. _P_ , _P_

@ An Internet search using the keywords 'Niccolò Machiavelli' will list websites with information about the man and his theories.

Passive forms

There are two basic types of passive construction: standard passive constructions, which use a form of the verb *be* followed by a past participle, and causative passive constructions, where the verbs *get* and *have* are usually followed by both an object and a past participle. Causative passive forms are used to describe situations where the subject is responsible for the action in some way but does not perform it.

Complete the following sentences with a form of *have* or *get*.

1 No one was surprised when Marcus __got__ offered a new job with one of our competitors.

2 We showed the designs to our supplier and __had__ a series of prototypes prepared.

3 One of the traders had been concealing certain transactions but eventually he __got__ caught by his supervisor.

4 Before we commit funds to the joint venture I think we should __have__ their accounts gone over in detail.

5 Call the supplier immediately and __have/get__ an estimate for the repairs faxed through.

 For more information, see page 158.

Practice
1 Read the text and complete the blanks with the appropriate active or passive forms of the verbs in brackets.

2 Read the text again. Are there any passive forms which could be shortened to past participles?

Workplace harrassment

Workplace harassment can (¹define) __be defined__ as a situation where an employee (²subject) __is subjected__ to unwelcome, threatening or offensive behaviour by a co-worker or co-workers. Normally you would expect such behaviour to (³bring) __be brought__ to the attention of senior managers who could then take appropriate action. However, a recent survey of more than 1,000 British workers, (⁴reveal) __reveals__ that almost one third of the workers interviewed said they felt that they would be unable to report or challenge unacceptable behaviour. More surprising is that more than three quarters of the companies and organisations selected for the survey openly (⁵support) __support__ a policy of diversity in the workplace. But how should employees (⁶react) __react__ when they feel that they (⁷victimise) __are being victimised__ by their colleagues or bosses? According to Naomi Agnew, an HR consultant, there are only really two options: making a direct request for the behaviour to cease or threatening (⁸have) __to have__ the issue referred to a senior manager or HR department. However, she also points out that, in some cases, neither of these approaches (⁹guarantee) __guarantees__ that the harassment (¹⁰bring) __will be brought__ to an end. 'I've seen situations where employees (¹¹render) __are rendered__ non-functional by this sort of behaviour and my advice to them was to look for a healthier work environment. If you (¹²humiliate) __are being humiliated__ on a daily basis, then you have to think of your own well-being and it may be best for you to leave your job before your boss (¹³get) __gets__ you sacked.'

Writing
You work for a supervisor who regularly uses abusive language when referring to you and your work. Write a letter HR to explain your situation and to ask for disciplinary action to be taken.

Narcissism refers to excessive self-love, based on self-image or ego. Read the text below which deals with bosses who suffer from this and answer the questions.

1 What information about most current bosses does Jim Collins' book present?

2 What did the authors of the study 'It's all about me' base their research on?

3 How does the narcissism of bosses affect the companies they run?

Narcissistic bosses

The brand of me

Is it bad for business when the boss is in love with himself?

1 "WHAT'S the difference between God and Larry Ellison?" asks an old software industry joke. Answer: God doesn't think he's Larry Ellison. The boss of Oracle is hardly alone among corporate chiefs in having a reputation for being rather keen on himself. Indeed, until the bubble burst and the public turned nasty at the start of the decade, the cult of the celebrity chief executive seemed to demand boss-like narcissism, as evidence that a firm was being led by an all-conquering hero.

2 Narcissus met a nasty end, of course. And in recent years, boss-worship has come to be seen as bad for business. In his management bestseller, "Good to Great", Jim Collins argued that the truly successful bosses were not the self-proclaimed stars who adorn the covers of Forbes and Fortune, but instead self-effacing, thoughtful, monkish sorts who lead by inspiring example.

3 A statistical answer may be at hand. For the first time, a new study, "It's All About Me", to be presented at the annual gathering of the American Academy of Management, offers a systematic, empirical analysis of what effect narcissistic bosses have on the firms they run. The authors, Arijit Chatterjee and Donald Hambrick, of Pennsylvania State University, examined narcissism in the upper echelons of 105 firms in the

computer and software industries.

4 To do this, they had to solve a practical problem: studies of narcissism have hitherto relied on surveying individuals personally, something for which few chief executives are likely to have time or inclination. So the authors devised an index of narcissism using six publicly available indicators obtainable without the co-operation of the boss. These are: the prominence of the boss's photo in the annual report; his prominence in company press releases; the length of his "Who's Who" entry; the frequency of his use of the first person singular in interviews; and the ratios of his cash and non-cash compensation to those of the firm's second-highest paid executive.

5 Narcissism naturally drives people to seek positions of power and influence, and because great self-esteem helps your professional advance, say the authors, chief executives will tend on average to be more narcissistic than the general population. How does that affect a firm? Messrs Chatterjee and Hambrick found that highly narcissistic bosses tended to make bigger changes in the use of important resources, such as research and development, or in spending and leverage; they carried out more and bigger mergers and acquisitions; and their results were both more extreme

(more big wins or big losses) and more volatile than those of firms run by their humbler peers. For shareholders, that could be good or bad.

6 Although (oddly) the authors are keeping their narcissism ranking secret, they have revealed that Mr Ellison did not come top. Alas for him, that may be because the study limited itself to people who became the boss after 1991 – well after he took the helm. In every respect Mr Ellison seems to be the classic narcissistic boss, claims Mr Chatterjee. There is life in the old joke yet. ■

The Economist

1 Work in pairs. Take it in turns to tell a 'business' joke. If you don't know any jokes, Student A can turn to page 136 and Student B to page 142 to find one.

2 We read in the text, 'great self-esteem helps your professional advance'. Work in pairs. Discuss whether you think this is true. What other characteristics or personality traits can help advance a career?

Career skills

Influencing

Effective influencing skills require a combination of interpersonal, communication, presentation and assertiveness skills. If you are the boss, you may try to exert your influence by relying on your legitimacy – referring to your position and pointing out that what you want done is company policy. You may also be coercive by using warnings and threats. You might even succeed in getting things done but that's more about getting people to do what you want them to do, sometimes against their own will. An alternative way to influence is to move things forward without forcing or pushing people to do things. If you use your influencing skills well, the 'influencees' will willingly carry out your requests while believing that they are acting in their own best interests.

Extensive research on influencing tactics has revealed the use of nine distinct tactics which are summarised below.

a regularly reminding the influencee of your request through clearly communicated verbal statements

b negotiating and exchanging benefits

c mobilising other people in the organisation to help you, thereby strengthening your request

d achieving the influencee's commitment by involving them in the decision of the change

e using the chain of command and outside sources of power; appealing to or threatening to appeal to the upper echelons *levels* of power to gain agreement

f using flattery, praise or friendly behaviour before or while making the request

g developing emotional commitment by appealing to the influencee's needs, aspirations, values and hopes

h appealing to the influencee to comply based on friendship with or loyalty to them

i relying on the presentation of data and information as a basis for a logical argument that supports a request

Read the list of tactics (a–i) and match them to the following headings.

1 Higher authority ____e____
2 Inspirational appeal ____g____
3 Reason ____~~h~~ i____
4 Assertiveness ____a____
5 Consultation ____~~h~~ d____
6 Bargaining ____b____
7 Coalition ____~~d~~ c____
8 Personal appeal ____~~f~~ h____
9 Ingratiation ____~~c~~ f____

What do you think of these tactics? Are there any that you would never use, under any circumstance? Why/Why not?

Influencing the boss

Work in pairs. Read the scenarios below. Discuss and analyse the situations and then answer the questions.

1 Your team leader is constantly putting pressure on the team to come up with ideas for new products and ways to expand into new markets. After every brainstorming session you report back to her with the team's suggestions. However, she always finds fault, refuses to take any risks and says 'no' to any further development of the idea. She is probably over-cautious because of past problems with her boss due to a string of failures proposed by her previous team. She also likes to control everything and resents it when the team takes too much initiative. The team is demoralised, unmotivated and desperate to get their latest idea past her and to the implementation stage. You need to persuade her. Job cuts are imminent and you know that she and her team will be the first ones to go if you don't have success soon.

2 You have been working in the field as a sales rep for your company for five years. You have built up an impressive client list and have had excellent sales results. Your manager doesn't want to lose you. You have applied to the marketing department for the position of assistant marketing manager. You really want this job. You never had any intention of staying in sales but saw it as a stepping stone to a marketing position. You know that the marketing manager is going to ask the sales manager for his opinion. You also know that they don't have much respect for each other and that the marketing manager has made life difficult for the sales manager on more than one occasion in the past. It is unlikely that the sales manager will want to cooperate with him by letting one of his top people move to his department. You need to convince him to recommend you for the job.

1 Which of the tactics on the opposite page are available to you when you are trying to influence your superior?
2 Which tactic(s) would you choose in each of the cases above?
3 Describe how you would handle the situation.

In pairs, choose one of the scenarios and write the dialogue that could take place between the influencers and their bosses. Then act out the dialogues for the class and compare your work with other pairs.

Listen to the two conversations and answer the questions.

1 Which influencing tactics did the speakers wishing to influence use?
2 Are these very different from the ones in your dialogues?
3 Did you find them effective?
4 Would they have persuaded you? Why/Why not?

Speaking up

The amount of influence subordinates can exert over their bosses depends on culture. In 'status cultures' it is generally not acceptable for subordinates to make suggestions or give advice to their superiors. They would be advised to use ingratiation and consultation tactics rather than assertiveness and personal appeal. Even in 'achievement cultures', where managers are more open to suggestions from all levels of the hierarchy, it takes courage to tell your boss that there is something he or she could do more effectively, or to offer help. Part of why it is 'lonely at the top' is because so few subordinates see that bosses need to learn and grow, too. The exchange of information about performance (or advice on how to improve it) in return for appreciation from the boss, can, therefore, be seen as a beneficial exchange in some cultures. How would that work in your culture?

Dilemma: Winning the rivalry game

Brief

Central Computers, a computer manufacturing firm, has been experiencing falling profit margins on hardware sales. They hope to make up for it by selling solutions and consulting services, so they appointed Carl Sagan to head a new services division. On the third day in the job Carl Sagan was approached by the company's most successful sales manager, Peter Arroway, who has the same management grade and reports to the same senior manager. Arroway is in his mid thirties, recently married and about to start a family.

Unprovoked, he insulted Sagan and threatened to have him removed from the company. He has also been undermining Sagan's credibility with his staff by spreading rumours. Sagan has discovered that Arroway is capturing his emails and that of other managers.

Arroway generates 40% of the company's turnover from one customer whose buyer is a close personal friend of his. Sagan knows that Arroway incurs high expenses on overseas trips that generate no new sales and that senior managers are aware of the dangers of depending on one customer.

Carl Sagan needs to defend his position, destabilise Arroway's and develop his service role. There are five options open to him:

1 Report Arroway's behaviour to their senior manager. Ask the director to solve the problem in the interests of morale and performance.

2 Ask Arroway for a meeting in which differences can be genuinely shared and discussed. Jointly negotiate a compromise and establish a working relationship.

3 Force him out slowly. Develop contacts and business with that one important customer. Feed damaging information about him to senior managers.

4 Refuse to get involved in power games. Concentrate on his team, ignore Arroway's tactics and get on with the job as best he can.

5 Put his new role to one side and play the game by Arroway's rules. Copy his methods. Capture his emails, spread rumours and damage his credibility with his own staff.

Task 1

In pairs or small groups, evaluate the advantages and limitations of each of the five options.

Task 2

Decide which one you would choose and why.

Task 3

Present your decision to the class.

Write it up

You are Carl Sagan. Write the agenda for a meeting with Peter Arroway.

For more information, see *Style guide*, page 3.

Decision:

Listen to Janet Haviland, a specialist in political conflicts, talking about this situation.

1 According to her, what are the conditions that create this type of political behaviour?

2 What is the most important thing to do in situations like these?

3 What does she say about each option?

Unit 9
E-marketing

www.longman-elt.com   www.economist.com

Keynotes

E-marketing, like conventional marketing, aims to create powerful messages which will engage consumers, build brands and drive sales. The difference is that it uses **digital technologies** to do so. Whereas traditional marketing has PR and advertising media such as TV, press, outdoor and radio as part of the marketing mix, e-marketing uses **websites**, **email** and **sms** to reach target markets. Other options are **pop-ups** or **banner ads**, which are graphic images used on websites to advertise products or services, and embedded videos. **Search advertising** is a form of Internet marketing where companies pay to increase the visibility of their websites in **search engine** result pages. **Social networking** sites provide marketers with an opportunity to tap into a huge market of specific consumer groups.

Talking to customers online

1 **Discuss the following questions.**

1 Which websites do you and your peers spend time on?
2 Do you have a web-based email account? If so, do you read the advertisements posted on it?
3 Do you read email advertising or do you treat it as spam and delete it without opening it?
4 Do you answer email surveys?
5 Have you ever bought anything online after clicking on a pop-up or banner ad?
6 Do you watch video clips and cinema trailers on the Internet?
7 Do you read texts from marketers on your mobile phone?

2 **Look at the marketing briefs and decide which campaign would suit each product.**

1 email promotions with interactive email surveys
2 banner ads on Yahoo's main page
3 ads streamed directly to the inboxes of MSN hotmail users

Product: Nissan 350Z
Target: 18- to 34-year-olds
Needs: increase traffic on Nissan 350Z's micro site
2

Product: B2B Marketing magazine
Target: marketing practitioners
Needs: gauge industry opinion and get regular feedback from customers
#1

Product: Sony's James Bond – Quantum of Solace
Target: 15- to 35-year-olds
Needs: generate interest in movie and DVD
2 x 3

Speaking Work in pairs. Discuss whether the e-marketing media used above would appeal to you as consumers.

Listening 1 Listen to Amy Masterson from Internet Plus, an advertising agency in the UK, talking about the key drivers for growth in online marketing and take notes under the following headings. How does she think each of these drivers will affect this marketing sector?

– Quality broadband   – Online audience
– Social networking websites – Wireless connections
– Catch-up and online TV

Speaking Do you have a Facebook, Myspace or other social networking page? If so, what kind of information about yourself and your friends do you post on it? How could this information be useful to marketers?

Reading 1 **Conversational marketing**

1 **Read the text on the opposite page and answer the questions.**

1 What is meant by 'conversational marketing'?
2 What conflicting views of the future of conversational marketing are presented in the text?

Glossary

piggyback ride on the success of, take advantage of

eavesdrop listen in on conversations

creepy scary

clutter untidy mess

Conversational marketing
Word of mouse

Will Facebook, MySpace and other social networking sites transform advertising?

1 Mark Zuckerberg, who is 23 and the boss of Facebook, a popular social networking website, recently announced to advertising executives that Facebook was offering them a new deal. "For the last hundred years media has been pushed out to people," he said, "but now marketers are going to be a part of the conversation." Using his firm's new approach, he claimed, advertisers will be able to piggyback on the "social actions" of Facebook users, since "people influence people".

2 Mr Zuckerberg's language was strikingly similar to that of Paul Lazarsfeld and Elihu Katz in their book "Personal Influence", a media-studies classic from 1955. They argued that marketers do not simply broadcast messages to a passive mass audience, but rather that they target certain individuals, called "opinion leaders". These individuals then spread, confirm or negate the messages of advertisers through their own "social relationships", by word of mouth or personal example.

3 Messrs Lazarsfeld and Katz, of course, assumed that most of these conversations and their implicit marketing messages would remain inaudible. That firms might be able to eavesdrop on this chatter first became conceivable in the 1990s, with the rise of the Internet.

4 In the past decade the Internet has already produced three proven advertising categories. First came "display" or "banner" ads, usually in the form of graphical boxes on web pages, now often with embedded videos. Today these account for 32% of online advertising revenue. Next are classified ads, now 17% of the total. The third, and now largest, category is search advertising, with 41% of the total. Proven though not invented by Google, the biggest search engine, these are the text snippets that appear next to search results for a specific keyword.

5 From the point of view of marketers, these existing types of online ads already represent breakthroughs. In search, they can now target consumers who express interest in a particular product or service by typing a keyword; they pay only when a consumer responds, by clicking on their ads. In display, they can track and measure how their ads are viewed and whether a consumer is paying attention (if he turns on the sound of a video ad, say) better than they ever could with television ads. The goal of observing and even participating in consumers' conversations – true conversational marketing – now appears within reach.

6 The first step for brands to socialise, or converse, with consumers is to start profile pages on social networks and then accept "friend requests" from individuals. On MySpace, brands have been doing this for a while. For instance, Warner Bros, a Hollywood studio, had a MySpace page for "300", its film about Spartan warriors. It signed up some 200,000 friends, who watched trailers, talked the film up before its release, and counted down toward its DVD release.

7 Facebook also lets brands create their own pages. Coca-Cola, for instance, has a Sprite page and a "Sprite Sips" game that lets users play with a little animated character on their own pages. Facebook makes this a social act by automatically informing the player's friends, via tiny "news feed" alerts, of the fun in progress.

8 In many cases, Facebook users can also treat brands' pages like those of other friends, by adding reviews, photos or comments, say. Each of these actions might be communicated instantly to the news feeds of their clique. Obviously this is a double-edged sword, since they can just as easily criticise a brand as praise it.

9 Facebook even plans to monitor and use actions beyond its own site to place them in a social context. If, for instance, a Facebook user makes a purchase at Fandango, a website that sells cinema tickets, this information again shows up on the news feeds of his friends on Facebook, who might decide to come along. If he buys a book or shirt on another site, then this implicit recommendation pops up too.

10 There are plenty of sceptics. Some people may find all this creepy, so Facebook will allow people to opt out of sharing their information. Another problem, says Paul Martino, an entrepreneur who launched Tribe, an early social network, is that the interpersonal connections (called the "social graph") on such networks are of low quality. Because few people dare to dump former friends or to reject unwanted friend requests from casual acquaintances, "social graphs degenerate to noise in all cases," he says. If he is right, social-marketing campaigns will descend into visual clutter about the banal doings of increasingly random people, rather than being the next big thing in advertising. ■

2 **Read the text again and answer the questions.**

1 What did Mark Zuckerberg of Facebook promise marketers?

2 How is this similar to the classic media study by Lazarsfeld and Katz?

3 What are the three forms of Internet advertising?

4 How do brands intend to socialise with consumers through social networking sites?

Vocabulary 1 **Match the words from the text with their meaning.**

1	word of mouth (para 2) C	a	a brief listing of products and services for sale
2	classified ads (para 4) a	b	a format used for providing web users with frequently updated content
3	snippets (para 4) f	c	information gained verbally, by someone telling you, rather than written
4	profile page (para 6) e	d	an exclusive group of people
5	news feeds (para 7) b	e	a place where you post details about yourself on the Internet
6	clique (para 8) d	f	a two-line summary that appears along with a link to a website

Vocabulary 2 ## Word clusters

Many words have a 'cluster' of derived words and idiomatic expressions that all stem from the original word or 'base form'. For example, in the text the noun *breakthrough*, which means a sudden, unexpected discovery, is derived from the verb *break*, and the adverb *through*.

1 Study the spidergram on page 141, which shows other derived forms of *break*. Where would you insert the following words?

breakable	break the law	break-even *adjective*	break up

2 Complete the sentences below with forms of *break*. Then make your own word cluster diagram with *back, do, draw, light, set* or *take*.

1 With over 1 billion websites in existence, it is getting harder for companies to break into the select group of the 20,000 most visited sites.

2 After investing massively in their online operations, it took major retailers several years just to break even (v+av) and they only started to become profitable in 2003.

3 Most web advertising companies provide extensive data which gives a breakdown of all Internet users who have clicked on their adverts.

4 Many Internet users do not have sufficient antivirus protection and are therefore vulnerable to outbreak of spam attacks.

5 For people who spend long hours working on their computers, it is recommended that they take a break of at least ten minutes every hour.

6 In some counties, a website that doesn't display its privacy policy about data-gathering is considered to be breaking the law.

Speaking **Does the idea of marketers monitoring your life through your social network page scare you? Would you opt out of 'sharing' information about your life with marketers?**

Puns

In the title 'Word of mouse', *mouse* is used instead of *mouth* to create a pun. Journalists often use puns in headlines to grab readers' attention. Advertisers use similar techniques to make their slogans memorable.

1 **Each of the examples below contains a pun. Identify the pun and say what you think the original word was.**

a I think therefore I BM (IBM) *

b Taste not waist (Weight Watchers frozen meals)

c These are Wright for me (Frank Wright Shoes)

d It 'asda be Asda! (Asda)

e Burton's menswear is everywear (Burton's menswear)

2 **Match the idiomatic expressions (1–4) with their meanings (a–d).**

1	So far so good.	a	Lots of bad things happen all at once.
2	It never rains but it pours.	b	Always try to adapt to a new culture.
3	When in Rome (do as the Romans do).	c	Don't say anything about it to anyone.
4	Mum's the word.	d	For the moment things are going OK.

3 **Which of the expressions above is referred to in these slogans? Which ones are the most effective? Can you think of similar examples in your own language?**

a So Farley's so good (Farley's baby food)

b Cell phones cost when in Roam (cell phones)

c When it pours it reigns (Michelin tyres)

d One word captures the moment. Mumm's the word (Mumm's champagne)

Google clicks

Listen to Greg Stillman, a journalist specialising in digital technologies and the Internet, talking about how Google developed its advertising business. Decide whether the statements are true or false.

1 Google has been in business since 1998.

2 Advertising has always been an integral part of the company's business model.

3 Google's first use of advertising relied on traditional sales techniques.

4 Advertisers have to bid for keywords that they want to use in their ads.

5 Search engine companies approve of 'black hat' techniques.

6 Advertising is the only way to make sure that a web page is well ranked.

7 Google has failed to diversify into areas other than Internet searches.

8 Google is preparing to pay users for information it gathers about them.

Some researchers have suggested that the online world is becoming dangerous for young people because they perceive their offline lives as being comparatively boring and unstimulating. Do you agree? Do you think that people will spend more or less time online in the future?

 An Internet search using the keywords 'Google labs' will show links to Google's research projects. Choose one of these to discuss with a partner.

Word order: adverbs

In English, adjectives generally appear before nouns and adverbs after verbs. However, the positions of words or phrases can vary depending on the context and on the style or register of what is being said. Adverbs, in particular, may appear in different positions depending on their function.

1 Match the adverbs in italics in the text to categories 1–6 below.

Basic email marketing

Email marketing is *rapidly* becoming an essential tool for businesses to reach their audiences *wherever* they happen to be. In its simplest form it works like this: Rebecca is a typical customer who *frequently* buys online. *Recently* she bought several items from a retailer's website and *subsequently* received an e-mail with a special offer of a reduction on her next purchase. *Even* if she doesn't take advantage of the offer, she will most *likely* receive a string of similar mails *regardless* of any action she may take. That is an example of first generation e-mail marketing: *relatively* simple but not *exactly* dynamic.

1 adverbs of frequency (e.g. *sometimes, periodically*) ___frequently___
2 adverbs of time (e.g. *soon, afterwards*) ___recently___
3 adverbs of manner (e.g. *easily, quickly*) ___radically___
4 adverbs of condition or attitude (e.g. *possibly, luckily*) ___likely___
5 adverbs that modify adjectives (e.g. *widely, highly*) ___relatively___
6 wh- adverbs ___wherever___

2 Which of the adverbs could be moved to alternative positions?

 For more information, see page 159.

For more information, see page 159.

Practice   **In the following passage the adverbs have been removed. Insert the adverbs into appropriate positions in each section of the passage. More than one position may be possible.**

Dynamic email marketing

radically	systematically	actually

Dynamic e-mail marketing uses a different approach, incorporating multiple components to determine the next marketing step by factoring in data obtained from user profiles and data about how the target client behaved when they visited a particular website.

previously	particularly	eventually

For example, let's suppose Christy returns to a retailer's website where she has made a purchase. She clicks on a couple of pages until she finds one that interests her. She spends some time taking a closer look at some items that interest her but leaves the site without buying.

already	precisely	really	highly	effectively

On her next visit, Christy is treated to an email offering her a discount – her user profile is in the system – on a necklace, promoting the style she spent the most time viewing. Now, that is dynamic marketing but the problem is that most companies do not have the sophisticated data management and communication systems that are required to use it.

Second Life

Read the text about Second Life, a virtual world where people interact using graphic representations of themselves, or 'avatars'.

1 What problems did the original investors in Second Life face?
2 Why is traditional advertising media ineffective with Second Life?
3 In what capacity was Joni West involved in Second Life?
4 What solutions did she find to attract companies back to Second Life?
5 How can brands benefit from being present in Second Life?
6 How have advertisers changed their attitudes to Second Life?

FAST COMPANY

| TECHNOLOGY | DESIGN | ETHONOMICS | LEADERSHIP | MAGAZINE \| NEWSLETTERS \| JOBS | Google™ Custom Search |

Marketing in the virtual world
The second life of Second Life

1 Online virtual world Second Life first got hot a couple of years ago. Companies moved in and started to build their own virtual spaces. However, maintaining these areas required a lot of resources. Of course, if customers had followed, there would have been no problem. But they didn't, and dozens of companies scrambled to staunch their bleeding Second Life budgets. Second Life was over before it had begun.

2 At the same time, Joni West, a San Francisco-based fine artist and business-development consultant, stepped into the breach. "I saw all these huge virtual spaces – Adidas, Starwood Hotels, Dell – and they were all empty," says West, 47. "It was ridiculous."

3 In just two years, West has rewritten the rules of corporate marketing on Second Life. An avid user of the site, she realised that billboards, commercials, and streaming video fell flat among hyper-creative users who wanted to interact. Instead, she concluded, companies should try to spark user-to-user discussion – a surprisingly cost-effective option on Second Life. This insight has produced successful initiatives for clients such as Sun Microsystems, Overstock.com, and Nestlé, and made West's firm, This Second Marketing, the leader in shepherding name-brand companies back to the virtual world.

4 West stumbled into the business potential of Second Life while pursuing her passion for fine art. "I thought it would be fabulous to create a virtual art gallery where I could bring people from all around the world," she says. One day, she was sitting on a Second Life art gallery couch, doing just that – talking to people from various countries – and she had their rapt attention. "At that point, I realised how powerful one-on-one engagement could be in Second Life."

5 West used techniques gleaned from 25 years of marketing experience, including digital and email campaigns, to woo potential clients. She calmly explained that the previous failures of Second Life were a result of not harnessing the medium appropriately to reach its 14 million users, up to 66,000 of whom are present at any time. "I describe the mistake companies made like this: Imagine you've never been to Manhattan. You cross the George Washington Bridge, and someone hands you a guidebook. The first place you're going is not the Reebok store."

6 Translation: Second Life is not a place to make sales. It's also a venue where large companies don't have to spend $3 million to build an elaborate space when $10,000 to $100,000, used judiciously, can have a much larger impact.

7 For an early campaign with Colgate, for example, West's staffers fanned out in the virtual world to give out about 35,000 Colgate smiles, along with a list of 10 cool places that make you smile. "Avatars aren't born with smiles, and people often don't know where to go in Second Life," she says. "Users want companies to bring something relevant to the community."

8 West's work has started to inspire other high-profile, higher-budget efforts. The Weather Channel has developed an attraction that lets users play sports in varied terrains with highly challenging weather conditions (tsunamis, avalanches, flash floods). Users spend an average of 30 minutes per visit, and the attraction draws a crowd around the clock. "It's not like a commercial, where maybe they watched and maybe they didn't," says Drew Stein, CEO of developer Involve 3D, which built the Weather Channel's virtual experience. "You're talking about a user actually paying attention, and you can time it. That's hard to replicate in any other medium."

9 The upshot is that the virtual world has survived the media spin cycle. "I think at first, everyone was there strictly for the hype and sunk their money into 15 minutes of fame," Involve's Stein says. "Now they're analysing what they're doing and seeing how Second Life breathes." And in the process, breathing into it a second life.

Career skills

Decision making

Making choices is an integral part of the decision-making process. Leaders who make good choices without wasting time are seen as decisive, insightful and successful. Leaders who stall and who can't make up their minds have difficulty motivating and inspiring their teams.

In everyday life, we generally have to make snap decisions about choices. In such situations the best strategy is to keep our goals in mind and trust our intuition to make the right choices. However, when time is available, the following techniques can help make the most appropriate choice.

a Consider the consequences.
b Go for it!
c Narrow down the options.
d Evaluate the outcome.
e Get the facts.
f Set your goal.

Read the list of techniques and match the headings (a–f) to each of the points below (1–6).

1 _____ f _____

You need to clearly identify and define the reason and purpose for the decision you are about to make. To do this you can ask yourself the following questions:

- What exactly is the reason for making a change?
- What do we hope to obtain from the outcome?
- If you never lose sight of the answers to these questions, you will be more likely to make the best choice.

2 _____ e _____

Find out what options are open to you and collect as much data and information as you can about each option. Asking for advice isn't a weakness – it can be very beneficial to learn from other people's experience.

3 _____ a _____

List and brainstorm all the pros and cons of every option. Consider all the angles, which could include cost, energy, time, etc. Consider whether positive outcomes can outweigh any losses.

4 _____ c _____

If there are several alternatives open to you, try to reduce them to a limited few and reconsider the situation with these restricted choices.

5 _____ b _____

There always comes a time to stop talking and start acting. Make your choice and start a plan of action to be executed.

6 _____ d _____

When the action has been put into place ask youself what lessons can be learnt [*learned*] from the decision making procedure used. This is an important step for further development of your decision-making skills and judgement.

When brainstorming the pros and cons of an option you can use a table or grid to help you to organise your thoughts. You can also give each point a weighting by giving it a plus or minus score out of five or ten.

Work in pairs. Study the table below which shows the advantages and disadvantages of producing an e-catalogue instead of a paper one. In this case the scores for and against are very close. What do you think the company should decide to do? Can you think of any more pros, cons and outcomes to add to the table?

Pros	Cons	Possible outcomes
Cheaper to produce in the long run. +5 Easier and cheaper to distribute by email. +5 A majority of customers will be happy and comfortable with an e-version of the catalogue. +4 Sales force could show the catalogue on their laptops. +2 Total +16	Need specialised staff or train existing staff to produce an e-catalogue, the first year. −5 Some customers may not want to download the catalogue. −4 Some customers prefer a paper support. −3 Sales force will have no paper support to show customers. −5 Total −17	It will make the catalogue more expensive in the first year. −2 Customers may print out the catalogue anyway, and resent the cost. −3 Customers may get used to it in time and see the point. +3 Some ecologically-minded customers might be impressed with the move on ideological grounds. +4 Total +2

Listening 3 ⊙ **Listen to two people talking about the problem and answer the questions.**

1 What is the most important argument for the first speaker?
2 What is the most important argument for the second speaker?
3 What choice did they make in the end?
4 Do you think they made the right choice?

Speaking **Work in pairs. Use the technique shown in the table above to make a decision about one or more of the following.**

- buying your new camera in a shop or over the Internet
- buying a new car or keeping your old one
- changing jobs or staying in your current one
- applying for a job in a small business or in a large corporation
- investing money in the stock exchange or in property

Discuss your choices with other pairs.

Culture at work **Taking action**

In some cultures it is considered positive to take your time when making choices. In cultures like these, choices are based on logical, rational and sound arguments. Business people will spend a lot of time thinking about the outcome of each possible move and will be slower to take action than in cultures where intuition is valued and time is considered a scarce commodity. These cultures prefer to act quickly even if it means making a mistake and going back to the drawing board later. What is closest to your culture?

Dilemma
 &Decision

Dilemma: Creative showcase

Brief

IAB (Internet Advertising Bureau) have a monthly award for cutting-edge creativity in the online advertising sector. Anyone can enter as long as their campaign is targeted at a UK audience. The work is judged by senior online creatives and the winners, plus two runners up, have their work published in *Marketing Week*. Recently, the following campaigns were shortlisted for the prize.

In one take, on one tank

Tribal DDB's 'in one take, on one tank' concept for Volkswagen showcases the amazing fuel efficiency of the new Bluemotion Polo in a clear, engaging way. To create it, the team drove the car from London to the Geneva motorshow on a single tank of diesel and filmed the journey in a single take – 36 hours of footage which was edited down and incorporated into a site that enabled the viewer to participate interactively in the drive and review statistics relating to CO_2 output, cost and fuel consumption. The end result is a vivid demonstration of the car's unique capability.

Task 1

Work in groups. Discuss what you think of each of the campaigns. Which one appeals most to you personally?

Task 2

Discuss each of the campaigns in terms of the criteria below. Weight each one by giving it a score out of ten.

- Brand fit: how well does the campaign fit the brand image?
- The idea: how original is the campaign?
- Use of the medium: how many different media were used?
- Engagement: what is the quality of consumer interaction?

Task 3

Choose a winner.

Write it up

Write a press release to announce the winning campaign.

 For more information, see *Style guide*, page 24.

Decision:

Listen to Lars Vanderbilt, a creative consultant, talking about how the judges chose to distribute the prizes.

1 What does he think of the campaigns?
2 Does he agree with the judges' decision?
3 What reasons does he give?

Fill the Indigo

O2, the telecoms company, asked Archibald Ingall Stretton to raise awareness of their music credentials and deliver a real experience for the brand slogan – 'We're better connected'. They hired the Indigo2 venue, generally used for live music. Then they told people 'If you can fill it, you can win it.' Any person who could invite enough people to fill the stadium could have it for a private party! This was the ultimate test of popularity and social networking skills.

The X Factor Challenge

The X Factor is Europe's biggest singing contest, sponsored by Carphone Warehouse, a mobile phone retailer.The X Factor Challenge lets viewers sing and draw themselves for a chance to appear on TV during the show's ad breaks. The campaign uses TV, mobile and social media to engage the user at different levels, from simply watching someone else's performance to creating their own, sharing it via their mobile and, ultimately, starring on TV. Each week, contestants are picked from the website and their animations and singing performances are used as TV clips. They are seen by up to 12 million viewers during the Saturday night X Factor shows.

Review 3

Language check

Future perfect

Complete the management lecture with appropriate forms of the future perfect.

Many of you ([1] read) _____ last year's study which found no evidence of a connection between a boss's personality and company performance. Well, by now, I hope you ([2] also look at) _____ the notes I sent you about my personal research which, by the time it's finished, ([3] prove) _____ more or less the opposite and if by the end of today's class you don't believe there is a link, then I ([4] not achieve) _____ what I set out to do. Before publishing our results, both myself and a team of psychologists ([5] work) _____ day and night on this project. But I know we'll feel that ([6] be) _____ worth it in the end.

Active and passive

Are the underlined verbs active or passive?

The ever changing world of online advertising [1]<u>confuses</u> many business people about what really works. It seems that online video-based ads [2]<u>have been presenting</u> the biggest dilemmas. At a recent Ad Age Conference that very topic [3]<u>has been discussed</u>. What [4]<u>was brought</u> to the delegates' attention was the fact that only certain content works and that content should [5]<u>be designed</u> by professional content creators. Research shows that when businesses [6]<u>got</u> specialists to do the campaigns, the results were better. The only problem which seems [7]<u>to be looming</u> on the horizon is whether the novelty of online video advertising [8]<u>is wearing off</u> or not.

Have and *get*

Complete the sentences with a form of *have* or *get*.

1   They've just _____ the whole office redesigned.
2   Do you think she _____ the post of manager?
3   Why don't you _____ the books checked by an auditor?
4   They are thinking of _____ headhunters to do the new recruiting.
5   Thanks to his role in getting the new contract he _____ a pay increase.

Word order: adverbs

Are the adverbs in italics in the most appropriate place? If not, where should they be placed?

As [1]*frequently* alpha males are appointed to top jobs in the computer industry it surprised many [2]*probably* when Diane Green was appointed CEO of VMware. The company sells software that makes data centres more efficient and has [3]*quietly* become the world's fourth most valuable traded [4]*publicly* software company.

Ms Green has already made her management style clear to employees. Open communication is key to her method and she [5]*regularly* grants interviews in a glass walled office next to the entrance which she pops out of [6]*often* to greet passers-by.

Consolidation

Choose the correct word or form of the words in italics below.

Most people may drink [1]*periodically/ approximately* two litres of water a day but they [2]*actually/systematically* consume about three if the water that goes into their food is [3]*taken into account/being taken into account*. We need to [4]*get/have* the rich, who consume considerably more than the poor, to reduce their water consumption if a real crisis is [5]*to be avoided/to have been avoided*.

By the end of the coming decade farmers [6]*will have to have found/will have been finding* more efficient ways of using water if they want to continue producing enough food. Incredible as it sounds, by the end of the irrigation process as much as 70% of water used by farmers [7]*won't have made it/won't make it* to the crops, usually due to leaks.

But [8]*having/getting* farmers to use water efficiently is only one step to better yields. If Africa is to survive, it will [9]*have to have/ have to had* more decent seeds and enough fertiliser as well as [10]*radically/subsequently* improved pest control, storage and distribution by end of the next decade.

Vocabulary check

1 Put the words in the correct groups.

environment   carbon footprint   search
engine   subordinates   news feeds
harassment   scarcity   coaching   social
networking   Machiavellian   pop-ups
renewable   empowerment   snippets
sustainable

Resources	Power	E-marketing

2 Complete the text below with the correct form of some of the words above.

Politicians can no longer allow big polluters to operate on the [1]_____ theory that the end justifies the means. Producing short-term solutions with no concern for their [2]_____ and with little or no research being done to find [3]_____ solutions is creating nothing short of an [4]_____ disaster.

[5]_____ controllers, who feel intimidated by companies, to impose the penalties that are in place would be a start. Unfortunately many corporations consider regulations merely as unnecessary [6]_____ which prevents them from doing their business efficiently.

3 Which of the sentences below use *like* and *as* correctly? Make corrections where necessary.

1 Water is not *as* air, which is an endless resource. _____

2 They are looking for sustainable solutions *like* all companies should. _____

3 She acts *as* though she is the boss. _____

4 The company is sinking into financial ruin *as* a drowning man. _____

5 He runs the company *like* a military operation. _____

6 Facebook acts *as* an interface for marketers. _____

Usage

Proverbs

Complete the proverbs below.

1 Two _____ are better than one.
2 Don't judge a _____ by its cover.
3 _____ is the mother of invention.
4 All work and no _____ makes Jack a dull boy.
5 If at first you don't _____ , try, try again.
6 Scratch my _____ and I'll scratch yours.
7 Don't _____ your chickens before they're hatched.

Career skills

Influencing

Put the dialogue in the correct order.

☐ a Thanks. Listen, to be perfectly frank I'm still not keen on that idea we were discussing.

☐ b Where did you get hold of that information?

☐ c No problem, but I haven't a lot of time.

☐ d Thanks for agreeing to meet with me.

☐ e On the golf course! So if you bring it up at the next meeting ...

☐ f But I have it on good authority that management are!

☐ g Great tie, by the way!

Debating

Correct the mistake in each sentence.

1 Welcome to tonight's debate which I have the honour of moderation. _____

2 We are lucky having a distinguished panel of speakers. _____

3 Allow me to introduce the speakers who will be participating at today's debate. _____

4 The health and well been of the citizens of our country are under discussion. _____

5 We take many resources as granted. _____

6 Perhaps the most important of those resource is water. _____

7 I'll start my argument against this motion by putting some facts out. _____

Unit 10
Risk

www.longman-elt.com   www.economist.com

Facing the odds

Keynotes

Risk is a part of business. Managers have to **identify** risks and then analyse their **risk exposure** in terms of the **probability** or **likelihood** of a risk occurring and the seriousness of the **impact** that could result. Using **risk management**, companies can put in place systems and procedures to **assess**, reduce and **mitigate** the risks they face. The main areas of business risk are: **strategic risk** (customer and industry changes, for example), **operational risk** (such as regulatory, cultural and supply chain issues), **financial risk** (from exchange rates and interest rates, for example) and **hazard risk** (such as environmental events). **Contingency planning** refers to plans that are agreed upon and can be implemented if a risk actually happens. Businesses can also protect themselves against risk by using **insurance** and **hedging**.

Risk profiles

Some managers try to avoid situations where there is a high degree of uncertainty, while others feel stimulated by risk and are more willing to live with uncertainty. Your risk profile shows what your attitude is to taking risks.

1 What is your risk profile? Are you risk-inclined or risk-averse? What is the biggest risk that you have ever taken?

2 Assessing the degree of risk that you are exposed to is the starting point for risk management. The following list of statements is designed to help employees evaluate the risk of being made redundant. Put them into two groups according to whether they increase or decrease the risk.

a Your company would have to use a headhunter to find someone to replace you.

b You have no direct dealings with customers.

c The department you work in is well staffed.

d Your company is currently restructuring.

e You are approaching retirement age.

f Your boss resigned but you were not offered the position.

g Your salary is at the high end of the scale for your profession.

h The work you do is not very demanding.

3 Look at the following situations. How would you weigh the risks in each case? What decision would you make?

1 You have been given the chance to manage an overseas subsidiary that has been underperforming. The previous manager was transferred after antagonising the unions with a plan to reorganise work procedures. If you succeed in this assignment, your long term career prospects will be very promising. Would you accept the post or not?

2 Your company has recently patented a new technology. However, developing the technology would be extremely expensive and there are concerns that it could produce negative health impacts on users. Would you go ahead or not?

3 You have been contacted by your HR director, who is offering you a one year overseas assignment in a developing country. You would have to move to the country with your spouse and children. Would you accept or not?

Uncertainty

The text on the opposite page deals with the controversial ideas of Nassim Nicholas Taleb.

1 What does he say today's forecasters and planners fail to take into account when planning for the future?

2 What do we learn about:

- Mr Taleb?

- his theory of 'black swans'?

- the relevance of this theory to the business world?

Glossary

churn out constantly produce

charlatan a fake or imposter

maverick non-conformist and independent thinker

mainstream the current of thought of the majority

laureate a person who is given an award for outstanding achievement

Uncertainty
The perils of prediction

Let forecasters beware

1 "IT'S tough to make predictions, especially about the future," said that great baseball-playing philosopher, Yogi Berra. And yet we continue to try, churning out forecasts on everything from the price of oil to the next civil war. Nassim Nicholas Taleb, a professor of the sciences of uncertainty (who gave us "known unknowns") and author of *The Black Swan: The Impact of the Highly Improbable* (2007), has no time for the "charlatans" who think they can map the future. Forget the important things: we can't even get it right when estimating the cost of a building – witness the massively over-budget Sydney Opera House or the new Wembley Stadium.

2 The problem is that almost all forecasters ignore large deviations and thus fail to take account of "Black Swans". Mr Taleb defines a Black Swan as an event that is unexpected, has an extreme impact and is made to seem predictable by explanations concocted afterwards. It can be either positive or negative. Examples include the September 11th 2001 attacks and the rise of the Internet. Smaller shocks, such as novels and pop acts whose popularity explodes thanks to word of mouth, can also be Black Swans.

3 Humans are bad at factoring in the possibility of randomness and uncertainty. We forget about unpredict-ability when it is our turn to predict, and overestimate our own knowledge. When researchers asked a group of students to choose a range for the number of

lovers Catherine the Great had had, wide enough to ensure that they had a 98% chance of being right, a staggering 45% of them got it wrong.

4 Why didn't they guarantee being correct by picking a range of none to ten thousand? After all, there were no prizes for keeping the range tight. The answer is that humans have an uncontrollable urge to be precise, for better or (all too often) worse. That is a fine quality in a watch-repair man or a brain surgeon, but counter-productive when dealing with uncertainty.

5 Mr Taleb cut his philosophical teeth in the basement of his family home in Lebanon during the long civil war there (another Black Swan), devouring books as mortars flew overhead. By the time he began work as a financial-market quantitative analyst in the 1980s, he had already become convinced that the academic mainstream was looking at probability the wrong way. He remains a maverick, promoting the work of obscure thinkers and attacking Nobel laureates. All he is trying to do, he says, is make the world see how much there is that can't be seen.

6 Why, he asks, do we take absence of proof to be proof of absence? Why do we base the study of chance on the world of games? Casinos, after all, have rules that preclude the truly shocking. And why do we attach such importance to statistics when they tell us so little about what is to come? A single set of data can lead you down two very

different paths. More maddeningly still, when faced with a Black Swan we often grossly underestimate or overestimate its significance. Take technology. The founder of IBM predicted that the world would need no more than a handful of computers, and nobody saw that the laser would be used to mend retinas.

7 Nor do we learn the right lessons from such eruptions. Mr Taleb argues that the spectacular collapse in 1998 of Long-Term Capital Management was caused by the inability of the hedge fund's managers to see a world that lay outside their flawed models. And yet those models are still widely used today. This is ridiculous but not surprising. Business is stuffed full of bluffers, he argues, and successful companies and financial institutions owe as much to chance as to skill.

8 That is a little unfair. Many blockbuster products have their roots in bright ideas, rigorous research and canny marketing, rather than luck. And corporate "scenario planners" are better than they used to be at thinking about Black Swan-type events.

9 Taleb suspects that crises will be fewer in number but more severe in future. And he suggests concentrating on the consequences of Black Swans, which can be known, rather than on the probability that they will occur, which can't (think of earthquakes). But he never makes professional predictions because it is better to be "broadly right rather than precisely wrong". ■

Vocabulary 1 Match the definitions below to words and expressions in the text.

1 to calculate approximately (para 1) _estimate_
2 not likely to happen (para 1) _improbable_
3 prediction (para 1) _forecast_
4 to take into consideration x2 (para 2 and para 3) _take account of, factor in_
5 uncertainty x2 (para 3) _randomness, unpredictability_
6 scholarly or scientific investigators (para 3) _researchers_
7 achieving the opposite result to the one desired (para 4) _counter-productive_
8 take too lightly (para 6) _underestimate_
9 fakers or pretenders (para 7) _bluffers_
10 runaway success (para 8) _blockbuster_

Vocabulary 2 ## *Chance* and *luck*

Chance and *luck* are sometimes used synonymously but also have different meanings. Look at the examples from the text.

*... a 98% **chance** of being right ...* (para 3)

*Many blockbuster products have their roots in bright ideas, rigorous research and canny marketing, rather than **luck**.* (para 8)

Chance generally relates to the odds of something occurring, without any suggestion of preference. *Luck*, on the other hand, can be either good or bad.

1 Match the examples (1–7) with the appropriate definitions (a–g).

1	Chance will determine the outcome. b	a	a random or unplanned event
2	The chances of us meeting the deadline are good. f	b	a force assumed to cause events that cannot be foreseen or controlled
3	Is there any chance that you could replace me? d	c	a favourable set of circumstances; an opportunity
4	It was pure luck that nobody was injured in the accident. a	d	possibility
5	She took a big chance when she launched the business but it really paid off. e	e	a risk or hazard; a gamble
6	We tried to find a cheaper supplier but we had no luck. g	f	the likelihood of something happening
7	Don't make the same mistake again. This is your last chance. c	g	success

2 Complete the sentences below with the appropriate form of either *luck* or *chance*.

1 I couldn't believe my _luck_ when I got the transfer to head office.
2 What's the _chance_ of succeeding, do you think?
3 I jumped at the _chance_ of going to the States, I'd always wanted to.
4 As _luck_ would have it, my computer crashed and I lost the file.
5 I'm not leaving anything to _chance_ I've double checked everything.
6 What _luck_ to find you here, I was hoping we'd meet today!
7 Is this by any _chance_ what you were looking for? I found it on my desk.

Loanwords

Loanwords are words adopted into English from other languages, such as the French words *charlatan* and *laureate* in the text. The following loanwords are commonly used in business English. Put them into the appropriate columns. What do they refer to?

bonanza	embargo	glitch	imbroglio	mogul
per capita	tycoon	status quo	pundit	pro rata

People or situations	Problems and obstacles	Rates	States of affairs or situations
mogul 大亨 tycoon pundit	embargo 禁止 glitch 失误 imbroglio	per capira pro rara	bonanza 大好 status quo 现状

@ An Internet search using the keyword 'loanwords' will list websites with examples of loanwords. What words from your language are used in English?

1 Look at some predictions made in the past by specialists. Which of the words in the box do you think they were referring to?

computers	telephone	television
paperless	vacuum cleaners	nuclear energy

1 'I think there is a world market for maybe five _____ .' Thomas Watson (President of IBM), 1943

2 'This _____ has too many shortcomings to be seriously considered as a means of communication.' WIlliam Orton (President of Western Union), 1876

3 '_____ won't be able to hold on to any market it captures after the first six months.' Darryl Zanuck (Hollywood film producer), 1946

4 'By the turn of this century, we will live in a _____ society.' Roger Smith (Chairman of General Motors), 1986

5 'Nuclear-powered _____ will probably be a reality within 10 years.' Alex Lewyt (inventor and manufacturer), 1955

6 'There is not the slightest indication that _____ will ever be obtainable.' Albert Einstein (physicist), 1932

2 Make predictions about what will happen in the future.

Risk management

Listen to an interview with risk manager Diederik Van Goor.

1 What is Mr Van Goor's professional background?

2 List the four types of risk that he mentions and give an example of each.

3 What can a consultant do to help a company to manage its risks?

4 What examples are mentioned of companies that failed to manage their risks?

5 What are the potential consequences for a business that fails to manage its risks?

6 How are some companies going about improving their risk management?

Diederik Van Goor

Probability and possibility

When we refer to probability and possibility we use the modal verbs *can,* *could, may, might, ought to, shall* and *should* to indicate how likely an event or situation is to occur. The modal verbs *must, will* and *would* are used when we are referring to events or situations that are certain to take place.

you have choice or no choice

The past forms *could, might, should* and *would* are mainly used for reporting statements. The past perfect forms *should have, would have, could have, might have, must have* are used to talk about possibility, impossibility and probability in relation to past events or situations.

Other words that can be used to refer to probability or possibility in the present, future and past include the following:

Verbs: *expect, forecast, plan, predict*

Adjectives: *bound, certain, (un)likely, (im)possible, (im)probable, (un)sure*

Nouns: *odds, chance, likelihood*

For more information, see page 160.

1 **Indicate which of the alternatives in the text is not possible.**

Initially we were all [1] *certain/bound/sure* that the project [2] *could/might/would succeed* and none of us [3] *could/would/may* ever have imagined that that [4] *might/would/will not* be the case. The problem was that we hadn't factored all of the risks into our projection. Originally we [5] *had forecast/had expected/had planned* to spend six months on development. When we realised that we [6] *couldn't/shouldn't/wouldn't* meet that deadline, we had to review our cost projections and that's when we decided to abandon the idea. Whose fault was it? Well, the engineers [7] *can't have/ may not have/couldn't have* been informed of certain changes to the specifications so I suppose you [8] *can/could/may* say that it was a combination of factors.

2 **Complete the text with the appropriate modal or other form of the verbs in brackets.**

SPACE AND RISK

The recent collision of two satellites in space ([1] have) *might have* serious consequences for the future development of commercial space programmes. When an American and a Russian satellite smashed into each other, the result was a shower of space debris that ([2] undoubtedly remain) *will undoubtedly remain* on radar screens for many years to come. What's even more surprising is that the operators of the American satellite ([3] avoid) *could have avoided* the collision by changing the trajectory of their craft. There are already 17,000 pieces of highly dangerous debris in space and this latest incident ([4] make) _____ matters worse. Until *might make*

now, a catastrophe has been avoided – but that ([5] change) *could change* according to some specialists who say that more incidents like this ([6] be) *are* likely to happen. One way to deal with the problem ([7] be) *could be* to redesign spacecraft. But without an international agreement it seems unlikely that the issue of space debris will be resolved any time soon. The one lesson that space nations ([8] learn) *will learn* from the collision is that they ([9] have) *will have* to work together to mitigate space risk. If they don't, then space ([10] become) *will become* an even more dangerous place than it already is.

Speaking

Discuss with a partner how likely the following things are.

- Rapid long distance air travel will be made possible by space planes.
- Earth will be hit by an asteroid.
- Space rockets will be replaced by a giant space lift.

@ An Internet search using the keywords 'world space risk' will list proposed initiatives to protect our space environment. Choose an example of one such initiative to discuss.

1 Read the text below. What did the Cambridge researchers conclude about traders?

guardian.co.uk

Search | guardian.co.uk ⬍ | Search

News | World Cup | Comment | Culture | Business | Money | Life & style | Travel | Environment | TV | Video | Community | Jobs

News ⟩ Science ⟩ Medical research ⟩

Scientists find secret ingredient for making (and losing) lots of money – testosterone

1 Money doesn't make the world go round: it's testosterone. The more that traders have, the richer they'll become – up to a point.

2 John Coates, who used to manage a trading floor at Deutsche Bank on Wall Street but is now at the Judge Business School at Cambridge University, and Professor Joe Herbert, a neuroscientist, set out to study the brains of City traders to discover what makes them tick.

3 They measured levels of testosterone and cortisol (a stress hormone) in 17 traders at a City of London bank for eight consecutive business days. They found that those traders with higher testosterone levels in the morning were most likely to make money on the day's trading. One trader hit a six-day "winning streak" during which he made more than double his daily profit. During that time his testosterone levels went up 74%.

4 The team also found that cortisol levels among the traders increased when their takings became more volatile and the market generally was less stable. "You can get this positive feedback loop between winning, testosterone, greater confidence and risk taking," Coates said.

5 He believes his work taps into the "winner effect" that scientists have found in numerous competitive situations, from fighting male animals to human athletes. In one-on-one competitions, men gain a testosterone boost when they win. This gives them an advantage in the next bout and if they win that they get a further advantage. And so on. Coates' study suggests that this is happening even in the world of financial derivatives trading.

6 But he admitted it is not that simple. "My great fear is that people will walk away with the idea that if you want to make money in the markets you had better have a lot of testosterone," he said.

7 He thinks there comes a point when traders have too much testosterone and so start to take irrational risks. That is when the bubble bursts and the market crashes. At this point, the stress hormone cortisol becomes significant. Coates believes that prolonged high levels of cortisol – triggered by a rapidly falling market – lead to anxiety and clouded judgment. "You tend to see danger everywhere rather than opportunity. In that situation you don't do anything.

8 "People get paralysed by the fear. [It] takes over so they are no longer thinking rationally. They are no longer doing the things that they should be doing to make money." So, for every boom it creates, testosterone is most likely behind every bust too. "During the dotcom bubble I became really curious about the behaviour of people who were caught up in the bubble. They weren't acting in a way that accorded with any of the predictions of economics or finance. I thought these people were on a drug. They weren't themselves."

9 He believes the traders, who are almost all young men, were profoundly influenced by the testosterone hit they get from the job. But, he said, primeval brain mechanisms activated by the hormone can also lead them to irrational risk-taking. "I think this molecule is partly responsible for financial instability."

10 Among lessons Coates draws is that trading floors need more women and older men who have lower testosterone levels and cooler heads.

Glossary

makes them tick makes them behave as they do

winning streak a continuous series of successes

bout a fight or competition

derivatives financial instruments based on contracts and not on assets

2 Read the text again and answer the questions.

1 How was the experiment conducted?

2 What were the findings about (a) testosterone and (b) cortisol?

3 What is meant by the 'winner effect'?

4 What does Professor Coates believe are the negative consequences of too much testoserone?

5 What example does he give to illustrate his fears?

6 According to Professor Coates, what lessons can be drawn from the study?

Speaking Some people believe that the financial markets would operate better if more women worked there. What is your opinion?

Career skills

Know what you want.

Know what your counterpart want.

Know the concessions you are willing to make.

Know your options.

Know your counterpart and the subject matter.

Rehearse.

Negotiating

Good negotiating isn't about one person or side winning and the other losing. It is about both sides leaving the negotiation table feeling they got what they wanted, or at least feeling better off than when they went into the negotiation. Unsuccessful negotiation is when one side or the other feels they've compromised too much and made sacrifices they didn't want to. In an ideal situation, you will find that the other person wants what you are prepared to trade, and that you are prepared to give what the other person wants. If this is not the case, and one person must give way, then this person might try to negotiate some form of compensation for doing so. Ultimately, if the agreement is to be considered 'win-win', both sides should feel comfortable with the final solution. One of the keys to success is preparation. The following checklist should help to prepare a negotiation.

1 It's not enough to have a general idea of what it is you are trying to achieve through the negotiation. It may be a good idea to write a paragraph describing in detail what you want to get out of the transaction. Then you can extract from this a precise list of points about which you must stay focused during the discussion. You must be very clear on your objectives and how you mean to achieve them before going into any negotiations.

2 The next step is to make a list of what you think your opposite is looking for and seeking to avoid. Knowing your counterpart's goals, objectives, and sought after results helps to identify common points that may lead to creative solutions.

3 Consider the following: what must you absolutely achieve to conclude a successful bargain? What terms, conditions, extras could you live without? Try to identify something extra which you can offer which is of little value to you but of great value to your counterpart.

4 Knowing there are alternatives can give you confidence and can influence the negotiation in your favour.

5 People can view the same facts and appeals differently. It is possible to get some insight into how your counterpart might react by thinking about his/her personality, studying body language, considering culture, position in the hierarchy, etc. Your knowledge of the person will influence how you bargain with them. It is also important to understand the area under discussion thoroughly or you will almost certainly lose more than someone who does know it.

6 To prepare for a particular negotiation, you could ask a friend or colleague to role play with you. You could give them the description you wrote in stage one of this process to help them prepare for the practice run through.

Match the headings (a–f) to each of the descriptions (1–6) above.

a Know your options. _____4_____

b Rehearse. _____6_____

c Know your counterpart and the subject matter. _____5_____

d Know the concessions you are willing to make. _____3_____

e Know what you want. _____1_____

f Know what your counterpart wants. _____2_____

Stages of negotiations

When the actual negotiation takes place, it is usual to make some small talk or general conversation first as an 'ice breaking' exercise. Then there will probably be an exchange of proposals and refusals, followed by counter proposals. It may be that some conditions will be imposed and/or some concessions made before a final agreement is reached.

Listening 2 ⊙ **Listen to a negotiation between a boss and an employee and answer the questions.**

1 What is the subject and outcome of the negotiation?
2 What proposal is made?
3 What counter proposal is put forward?
4 What argument is given for imposing conditions?
5 Which speaker is best prepared for the negotiation?
6 If the other person had also prepared well, what might the outcome have been?
7 Could you describe this as a win-win negotiation?

Speaking

1 In pairs, prepare some strong counter arguments for Paul and what the boss could say to him and role-play the situation again to arrive at a different outcome. Use the preparation techniques opposite to help you. Think about:

- his marital status
- whether or not he has children
- if he has plans for the office
- improvements he could make here if he has other job options.

2 Work in pairs. Student A is in a well paid, secure job. Student B has invited him/her to a meeting to try to convince Student A to leave his/her job and to invest his/her savings in a start-up and help run it.

Student A: Turn to page 139.
Student B: Turn to page 140.

Read your profiles. When you have fully prepared the negotiation, meet and act it out.

Culture at work

Striking a bargain

There is an argument that maintains that as long as a proposal is financially attractive it will succeed in every culture. On the other hand, there is evidence that being sensitive to culture can make a difference when there are two people putting forward identical proposals and packages. If you are sensitive to the culture you are negotiating in, you can prepare properly and you won't be thrown off by surprises. For example, in some cultures negotiators may discuss issues simultaneously rather than approaching topics sequentially. Some cultures will negotiate in teams and decisions will be based upon consensual agreement. In others, decisions can take a long time due to the need to analyse information and statistics in great depth. Pressure tactics and imposing deadlines are ways of closing deals in some cultures whilst in others this would backfire. Which of the above points correspond to your culture?

Dilemma &Decision

Dilemma: Wildcat strike

Brief

Lonsdale Fuels plc is a major petroleum refiner and distributor with operations in several countries. As part of its strategy to reduce production and operating costs, the company has embarked on a five-year plan to renovate key parts of its refining plants by introducing more cost-effective technologies. The first plant that is scheduled for renovation is the ageing Kirkby refinery on the East coast of the United Kingdom.

Janet Fraser Darling, the plant manager of the Kirkby refinery, has the challenging task of overseeing the implementation of the first phase of the company's modernisation plan which is due to start in one month's time. She knows it won't be easy but she is confident that she has fully analysed all the risks that will be involved.

And as Janet drives in to work on Monday morning she is already mentally going through the list of tasks that she still has to deal with before the project starts up. At the motorway exit she is surprised to see so many police vehicles but it's only when she reaches the refinery itself that she realises that something is wrong. Just outside the main gate she sees a line of police officers in yellow DayGlo jackets and immediately behind them a large group of Lonsdale employees on strike. The strikers have positioned several large trucks across the entrance and it's clear that access to the plant is blocked. At the head of the group of strikers, Janet recognises Bob Leighton, the outspoken leader of the CPW – the Confederation of Petroleum Workers. Janet parks her car and strides over to talk to Mr Leighton. She knows that if she doesn't find a solution to whatever the problem is, production could be stopped and the renovation plans could be brought to an indefinite halt.

Bob Leighton gets straight to the point. Members of his union have informed him that Lonsdale Fuels is planning to use subcontractors from overseas for the renovation work at the plant. According to reports, 200 foreign workers will be arriving later in the week to start work on the project and they will be working under contracts negotiated in their home countries. None of these jobs has been advertised in the UK. The union suspects that Lonsdale is aware of this and has called its workers out on strike in protest. It looks as if Janet and Bob have some serious negotiating to do.

Task 1

Divide into two groups. Student A will represent Bob Leighton and Student B will represent Janet Fraser Darling. To prepare the negotiation, Student A should use the information on the page 141 and Student B on page 142.

Task 2

Work in pairs. Meet a representative of the other side and hold the negotiation.

Task 3

Compare the outcome of your negotiation with that of another pair.

Write it up

Write a short report for either the head office of Lonsdale Fuels or that of the CPW, summarising the outcome of the negotiations. You may want to conduct further Internet research on the subject.

 For more information, see *Style guide*, page 22.

Decision:

Listen to Dennis Cooper, a risk manager, talking about the events at the Kirkby plant. What does he have to say about the risks of 'impatriation'?

White collar fraudsters

Keynotes

In today's electronic age, many illegal acts such as **credit card fraud**, **money laundering** and **identity theft** have been made easier due to the increase in business transactions over the Internet. In more traditional business organisations **fraudulent** acts, when they occur, can range from relatively minor **expense account fraud** to more serious **embezzlement** and huge **misappropriation of funds** through **creative accounting**. Other **white collar crimes** include **tax evasion** and **bribery**. Most **fraudsters** are caught following **whistleblowing** (colleagues revealing the wrongdoing of peers or seniors to outside authorities), rather than through **internal controls**. Recently, regulatory bodies such as the **FSA** and **SEC** have filed **law suits**, and some executives have been found **guilty**, **fined** and even been given a **prison sentence**.

Ivan Boesky

Dennis Kozlowski

Preview — Crime and punishment

1 Work in pairs. Look at the following examples of acts which are considered to be dishonest, or are even illegal, in many countries. Rank them in terms of how serious *you* think they are.

- ⑦ demanding cash in return for securing contracts ___3___
- ④ using company funds to buy a new laptop ___5___
- ③ depositing money you earned in cash in a country with fewer banking regulations ___4___
- ① taking home company stationery ___6___
- ② photocopying a chapter from a management book to distribute at a meeting ___7___
- ⑥ asking a friend who is a policeman to cancel parking fines that your sales team have accumulated ___2___
- ⑤ buying shares on the basis of secret information given to you by a friend ___1___

2 Match the acts in exercise 1 with the types of misconduct below.

1 petty theft _____
2 copyright infringement _____
3 tax evasion _____
4 embezzlement and misappropriation of company funds _____
5 insider trading _____
6 corruption _____
7 racketeering 羿圆凶②

Speaking

Do you think people should go to prison for any of these acts? If not, how should they be punished, if at all? If you discovered your boss or colleague was involved in similar activities, would you contact the appropriate authorities? Why/Why not?

@ An Internet search using the keywords 'Ivan Boesky' and 'Dennis Kozlowski' will list websites with articles about each man. Which of the above crimes were they convicted of? Do you agree with the sentences they received?

Reading 1 — Punishable by prison

Read the text on the opposite page and answer the questions.

1 Which type of business group is involved?
2 What have they been accused of doing?
3 What kind of punishment are the executives facing?
4 How are other 'sins' against competition punished?
5 Does the author think that Steve Ballmer should have gone to jail?
6 Why is the author against heavy sentences in antitrust breaches?
7 According to the author what is the effect of giving fines to managers?
8 Why is it important to threaten jail?

most serious   1   2   3   4   5   6   least serious   7

Glossary

carve up divide and share

cartel a group of businesses who have joined together to reduce competition

plea-bargain a deal made when someone admits guilt in return for less punishment

antitrust opposing monopolies in order to promote free competition

pact agreement or bargain

breach break an agreement

trustbusters people who prosecute or dissolve business trusts

create a stir get a lot of attention

larceny stealing personal property

Well-dressed thieves

Punishable by prison

Why the threat of prison is necessary to deter cartels

1 GRIMSBY lies on England's east coast. It is an unlikely location for a landmark white-collar crime. Yet three executives, from there, two of them former employees of Dunlop Oil and Marine based in Grimsby, are going on trial in Britain for their role in a global price-fixing cartel.

2 The three have already pleaded guilty in America to their part in a conspiracy that carved up the market for marine hose – used to funnel oil from tankers to storage facilities. The defendants face jail under the terms of a plea-bargain with American prosecutors. Time served in British prisons will be knocked off the sentences handed down in America.

3 Cartels have long been prohibited, but many countries have recently adopted criminal sanctions. Conspiring to rig markets is punishable by prison in Germany, France, Ireland, Japan and Canada, as well as America and Britain. Australia is about to join the club too.

4 What explains the demand for harsher penalties? After all, other sins against competition are usually dealt with by an order to desist or a fine. When European Union courts upheld the case against Microsoft for abuse of its dominant position the firm had to pay a hefty €777m ($990m). But Steve Ballmer, the software giant's CEO, was never threatened with prison.

5 That is just as well. Antitrust breaches such as the ones that Microsoft was convicted of – using its monopoly in desktop operating systems to hinder rivals in related markets – are hard to distinguish from robust competition. One of the firm's misdeeds was to bundle its media player with Windows. Yet bundling is a common business practice that can be entirely legitimate.

6 It is often tricky to draw the line between healthy discounting and predatory pricing too. Loyalty discounts are widely used in business and have benefits for consumers and suppliers alike. But such schemes can be used to keep rivals out of a market and preserve a monopoly position. It is hard to say for sure whether a firm's actions are harmful to consumers. The immediate benefits of lower prices have to be weighed against uncertain longer-term costs. Firms may be genuinely unclear on what is permissible and heavy sentencing may make them wary of competing aggressively.

7 However, for sophisticated firms, entering into an agreement to fix prices is a clear and knowing conspiracy against consumers. And because such pacts are secret and hard to uncover, harsher penalties are needed if the expected costs of price-fixing are to exceed the likely benefits. In principle, a big fine might suffice. But in practice a fine large enough to work as a deterrent would financially cripple a company, further impairing competition and harming innocent bystanders, such as suppliers and workers. Sanctions against culpable executives ought to be more effective. Fining managers, however, has some of the same problems as fining firms.

Because there is only a small chance of being caught, a penalty big enough to put off a potential price-fixer may be many times his wealth – and hence unpayable.

8 A survey carried out for Britain's Office of Fair Trading (OFT) asked executives to score the deterrent effect of five sanctions. Fines ranked fourth and private damages fifth, behind bad publicity and being disqualified from doing business. The most feared punishment was prison.

9 The threat of jail also helps with the detection of cartels. Trustbusters rely heavily on the promise of amnesties to crack price-fixing conspiracies. Immunity for whistleblowers strikes at the heart of a cartel, because each conspirator is aware one of the others could report offenders to the authorities and escape punishment. The harsher the penalty, the greater the rush to be first to confess.

10 In Australia Visy was fined A$36m ($32m) for fixing the price of cardboard. The case created a stir because of the record fine and because the judge said that every Australian had been harmed by the cartel each time they bought goods that had been moved in cardboard boxes. Or to put it more bluntly: consumers were robbed. As Australia's chief trustbuster, Graeme Samuel, noted after the trial, "Cartels are theft – usually by well-dressed thieves". Today the belief that the punishment should fit the crime is gaining ground. Secret deals with rivals, such as the ones made in Grimsby, are larceny and should be treated as such. ∎

1 Match the nouns from the text with their definitions.

1	conspirator	e	**a**	a government official who conducts criminal cases on behalf of the state
2	defendant	c	**b**	a person who brings an action to a court of law
3	litigant/litigator	d	**c**	a person being sued or accused (sometimes called 'the accused')
4	plaintiff	b	**d**	someone involved in a court case (both the accused and the person bringing the action)
5	prosecutor	a	**e**	a member of a group who agrees to perform illegal acts together

2 Group the vocabulary in the box under the appropriate heading.

cartel   cripple   fines   harm   impair   jail sentence   larceny
market rigging   monopoly   penalties and sanctions   price fixing   trust

1 Organisation	2 Misdeeds	3 Damage	4 Punishment
cartel	larceny	harm	fines
monopoly	market rigging	impair	jail sentence
trust	price fixing	cripple	penalties and sanctions

Idioms and phrasal verbs with *draw*

1 In the text we read 'It is often tricky to draw the line between healthy discounting and predatory pricing', meaning that it is difficult to decide the limit between different things. Using words from the box, complete the text with other expressions with *draw*.

blank   conclusion   line   strength   veil

The shareholder meeting tried to draw a ¹ _veil_ over the whole sorry issue. It was difficult to face the fact that the judge would probably draw the same ² _conclusion_ as they themselves had. It seemed inevitable that senior management was involved in the fraud, even though the preliminary investigation proved nothing and the regulatory bodies had drawn a complete ³ _blank_ , failing to find any incriminating evidence. Initially the shareholders had drawn ⁴ _strength_ from that but the reality was that everyone suspected the worst. One spokesperson said, 'As shareholders of course we want to make money at all costs but we draw the ⁵ _line_ at illegal practices.'

2 Match the phrasal verbs to their definitions.

	Phrasal verb		Definition
1	draw back	f	**a** approach
2	draw down	d	**b** prolong or induce to speak freely
3	draw near	a	**c** compose, write up or set down
4	draw out	b	**d** deplete by consuming or spending
5	draw up	c	**f** retreat

Bernard Madoff

Bernard Madoff

Charles Ponzi

1 Listen to an interview where Jackie Coleman, a specialist in corporate crime, talks about the Bernard Madoff affair. Describe the events that occurred in these years and say how they affected his career.

1	1960	_____
2	1975	_____
3	1990	_____
4	2005–07	_____
5	2009	_____

2 Answer the following questions.

1 Which financial scandal does the speaker suggest is comparable to the Bernard Madoff affair? What do they both have in common?

2 What trading innovations were introduced by Bernard Madoff's company?

3 What new business activity did Bernard Madoff start in addition to stock trading? What services did it offer?

4 Why did investors consider Bernard Madoff to be so trustworthy?

5 Give examples of three crimes that Bernard Madoff committed.

Usage

Euphemisms

Euphemisms are words or expressions that we choose to use in place of others which might be considered negative, offensive or embarrassing.

1 In the interview the speaker refers to the euphemism 'incompletely documented payments'. What does she suggest might be a more appropriate term? *Concealed or falsfied information*

2 Look at some examples of euphemisms that are used in business. Match them with the words that best reflect their meaning.

1 It's true that over the last quarter our results have been <u>in negative territory</u>.

    a stable   (b) decreasing   c fluctuating

2 The directors say that our company is in for some <u>rightsizing</u>.

    a expansion   (b) cutbacks   c liquidation

3 One solution would be to <u>repurpose</u> some of our existing products.

    a redesign   b repackage   (c) modify

4 It's possible that our sales may <u>flatline</u> during the coming months.

    a increase   b fall   (c) remain stable

5 We've seen some considerable <u>value migration</u> in our sector this year.

    (a) lower returns   b money laundering   c new competitiion

6 Setting up an interactive website would be fine if we could find a way to <u>monetise</u> it.

    (a) make money   b finance   c publicise

7 We won't be <u>originating</u> any new materials for this project.

    a purchasing   b outsourcing   (c) creating

3 What other euphemisms do you know? Do you think that using euphemisms is acceptable or is it better to be more direct?

Reporting

When we refer to what other people have said we can either reproduce their actual words in direct speech or we can reword as indirect speech. Direct speech is used in specific contexts such as newspaper articles where it is important to quote exactly what was said. We use indirect speech more often, especially when there is no need to focus on the speaker's exact words. The most common verbs used in indirect speech are *say, tell* and *ask*.

Look at the following examples of direct and indirect speech. What changes have been made?

1   'What do you think of the new security procedures?'

    She asked me what I thought of the new security procedures.

2   'I'm sorry but I really don't have the time to help you with that right now. I'm just too busy.'

    He said that he couldn't help because he was too busy.

Reporting verbs

We use reporting verbs to summarise or interpret what has been said without referring to the actual words that were spoken. There are different types of reporting verbs: verbs that refer to what we suppose the speaker was thinking (e.g. *assume, believe*), verbs that interpret the intention or attitude of the speaker (e.g. *blame, claim*), and verbs that refer to the function of what was said (e.g. *add, explain*).

 For more information, see page 161.

Look at the following comments from a talk. Report what was said, using some of the verbs from the list on page 161.

1   Cybercrime is already costing companies $100 billion dollars a year and if you don't give this your full attention then you could find yourselves in very serious trouble.

_____

2   Looking towards the future, it's pretty clear that more and more transactions will be web based, so I would expect to see more attacks against online banks.

_____

3   To understand just how serious the threat is, consider this: during the last three years 240 million people have been affected by the unauthorised disclosure of confidential information.

_____

4   Although I do know the answer to your question about which institutions have lost the most money to cyber criminals, I'm afraid I can't comment on that in public.

_____

Have you ever experienced problems with viruses or been targeted by computer criminals? How secure is your computer?

Work in pairs and interview each other about your experiences with the Internet. Prepare a short summary of your interview using indirect speech and present it to another pair.

1 Read the text and write a short description of each case of insider trading described.

The Economist

Glossary

ring gang/group

scam a dishonest business scheme

get away with succeed in doing something you shouldn't

file a suit against take to court

buck dollar

intent meaning to commit a crime

sounding out trying to understand someone's opinions and attitudes

smoking gun concrete evidence

nosy curious

Disclosure
Hints, tips and handcuffs

American regulations have declared war on insider trading

1 A WHISPERED aside in a bar, an indiscreet remark in an email – this is how insider trading thrives. But Blue Bottle, a Hong Kong firm pointed at on February 26th by America's markets watchdog, the Securities and Exchange Commission (SEC), took things a bit further than that. It earned $2.7m trading on information it had gathered by hacking directly into computers to view press releases before they were published.

2 This is not the worst insider-trading case of recent times. That prize goes to a ring of 13 bankers and fund managers, including ex-employees of UBS, Bear Stearns and Morgan Stanley. They were busted by the SEC for illegally trading ahead of analysts' stock-tips. What started out as a way to repay a $25,000 debt apparently grew into a lucrative scam as colourful as it was criminal. Mobile phones were thrown away to cover their tracks and cash passed around in Doritos packets. Some say the bust was the biggest blow against insider trading since Ivan Boesky was jailed and fined $100m.

3 The commission must prevent any "buzz in the markets that you can get away with it," says one of his officers,

Walter Ricciardi. "Nothing paints a picture as well as people being led away in handcuffs."

4 The SEC will act even when it has no one to put the cuffs on. It filed a suit against unknown investors who had profited in the options market before the announcement of a takeover of TXU, the Texan utility. Over $5m of profits from these options has been frozen while investigators try to identify who bought them.

5 Insider trading is hard to quantify, but regulators see evidence that it is alarmingly common. The boom in mergers provided more opportunities to make a dishonest buck ahead of deals.

6 A few, including the late Milton Friedman, a Nobel laureate in economics, think there is no sin to escape. He argued that insider trading should be legal, because it benefits all investors by quickly introducing new information to the market. Why should everyone have to wait for a company's press release?

7 This is not, of course, the defence the hedge funds themselves are making. Some are tightening restrictions on outside contacts, others hiring compliance officers, all in the hope of preventing

fresh calls for regulation. But as Friedman might have pointed out, the issue of insider trading is highly imprecise. At what stage, for instance, does sounding out interest among institutional clients for an upcoming corporate financing become something sinister?

8 These unclear areas are one reason why cases against insider trading are so hard to build. It is rare to find a smoking gun. The SEC and others use specialised software to catch unusual peaks and valleys in trading. But says Mr Ricciardi proving intent, requires plenty of "good old-fashioned detective work."

9 Even the most obvious misconduct can be hard to turn into a watertight prosecution. For instance, when a retired, unknown Croatian dressmaker earned over $2m from a series of sophisticated options trades in advance of Reebok's takeover by Adidas-Salomon, the authorities were obviously suspicious. But building a case against the conspirators, led by a Merrill Lynch analyst, took many months of examining thousands of emails, brokers' statements and telephone records.

10 No doubt uncovering all the dirt in cases will prove difficult. Perhaps investigators should hire some of Blue Bottle's nosy techies to help them. ∎

The Economist

2 Do you agree with Milton Friedman that insider trading should be legal? Why/Why not?

Career skills

Making ethical decisions

Business people regularly have to make ethical decisions, such as whether to lay off workers in order to enhance profit, or whether to cut corners in order to meet a deadline, etc. Time pressures may not always allow the luxury of reflection and high stakes may sometimes tempt business people to compromise on certain values or ideals. Most people, however, believe that they have a natural ethical outlook that kicks in automatically. It is important to remember, though, that different cutures and religions do not always agree on what constitutes an ethical outlook.

Generally speaking there are two major approaches that philosophers recommend when solving ethical dilemmas. The first focuses on the practical consequences of the decision taken and argues that the most ethical approach is the one that does the least harm. The second focuses on the actions themselves and claims that some actions are simply unacceptable. Even though each step may lead to conflicting points of view, the important thing is to find the right balance. When handling ethical dilemmas, it is useful to think of the approaches as complementary strategies for analysing and eventually resolving ethical problems.

Read the three-step strategy outlined below. Then read the questions that follow. Decide which questions are relevent to each step in the process.

1   Analyse the consequences

Consider the likely positive and negative outcomes of all the actions open to you before making a decision. Think about long-term as well as short-term consequences. A widely accepted position is that the most ethical action is the one that produces the greatest good for the greatest number of people for the longest time possible.

2   Analyse the action

Look at how an action measures up against moral principles like honesty, fairness, equality, recognising rights and the vulnerability of individuals who are weaker or less fortunate than others.

3   Make a decision and test it

Based on both steps of your analysis decide what is the most ethical decision and test it by preparing arguments you'd give if asked to defend your decision. Check the long term consequences by following up the situation at a later stage and record the consequences for future reference.

Points to consider during the ethical decision-making process

a   What actions are open to you?   1
b   How did it turn out for all concerned?   3
c   Who will win and who will lose by what I do?   1
d   Does this action go against my personal beliefs?   2
e   Even if not everyone gets everything they want, will everyone's rights and dignity still be respected?   1
f   If you had to explain your decision on television, would you be comfortable?   3
g   Does the issue go beyond legal or institutional concerns?   2
h   Would I think it was fair if someone did this to me?   2

Listen to a business woman talking about how she made an ethical decision and answer the questions.

1 What is the speaker's job?
2 What do some clients mean by 'legally'?
3 What ethical dilemma did she face?
4 What did she decide to do at first and why?
5 What decision did she make in the end?
6 What were the consequences?
7 Does she have any regrets?

Speaking

Work in pairs. Read the ethical dilemmas below. Decide what to do and then discuss and compare your decision with other pairs.

1 You work for a non-profit organisation that helps AIDS victims. You discover a government error that results in significantly higher funding for your organisation. Do you keep the money, which you know will go to a good cause, or do you report the error?

2 You discover that your immediate supervisor is taking bribes. You are uncertain whether to report it. The conflict is between your loyalty to your boss and your commitment to the greater good of the company.

3 You discover that you are paid more than a colleague who does the same job as you. You don't want to antagonise your boss, as you're next in line for a promotion at the moment, but at the same time you feel something ought to be done to bring your colleague's salary into line with yours. Speaking out may lose you any chances of promotion.

4 You are in charge of training the new intern who is on a six-week training course at the bank where you work. Your boss is considering offering her a full time job when she finishes her studies. You discover that since she's been with the bank, items of office stationery have been going missing. You think she is stealing them. Should you tell your boss?

Culture at work

Rights and wrongs

Although principles of universal ethics do not, in theory, rely on national cultures, it would be unrealistic to imagine that culture doesn't come into play when exploring ethical dilemmas. The accepted code of practice, or what is considered acceptable ethical behaviour in business, will differ from culture to culture. For example, the rights and conditions of workers can vary, usually according to the economic success of a country. Even if it wasn't illegal, it would probably be considered unethical not to pay overtime in developed countries. Indeed, it is often considered unethical even to allow people to work more than the required minimum number of working hours. However, in other countries it might be judged unfair to stop people, who need to earn as much as they can no matter how small the salary, from working as much overtime as the employer can afford to provide them with. Where does your national culture stand on the issue of paid overtime? Do you think your country has good ethical standards when it comes to workers' rights?

Dilemma & Decision

Dilemma: Just because it's legal doesn't mean it's ethical

Brief

Hellman's Plastics, Inc. hired Hans Hofferman as their environmental compliance manager to ensure that all legal requirements concerning pollution are met by their factories worldwide. His brief is to avoid sanctions, penalties, fines and negative publicity.

In one of their factories, the wastewater from the factory flows into a local lake which people rely heavily on for fish. The factory's emission level does not exceed current legal levels. However, Hans Hofferman knows that environmental regulations are lagging behind scientific evidence. In fact, a scientist from the local university has been quoted in the newspaper recently, saying that if emission levels stay at this level, the fish in the lakes and rivers in the area might soon have to be declared unsafe for human consumption.

Furthermore, the government may force companies to begin using new technology in the future and may also begin requiring monthly emission level reports (which would be both expensive and time consuming). But the company's environmental compliance budget is tight. This new technology would put Hofferman's department over budget, and could jeopardise the company's ability to show a profit this year. Hofferman will need to build a good case of both ethical and hard-headed business arguments to convince the board of management of the necessity of acting ethically now to avoid long-term problems.

Task 1

Work in pairs or small groups. Based on the information in the brief, prepare some sound business arguments for investing in the new technology now rather than later.

Task 2

Answer the following questions:

- Even if we are respecting the law, does this issue go beyond legal concerns?
- Can you think of other examples in business where perfectly legal practices have had dire consequences? (This could be useful to build a strong case.)
- What action will create the greatest good and do the least harm to all the people involved?
- How do the actions we want to take measure up to your basic moral values?

Task 3

Based on your answers to the above questions, prepare ethical arguments to present to the board. Add these to the arguments from Task 1 and present your case for investing in technology to the class.

Write it up

Write a report about this ethical dilemma to give to the board.

 For more information, see *Style guide*, page 22.

Decision:

Listen to Melissa Shaw discussing this dilemma.

1 Why is this a particularly difficult situation for a compliance manager?

2 Which arguments does she think Hofferman could put forward? Are they similar/ different to yours?

3 What does she think his chances of convincing the board are? Do you agree with her?

Unit 12
Development

www.longman-elt.com   www.economist.com

Lifelong learning

Keynotes

In today's business world, companies have to react rapidly to develop solutions to new challenges. In response to this, many organisations have become '**learning organisations**' where the collective knowledge of all the staff can be shared and developed through **knowledge management**. At the same time individual members of staff are encouraged to undertake **personal and professional development**. This can take different forms: formal **academic qualifications** such as an **MBA (Master of Business Administration)**, internal **training programmes** to develop specific skills, **coaching** and **mentoring** programmes to provide support to staff, and **e-learning programmes**. The objectives of learning organisations are to encourage all staff to view education as a lifelong process where new skills are continuously added and upgraded and new knowledge acquired. The more learning that is taking place inside an organisation, the greater its productivity.

Learning styles

People learn in different ways and learning can take place in different contexts. According to some researchers, there are four main styles of learning:

– active
– pragmatic
– reflective
– theoretical.

Each learning style can be represented by one of the questions or statements below. Which one matches each style?

1 How does this relate to that?
2 What's new? I'm ready for anything.
3 How can I apply this in practice?
4 I'd like some more time to think about this.
5 I believe learning is by doing.
6 I want to learn the things I know will be most useful to me.
7 I don't think people really learn without hindsight.
8 You can't learn something if you don't understand why it's important.

1 Which of the learning styles do you prefer? Which of the styles, or combination of styles, would be most suitable for learning the following? Discuss your preferences with a partner.

– to windsurf
– to play the game 'Go'
– to write a computer programme
– to communicate in sign language
– to manage a project
– to administer first aid

2 Tell a partner about something that you have learnt and explain how you learnt it.

Business education

1 Read the text on the opposite page and answer the questions.

1 According to the author of the article, what have been the main failings of managers in recent times?
2 What do Rakesh Khurana and Nitin Nohria suggest could be done to make managers more professional?
3 What are the most striking differences between the career paths of Bill Gates and Jeffrey Skilling?
4 Why is profit not necessarily a good indicator of a manager's performance?
5 Why might it be difficult to enforce universal standards of education and training for all business professionals?
6 Why does the author of the article suggest that businesses urgently need to address the problem of professionalisation?

Glossary

Hippocratic oath a promise made by doctors to respect the principles of their profession

wanting not good enough, inadequate, insufficient

iconoclast someone who attacks established ideas

rumblings comments that indicate emerging dissatisfaction

top-up extra, additional

Business education

First, do no harm

Do bosses need their own Hippocratic oath?

1 ALREADY the managers of many of the world's leading financial firms have been found wanting. Attention will now turn to managers of non-financial firms, to see if they are any better prepared for the rainy day that was bound to come sooner or later. It will be no surprise if soaring bankruptcies demonstrate that their risk management was just as inept, and just as focused on maximising short-term profits (and their pay packets) without thinking too hard about what would happen when the good times ended.

2 Why is this failure so unsurprising? In an article in the *Harvard Business Review*, Rakesh Khurana and Nitin Nohria, who teach at the Harvard Business School, argue that the problem is literally a lack of professionalism. Contrasting corporate managers with doctors and lawyers, the authors title their article with their argument: "It's Time to Make Management a True Profession".

3 As they point out, "unlike doctors and lawyers, managers don't need a formal education, let alone a licence, to practise. Nor do they adhere to a universal and enforceable code of conduct." Even if individual firms write and enforce corporate codes or value statements, "there's no universally accepted set of professional values backed up by a governing body with the power to censure managers who deviate from the code."

4 Implicit in this argument is a deep criticism of the MBA, a degree that Messrs Khurana and Nohria teach, and which many of today's failing managers hold. Indeed, there are already rumblings about the failure of the MBA courses that Wall Street's "finest" took before rising up the ranks of global finance – just as

there was after Enron went bust in 2001 (Jeffrey Skilling, Enron's chief executive, holds an MBA from Harvard).

5 Yet, as the professors point out, the desire to make management a profession like law and medicine was central to Harvard Business School in the first decades after it was founded 100 years ago. A start would be for management education to "adopt the more stringent knowledge and competency standards required by true professions," they argue. For instance, the Association to Advance Collegiate Schools of Business "could devise and administer an exam that all graduating MBAs would have to pass before they were licensed to practise". Managers could also be required to take top-up courses to retain their licences.

6 One question this raises, the authors concede, is just how essential management education is – indeed, the success of iconoclasts like Bill Gates might suggest that a lack of formal management training was a positive advantage in becoming a successful entrepreneur. Medicine and law have far fewer examples of top practitioners succeeding without professional training – despite the popularity of some alternative healers and upstart legal heroes such as Erin Brockovich. Messrs Khurana and Nohria propose that management jobs be classified according to the amount of professional training required in order to allow the market to make clear the value of such training, but it is hard to imagine the traditional entrepreneur educated in the university of life going out of fashion.

7 Perhaps more important than an educational standard may be a general agreement on what constitutes professional standards of behaviour. To

this end, the two professors propose a managerial version of the Hippocratic oath, to which all doctors must swear. "Codes create and sustain a feeling of community and mutual obligation that members have toward each other and toward the profession," they argue.

8 The management oath they propose covers issues including selfishness ("I pledge that considerations of personal benefit will never supersede the interests of the enterprise I am entrusted to manage") and transparency ("I vow to represent my enterprise's performance accurately and transparently to all relevant parties").

9 This lacks the simple clarity of medicine's "First, do no harm", largely because it is exceedingly hard to judge whether a manager is doing a good job until long after he or she has ceased to do it, if even then. The professors want managers to pledge "to serve the public's interest by enhancing the value [their] enterprise creates for society." But this is a difficult standard to judge; peers and the public tend to focus on the measure of performance they can see easily: profit. In business, profit can go up for years even when a manager is overseeing activities that neither maximise the long-term value of the company nor aid society. Going against the norms of the profession is not the route to success in medicine.

10 Yet, as the public and politicians increasingly look to blame business for the problems of the economy, the call for professionalism could hardly be more timely. If they are wise, today's business leaders and educators will see it is in their enlightened self-interest to take the goal of professionalisation seriously, and thus start to regain society's trust. ■

Bill Gates

Donald Trump

Warren Buffet

Steve Jobs

2 **Read the text again. Which of the following statements reflect the recommendations that Rakesh Khurana and Nitin Nohria have made?**

All business managers should:

1 prioritise short term profit.
2 only be allowed to practise after passing a degree in law.
3 have precise definitions of the training requirements of their jobs.
4 be fined for inappropriate behaviour.
5 undergo periodic retraining.
6 take a standardised exam before being allowed to practise.

Speaking

Look at the photos of some prominent business people. Who do you think completed a formal academic business qualification? How important do you think it is for business people to study management?

Vocabulary 1

1 **Match the words from the text (1–6) with a synonym–antonym pair (a–f).**

1	deviate	a	tough/lenient
2	supersede	b	follow/disregard
3	adhere	c	replace/precede
4	stringent	d	acknowledge/deny
5	concede	e	openness/opacity
6	transparency	f	diverge/conform

2 **What synonyms and antonyms can you find in the text for the following words?**

soaring	inept	a lack	implicit	criticism

Usage

Expressions with *go*

1 **In the text are several expressions with the verb go. Which ones have the following meanings?**

1 cease operating as a solvent business (para 4) _____
2 no longer be popular (para 6) _____
3 increase (para 9) _____

2 **Complete the sentences with the correct form of the following verbs or expressions with go.**

go ahead	go without	go about	go under	go into

1 A lot of time has _____ redesigning the training procedures.
2 The finance committee have finally given the _____ for the new recreation centre and construction will start next month.
3 When a business outsources critical processes like payroll, there should always be a back up plan just in case the service provider _____ .
4 This programme is designed to inform staff of the importance of fitness and to explain how they can _____ improving it.
5 The Internet has become such an important part of our lives that many people cannot imagine _____ it.

Speaking

The MBA

Imagine that you have decided to apply for an MBA course. Draw up a list of the criteria that you think are the most important. Discuss with a partner.

Listening 1

Listen to Judy Holland, an educational advisor, talking about MBA programmes. What does she say about the following?

1 the value of an MBA degree
2 the main motivations for taking an MBA
3 the cost of enrolling in an MBA course
4 the criteria used to evaluate business schools
5 the procedures for applying to a school
6 the most recent trends in business education

How many of the criteria that she mentions were on your list? Which criteria does she think are the most important?

@ Visit the websites of the schools that Judy Holland mentions. Which one has the most appealing website? Which of these schools would you choose to attend and why?

Writing

As part of your application to an MBA programme you have been asked to write a short essay (300–400 words) on one of the following subjects.

– What are your most substantial accomplishments, and why do you view them as such?
– What matters most to you, and why?
– What have you learnt from a mistake?
– Tell us about a situation in which you were an outsider. What did you learn from the experience?
– Please tell us about a time when you had a difficult interaction with a person or group. Describe in detail what you thought, felt, said and did.

Reading 2

Educate to rehabilitate

Read the text and decide if the following statements are true or false.

1 Mr Amaya has a 50% chance of returning to prison within three years of his release.
2 PEP was created by business students.
3 Catherine Rohr believes that people who can run a criminal operation can become successful entrepreneurs.
4 Graduates of PEP commit fewer crimes than other prisoners who have completed their sentences.
5 PEP is financed by local government.
6 Graduates of PEP receive financial assistance to start their own businesses.

Rehabilitating prisoners

A new deal

Finding promise in prisoners

SAM AMAYA began running drugs as a teenager, picking up consignments of marijuana and cocaine near the border with Mexico and selling them around Texas. With such a background, it is perhaps not surprising that Mr Amaya was arrested and is today, at 28, about to finish a long sentence for aggravated assault. Statistics suggest that he will be back before long: according to the Pew Centre on the States, more than half of released offenders return to prison within three years. In fact, Mr Amaya's future should be more cheerful than those numbers suggest.

2　Just before he is released, if all goes to plan, Mr Amaya will graduate from the Prison Entrepreneurship Programme (PEP), a remarkable effort to prepare some of Texas's harder cases for their transition back to freedom. The programme was founded in 2004 by Catherine Rohr, a venture capitalist who changed careers after visiting several Texas prisons.

3　Her premise is that many criminals are intelligent people with good heads for business and healthy appetites for risk, and that these traits can be put to productive use. She is particularly interested in people who have already demonstrated these skills – for example by running a successful drug business or achieving a high rank in a gang.

4　Since 2004 PEP has put hundreds of inmates through four months of business classes and study. They meet MBA students to develop business plans, and hundreds of businessmen have taken part in special events at the prison. About 40 graduates already have businesses up and running. The vast majority are employed. Fewer than 5% have reoffended. The programme is privately funded, and that success rate has helped it grow. In 2004 Ms Rohr used her savings to get things going; by 2008 the operating budget was $3.2m.

5　PEP's success is partly due to the fact that the programme takes only the most serious applicants. Prospective participants first fill out a lengthy questionnaire. Those that pass have an interview, where Ms Rohr claims she rumbles the fakers. Once selected, a participant can be booted out at any time for a variety of infractions, such as cheating or maintaining gang membership. The current class started with 87 members and is down to 39.

6　Participants say that PEP provides male role models, and helps them have hope for the future. Ms Rohr considers it her job to build character. "They're not in here because they were bad businessmen," she says. "They're in here because they were lacking moral values in their lives." She assigns them ethical case studies and leads discussions on everything from honesty to sexual relationships.

7　Texas is making its own efforts to improve results for released offenders, but released prisoners typically get just $100 and a bus ticket to Houston or Dallas. PEP picks up its graduates at the gate with packages of sheets, toiletries and business suits. It helps them find work and housing, and even offers a free trip to the dentist. According to Gregory Mack, a participant, all this makes a big difference. Mr Mack has been in and out of prison on drug charges for the past two decades. He completed a behaviour-modification programme in 2002 as a condition for parole, but its value was limited. "They really had nothing to offer outside the walls," he explains. By 2005 he was behind bars again. Mr Amaya now has a chance to avoid that fate. ■

Glossary

running drugs making illegal deliveries of narcotics

rumble uncover secret intentions

faker a person who is not what he/she appears to be

boot out eject someone from a group or institution

Speaking

Look at the following comments that Internet users have posted about the PEP programme. Which ones do you agree with? Share your opinions with a partner.

– I don't believe that ex-convicts make the best CEOs and I don't think a criminal background is good preparation for running a company.

– If this programme is such a success, why aren't more prisons running similar ones?

– I think we have enough white collar criminals already.

– Business is business: drug dealers are in it to make money and so are entrepreneurs.

Writing

Write a comment about PEP to post on a website.

Verb patterns

Verbs can be classified into different categories depending on whether or not they require an object. Transitive verbs are used for actions or events that affect another person or thing. They take a direct object, e.g. *The new programme has produced* **excellent results.**

Intransitive verbs refer to things involving only the subject. They do not require an object but may be followed by a complement such as a prepositional phrase, e.g. *The participants talked* **about their own experiences.**

Link verbs connect the subject to a complement, usually an adjective or a prepositional phrase, which gives more information about the subject, e.g. *Training* **is becoming** *increasingly important.* Link verbs include such common verbs as *be, get, seem.* Verbs of all three types can be followed by a variety of different structures: objects, complements, phrases and clauses.

For more information, see page 162.

Decide which sentences require transitive (T), intransitive (I) or link (L) verbs. Then complete them using the verbs below.

achieve	become	deteriorate	matter	owe

1   Postgraduate business qualifications _____ more and more popular these days.

2   Last year we invested a lot in quality training but despite that our performance still _____ .

3   I don't think it really _____ whether the course takes place here or at another location.

4   The success rate that we have _____ with this new programme is higher than we expected.

5   We still _____ at least £2,000 for the seminar that we organised.

Complete the text with the following object/complement phrases.

a   them to do

b   its training

c   some time attending

d   to gain some useful insights

e   from the advice

f   that they were not satisfied

g   a lot easier

h   to the following conclusion

i   the least exposed

The future of learning

Choosing the right training for your staff sounds ¹_____ than it really is. Before a business can optimise ²_____ it needs to know what employees need to learn. The results of a recent survey may help organisations ³_____ . Almost 60% of respondents said that they had spent ⁴_____ classroom training sessions; almost the same number said that they had benefited ⁵_____ of colleagues at least as much. In terms of quality, however, 30% of the respondents admitted ⁶_____ with the quality of the training. 41% claimed that they do not have time to learn because of the amount of work that their supervisors require ⁷_____ . Unsurprisingly, junior employees were the group that was ⁸_____ to training opportunities. The authors of the report came ⁹_____ : to be effective, training should be tailored to trainees' needs.

Have you ever followed a training course? Was it led by an instructor or computer-based? What did you think of it?

Career skills

Coaching

Organisations use coaching to enhance the development of their staff by providing support. A coach arranges regular meetings with the person he or she is coaching (referred to as the 'coachee'). Together they can discuss developments at work and focus on problem areas where improvements can be made. The coach builds a relationship of trust with the coachee and provides the insight and analysis to enable him or her to better understand and deal with the complexities of the work environment. Coaching can help staff to develop in both personal and professional terms and can lead managers to obtain better results and have greater confidence in themselves.

Speaking

Most people already have some experience of coaching even if they are not aware of it. Look at the following list of situations that involve coaching. Which ones have you already done? Which ones do you think you might have to do in the future? Discuss your answers with a partner and tell them about your experiences.

- Give advice to friends or colleagues.
- Listen to other people's problems to help and support them.
- Explain to other people how to do something better.
- Give feedback to other people.
- Train other people in new skills.

Listening 2 ⊙

Listen to an extract from a coaching conversation and answer the questions. How successful do you think this coaching relationship is?

1 What does the coachee want to achieve?

2 What is the scenario or context?

3 How does the coachee need to modify his/her behaviour?

Building rapport

Successful coaching can only take place if there is a rapport between the two people involved. One way to help people to develop their coaching skills is to use exercises and simulations to develop awareness of the key techniques. The following exercise focuses on how to build a rapport with the person who is being coached.

Work in pairs. Student A, read your instructions below. Student B, turn to page 142. When you have completed the exercise discuss the following questions.

- What did you learn from this experience?
- How could this exercise help people to become better at coaching?

Student A

You are going to have a ten-minute conversation with Student B on the following subject: 'Things that I like and things that I dislike.' Think of some examples that you could mention in your conversation. Be ready to explain the reasons behind your likes and dislikes.

Active listening

Coaches are skilled listeners and are able to focus on what is being said while at the same time encouraging the speaker to elaborate on what they are saying. To do this, coaches use 'active listening'. With active listening we use appropriate gestures, sounds or expressions to express interest in what is being said and we also include questions to ask the speaker to clarify what they are saying.

How is active listening different to the type of listening that you do in the context of an everyday conversation?

Work with a partner. Student A should think of one or more things in his/her life that he/she would like to change and be prepared to talk about this for ten minutes. Student B should play the role of an active listener, encouraging the speaker to reveal as much as possible about the changes that they would like to make.

After ten minutes Student B should give a short summary of what Student A has said, adding any comments that are relevant. At the end of the conversation Student A should give feedback to Student B by answering the following questions:

- Did Student B give you his/her full attention? Do you feel that he/she understood you?
- What effect did Student B have on you? Did he/she make you want to develop what you were saying?
- How did the exercise affect what you feel about the situation(s) that you would like to change?

Culture at work

Body language

Coaching involves a certain degree of intimacy as both the coachee and the coach will be in a one-to-one situation where they will be focusing on each other's words and body language (voice, facial expressions, gestures and posture). Body language is of particular importance in a coaching situation as it may reveal much about what is being said or left unsaid.

However, depending on the culture, body language may be interpreted in different ways. For example, in North America nodding the head up and down is interpreted as a sign of agreement whereas in other countries an upward nod may indicate disagreement and a downward nod agreement. Similarly, what is considered appropriate eye contact in one culture may be perceived as inappropriate in another.

What is regarded as normal in your country for the following things:

- personal space (the spatial distance between people when they are interacting)?
- physical contact (handshake, embrace, touching)?
- eye contact?

How might this lead to misunderstandings when dealing with people from another culture?

Dilemma &Decision

Dilemma: Keeping everyone motivated

Brief

When Zara Faulkner joined Wyndham Industries, a major industrial equipment distributor in the US, Ben Bradley, the company's coach, was confident that all would go well. Wyndham Industries was proud of its corporate culture of open and productive communication with a focus on work-life balance for all, and Zara had the perfect profile for the management team: an engineering degree followed by an MBA. What could go wrong?

At first everything went according to plan. Zara worked hard, responded well to feedback and had an excellent understanding of the technical issues. However, it soon became apparent to Ben that she was having problems communicating with her colleagues.

Due to her shyness she had problems relaxing with them. She also lacked the initiative to work alone on certain projects and was starting to be over-dependent on Ben. When he raised these issues with her in their regular appraisal and feedback meetings she didn't seem to grasp the problem. She strongly defended her technical knowledge and contribution, which are undeniably invaluable. However, her coworkers are complaining that it is unfair that they have to complete tasks that she hasn't been able to handle. Ben needs to resolve this problem in a way that does not damage either the motivation of Zara or the others who have been working harder to compensate for her weaknesses. There are four options open to him at this time.

- Cut the losses and dismiss Zara before her trial period is up. Even though the investment in her development has been high, Ben has spent hours coaching her, and the long-term cost of keeping her may be higher. She could find a job better suited to her personality and the staff will be happy that Ben took their complaints seriously.

- Empower Zara more by allocating her only the tasks that he is confident that she can perform well.

- Arrange for Zara to be transferred to another department where her technical knowledge will be useful and where fewer demands will be made on her communication capabilities.

- Commission a consulting and development firm to run a two-day communication and conflict management workshop for Zara and all her colleagues.

Task 1

In pairs or small groups, evaluate the advantages and limitations of each of the four options. Consider long-term as well as short-term solutions.

Task 2

Decide which of the options you think Ben Bradley should take and prepare to present your arguments to the other pairs or groups.

Task 3

Present your decision to the class.

Write it up

You are Ben Bradley. Write a memo to your senior director informing her of the decision you've taken.

For more information, see *Style guide*, page 18.

Decision:

⊙ Listen to Alessandra Baricco, who runs a consulting firm that provides coaching and advice on compensation and reward strategies, talking about the problem.

According to her:

1 What seems to have been the cause of this dilemma, at first sight?

2 What are the benefits and drawbacks of each option?

Review 4

Language check

Probability and possibility

Complete the text with words from the box.

unable	bound	likely	might	expect	will

While you are more [1]_____ to get a good job with an MBA diploma it is not a guarantee that you [2]_____ definitely start your career in a managerial position. On the other hand someone of the same age [3]_____ easily [4]_____ to find themselves in a managerial position simply through hard work and experience in the field. However, an extra qualification is [5]_____ to be taken into consideration by the hierarchy when they are [6]_____ to choose between equally experienced candidates for a promotion.

Verb patterns

1 Look at the following sentences. Which ones require transitive verbs (T) and which ones intransitive (I)?

Preliminary results from a new survey
[1]_____ (_____) by a business magazine last month [2]_____ (_____) fraud to be more prevalent and commonplace in the corporate world than was previously [3]_____ (_____). More than 86% of survey respondents [4]_____ (_____) that at least one organisation they had worked for in the past ten years had been a victim of some sort of fraud. While most of the reported losses were not overwhelming, this [5]_____ (_____) to a pervasive pattern which [6]_____ (_____) corporate leaders.

2 Complete the paragraph above with the verbs from the box in their correct form.

worry	find	believe	indicate
	conduct		point

Reporting

1 Match the reporting verbs to the prepositions.

accuse	about
blame	for
complain	with
congratulate	of
threaten	on

2 Look at the comments made to you by your company's insurance company. Transform them into indirect speech, using a suitable reporting verb from above.

1 We regret to inform you that the accident report that you sent was illegible.

2 We have been informed by the police that the person who was driving your vehicle at the time of the accident was not the policyholder.

3 You didn't take the necessary precautions to protect the goods therefore it is your fault and the risk isn't covered by your policy.

4 If there is another accident, we will increase your premium fees.

5 Well done, your new security measures look really effective.

Consolidation

Choose the correct verb forms in italics and indicate whether the underlined verbs are transitive (T), intransitive (I) or linking (L) in the extracts from a cover letter below.

My tutor recently informed me that you [1] *were/would be* looking for a sales representative in the near future. She said she [2] *believed/had believed* that my profile [3] *might/can* be of interest to you.

Formal training combined with practical experience [4] is becoming (T/I/L) increasingly important for sales people today which is why I feel that my background is [5] *likely/able* to interest you.

After consulting your website, [6] I am convinced (T/I/L) that I [7] *would/might* be able to successfully accomplish the tasks that are listed in the job description.

I am enclosing my CV and I sincerely [8] hope (T/I/L) that you will find it of interest.

Vocabulary check

1 Complete the text below with the correct form of the words in the box.

fear	bluff	chance	illegal	risk
accomplish	predict	fine		coach

Pushing the limits

When asked about their personal [1]_____ , business people often refer to the extreme sports they practise. They feel that it is proof that they can face [2]_____ with courage and that it helps them to learn how to deal with [3]_____ situations. The most dangerous is BASE jumping, where people jump off buildings, bridges or cliffs and it is impossible to make truly accurate [4]_____ about the outcome. 'This is no sport for [5]_____ ,' said Jeff Peters, one of the [6]_____ at BASE Challengers inc. 'In the 18-year history of the sport there have been 46 deaths!' Peters takes [7]_____ too. His customers sometimes make [8]_____ jumps off cliffs in National Parks. If they are caught, his company faces serious [9]_____ .

2 Use the correct form of *chance* or *luck* to complete the sentences below.

1 Don't make another mistake. We don't give second _____ .

2 I've had no _____ in my search for a new supplier.

3 What are our _____ of meeting the deadline?

4 I feel _____ today! I think I'll buy a lottery ticket.

5 I didn't get a _____ to talk to her at the meeting.

3 Complete the sentences with words from the box.

conclusion	veil	blank	strength	line

1 Heated arguments are tolerated at meetings but the chairperson draws the _____ when it comes to personal insults.

2 He asked me to draw a _____ over the conversation and forget that it had ever happened.

3 Young business people who can't afford an MBA may draw _____ from the fact that Bill Gates had no formal management training.

4 We have been trying to understand what happened but so far we've drawn a complete _____ .

5 She finally drew the _____ that she should give up and forget about the whole affair.

Usage

Expressions with *go*

Complete the sentences with the correct form of the expressions in the box.

go bankrupt	go ahead	go without
go out of fashion	go about	go into

1 The trial _____ even though two witnesses failed to turn up.

2 _____ luxuries is something jailed executives will have to learn to do.

3 Values like honesty seem _____ these days.

4 Despite the fraud investigation, the staff are _____ their business as usual.

5 Sales are so bad that the staff feel sure that the company _____ within the next few weeks.

6 A lot of thought and effort _____ the compiling of strict laws which are designed to reduce and even prevent fraud in the future.

Career skills

Making ethical decisions

Match the extracts from conversations (1–6) to the headings (a–c).

a analysing positive and negative outcomes

b examining moral principles

c defending the position taken

1 It would have gone against everything we stood for not to ... _____

2 I started by weighing up the consequences. _____

3 We have certain values and beliefs I want us to adhere to ... _____

4 I could see that on the one hand our reputation was at stake and on the other ... _____

5 We are looking at what is decent and honourable. _____

6 We followed our conscience. _____

Pairwork

Unit 1   page 16 **Dilemma: Student A**

Top-down employee performance evaluations

Subordinates meet face to face with their manager to discuss performance in terms of targets and goals. The manager is in charge of assessing the employee and he or she should be someone who knows the employee very well, who works with that employee every day and knows his or her strengths and weaknesses, and not a Human Resources manager who has only second-hand knowledge of an employee's performance. Ideally there should be an atmosphere of mutual respect and trust. It should be seen by the employee as an opportunity to make long-term development and career plans, and a chance to set realistic targets and work-loads for the future. Employees may also use this opportunity to discuss pay rises and promotion with their manager. However, in this 'top-down' structure, hierarchical differences are usually strictly observed and communication is not always open and honest.

Unit 7   page 80 **Dilemma: Team A**

Information in favour of nuclear power:
- Nuclear power plants do not produce greenhouse gases.
- Nuclear power allows countries to avoid dependence on foreign imports of fuel.
- The nuclear power industry has made significant progress in safety and has the best safety record for all the energy industries.
- Nuclear power is able to provide an uninterrupted supply of electricity, which is essential for economic activity.
- Nuclear energy costs less than energy produced by burning fossil fuels.
- New technologies are making nuclear energy much more attractive.

Unit 3   page 28 **Preview questionnaire**

Review your partner's questionnaire and write down the number of 'yes' answers to odd numbered questions. Give your partner the number he/she can use to place an X on the line below to see how averse or open he/she is to change.

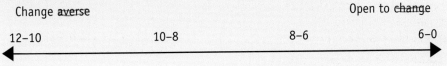

Change averse			Open to change
12–10	10–8	8–6	6–0

- The company is holding its own in the market as it is. Why tempt fate?
- The transition will be long and slow so that even if the changes work the company will have lost its market share before it starts to bear fruit.
- Resistance from managers, who will lose status, will be huge.
- Good managers will leave the company.
- Resistance from staff will also be great and cause complete havoc with work schedules. Lack of discipline will mean that teams won't meet deadlines.
- Staff were recruited for their experience manufacturing – they may not have the skills needed to create and design new products.
- People like routines and they will never adapt to these changes, which are too dramatic and will be the cause of the complete failure of the company in the long run.

Unit 4   page 48 **Dilemma**

The following information summarises the points of view of different organisations concerning the use of coal-fired power plants.

Government
The UK government is facing an increasingly difficult energy future. Supplies of petroleum and gas from the North Sea fields are now falling and the country needs to find alternative fuel sources to generate its electricity. The government has given its support to investments in sustainable energies such as wind power but it also favours investing in a new generation of more efficient power stations. It believes that this could also provide a business opportunity for developing new and cleaner technologies that could even be exported to other countries that rely on coal for their power needs.

Environmental groups
Most of the environmental groups are deeply opposed to the construction of a new generation of power plants because they believe that developing renewable energies is the only viable strategy in order to significantly reduce carbon emissions. Furthermore, they claim that none of the technologies that companies like Progenerra are proposing have actually been tried and tested. Some groups are also advocating a radical lifestyle change where people would be encouraged to reduce their consumption of energy and also to change their attitudes to mass consumption in general.

Progennera
The company will have to replace one third of its existing power stations within the next two decades as they become obsolete. Its directors believe that by introducing a new generation of more efficient power plants, they can make a positive contribution to the energy future of the country as a whole. The planned development at Marsdale will allow the company to develop and test new technologies which can then be applied to other new plants. They are forecasting that the new plant will be more efficient and will produce 20% less carbon emissions than the existing plant.

Unit 8   page 87 **Student A**

I'm not saying that the customer service at my bank is bad, but when I went in the other day and asked the clerk to check my balance ... she leaned over and pushed me.

Peer-to-peer employee performance evaluations

Peer-to-peer employee performance evaluations require employees at the same level to review each other. The thinking behind peer-to-peer employee performance evaluations is that nobody knows a worker's ability better than his or her coworkers. While this can be an effective review format for some groups of workers (for example, a team working on a research project together, where specific content knowledge is required), it can also cause controversy because of the way it affects future group dynamics. Members need to be very mature so that negative feedback from colleagues doesn't have a negative impact on the team's work. However, some feel this is a good system, particularly when they do not trust the management of a company to give a fair assessment of their performance.

Arguments in favour of taking the shareholders' advice:
- It is time to change the image of the stores and the company radically if we are to survive.
- A new CEO could help change the image and bring new, fresh ideas.
- It will be impossible to change family traditions if Ed McKenna remains CEO.
- We need to devote all management's resources and energy to the retail operation if it is to work.
- This will never happen as long as we can always rely on the subsidiaries to cover our losses.
- The figures from the past ten years prove this.
- The core retail business desperately needs a cash injection if it is to survive in the long run.
- This may be our only chance of saving the retail business.

Information against nuclear power:
- The costs of nuclear power are notoriously difficult to calculate: insurance costs can be very high and the costs of waste disposal are unknown as no solution has been adopted for the disposal of nuclear waste.
- The risks of a catastrophic nuclear accident are considerable. There have been alerts in several countries where nuclear accidents have only been narrowly avoided. In some cases nuclear power stations have released radiation into the atmosphere.
- The construction costs of nuclear power stations are almost always higher than expected.
- Once a nuclear power station has reached the end of its life it is extremely expensive to deactivate it.
- There are no safe solutions for disposing of nuclear waste.
- Nuclear power technology can be used by some countries as a means to develop nuclear weapons.
- There is a shortage of trained staff to manage and operate nuclear facilities.
- Nuclear reactors are expensive to build and are rarely delivered on time. The current cost of a nuclear reactor is 6,000 USD per kilowatt compared to 3,000 USD for a coal-fired plant.

Unit 3 — page 36 **Dilemma: Student B**

- The company has to find an area where it can compete with leading electronics companies.
- Managers can move around from project to project making their professional lives more interesting while building new competencies.
- Staff will be more motivated and will feel trusted and valued and will therefore work harder and come up with innovative products.
- Training will be provided to help staff acquire the new skills needed.
- Face to face informal communication leads to better team working conditions.
- People like the freedom to tackle exciting and challenging tasks.
- The company will produce new, innovative products thanks to the mass pooling of resources and information.
- These changes, though dramatic, are the company's only chance of survival.

Unit 5 — page 58 **Dilemma: Student B**

Arguments against taking the shareholders' advice:
- Analysts predict that stock will double in value, if we sell our financial companies, so obviously greedy shareholders will advise us to do so.
- If we sell off our only profit making businesses, we might not survive at all.
- Many of our loyal customers like our traditional image and trust our family-style management values.
- We have customer feedback to prove this.
- We could introduce lower prices to compete with discount stores.
- We could introduce high quality brands alongside our traditional home labels to make up profits.
- We could sell our prestigious headquarters building and move to smaller offices to raise capital.
- We should put the above suggestions in place and see if they work before listening to our shareholders.

Unit 1 — page 16 **Dilemma: Student C**

360-degree performance reviews

In 360-degree performance reviews, many different types of people are consulted about an employee's performance. This includes customers, suppliers, peers and direct reports. In the case of a manager, employees are often asked to give 'upward feedback' on how well they are being managed. Employees are encouraged to talk about any problems they are encountering and to explore ways of solving those problems. While the benefits of multiple points of view are obvious, there are also some challenges. Employees almost never give 'true' feedback about their managers and outside contacts may be simply too busy, or unqualified to effectively rate a specific employee. However, it does encourage the opening up of all lines of communication. A Human Resources manager should coordinate the process, so that employees are assured that their performance reviews of their managers are kept anonymous.

The statements in the quiz are designed to identify key character traits that are associated with successful entrepreneurs.

1 Entrepreneurs often have to face critical situations where they may have to bend the rules in order to survive. Agreeing with this statement shows that you have the necessary resourcefulness.

2 Imagination and creativity are an important part of setting up a new business venture. Daydreaming is a sign of creative thinking and shows that a person is able to disconnect from the outside world in order to focus on a train of thought.

3 Logic is important for designing systems and procedures. However, approaching all things in a logical manner will not leave room for intuition and spontaneity which are essential for all entrepreneurs who often have to deal quickly with unexpected developments.

4 Being able to take a position that goes against conventional wisdom is essential for an entrepreneur. If you are too sensitive to the judgements of other people, you may not have the right attitude for running your own business and you may lack the necessary perseverance.

5 Your position or status in the eyes of other people should not be the main motivation for starting a business. So what people think of you should not overshadow your desire to achieve what you have set out to do.

6 Teamwork is an important part of starting a business. However, being an entrepreneur also means that you will have to make important decisions without being able to consult others. Successful entrepreneurs tend to be people who are self reliant and who do not require the approval or agreement of others before taking decisions. ¹¹ making

Many head hunters have tried to recruit you but you've never been tempted to move jobs. They were offering more or less the same type of job with similar promotion prospects and every time you mentioned this to your present boss the company reacted quickly by increasing your salary in order to keep you. But you are getting bored with your job now.

Your husband/wife also has a good position in the same company and you sometimes think it might be better for the relationship if you moved jobs. You've saved a lot of money over the past few years and you are looking for an investment which will give you high returns. You like risk! At weekends you go sky diving and you generally go mountaineering and rock climbing on holidays.

You haven't made up your mind fully but you are very tempted. If you accept, you will want full control over the running of the business and you intend to bargain for an excellent salary and conditions so you prepare your bargaining strategy carefully. You don't intend giving your final answer at this meeting unless under pressure. You think you'll be in a stronger position if you make Student B wait another week while you give this some more consideration.

There is no doubt that Student A is the right person – having the perfect professional expertise and some extra cash to invest. You really need Student A so you've made it your business to learn as much as possible about his/her personality.

You know that he/she enjoys high risk sports (sky diving and mountaineering). This might be a good ice breaker. The project means giving up security and taking a real risk professionally. Perhaps this aspect will appeal to rather than repel Student A.

You know that Student A works in the same company as his/her life partner. You used to work in the same company as your husband/wife and you think it was one of the reasons for your divorce! You know that many companies have already unsuccessfully tried to recruit Student A and you suspect that he/she is waiting for a more interesting offer.

You want Student A to take care of the day-to-day running of the business but you want weekly feedback meetings and you want to be involved in all major strategy development.

You believe that the money Student A invests in the company will have a high return as soon as the business takes off the ground. You'd like things to get moving so you are going to tell Student A that you have other people lined up who are willing to take up the position but you'd like to give him/her first refusal. You need a definite answer today or tomorrow.

Unit 3 page 31 **Change framework**

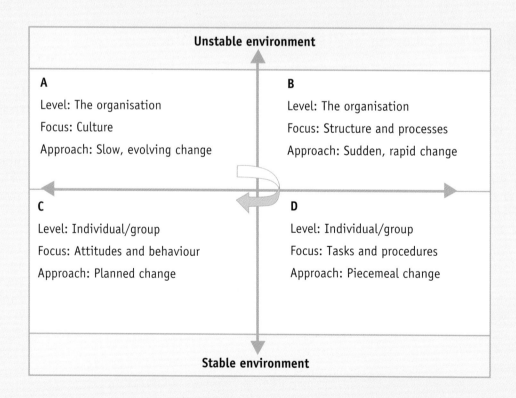

Unstable environment

A

Level: The organisation

Focus: Culture

Approach: Slow, evolving change

B

Level: The organisation

Focus: Structure and processes

Approach: Sudden, rapid change

C

Level: Individual/group

Focus: Attitudes and behaviour

Approach: Planned change

D

Level: Individual/group

Focus: Tasks and procedures

Approach: Piecemeal change

Stable environment

Student A: Bob Leighton

You represent the CPW. The majority of the employees at the Kirkby plant of Lonsdale Fuels are members of the CPW. The current crisis has caused a lot of resentment among your union members who feel that management has betrayed the relationship of trust that had existed until now by allowing subcontractors to bring in foreign non-union workers. Your members want you to obtain an assurance from management that the jobs that are being created will be advertised locally so that local people can apply. Ideally you would like all of the 200 jobs to be offered to local people but you would be prepared to negotiate a settlement if management guarantees that a significant proportion of the jobs will be filled locally. You would also like the company to make a clear policy statement which would apply to all Lonsdale operations in the country. If you fail to reach agreement with management, the CPW will consider extending the strike to Lonsdale's three other UK refineries which would stop all production in the UK.

Unit 9 · page 94 **Spidergram**

phrasal verbs

break away
break down
break even
break in (into)
break through
break off
break out

idioms with verbs

take a break
break the deadlock
break the ice
give someone a break
break the law

nouns

break
breakage
breakthrough
breakpoint
breakdown

prefixed nouns

outbreak

break
(verb)

adjectives

breaking   *break-even*
breakaway
breakneck
unbreakable
breakable

Unit 8 page 87 **Student B**

A young executive was leaving the office late one evening when he found the CEO standing in front of a shredder with a piece of paper in his hand.

'Listen,' said the CEO, 'this is a very sensitive and important document here, and my secretary has gone for the night. Can you make this thing work?'

'Certainly,' said the young executive. He turned the machine on, inserted the paper, and pressed the start button.

'Excellent, excellent!' said the CEO as his paper disappeared inside the machine.

'I just need one copy.'

Unit 10 page 112 **Dilemma: Student B**

Student B: **Janet Fraser Darling**

You are surprised at the reaction of the CPW which is much more virulent than you had expected. You thought that all employees had understood that Lonsdale Fuels needs to cut costs in order to remain competitive and you see this as the only guarantee for the future of the group's employees. You have discussed the situation with the senior management of Lonsdale Fuels and they have briefed you for the negotiation with the CPW. The CPW leader will try to persuade you that all of the 200 jobs should be filled by local applicants. You know that the local workforce cannot provide enough skilled technicians to fill the positions so you cannot agree to such a demand. Your management has authorised you to negotiate a quota of jobs that will be reserved for local people but they have hinted that this should be as low as possible. They have also said that they do not want to see an escalation of the crisis and that they want the Kirkby plant reopened as soon as possible.

Unit 12 page 130 **Career skills: Student B**

Student B

You are going to have a ten-minute conversation with Student A on the following subject: 'Things that I like and things that I dislike'. Student A has received instructions to prepare a list with some examples of his/her likes and dislikes and will explain some of the reasons behind them. However, your role in this conversation is quite different. During the conversation you should follow the four steps outlined below:

1 Begin the conversation by asking your partner some questions about the subject. Pay careful attention to your partner's body language: posture, gestures, breathing and voice.

2 As the conversation develops, you should begin to match the body language and tone of voice of your partner as closely as possible. If he or she places their hands in a particular position or speaks slowly and softly, you should do the same, etc. Do this for two or three minutes.

3 Continue the conversation but instead of matching the body language of your partner, you should mismatch: adopt a different body language and tone of voice. Do this for two or three minutes.

4 Now tell your partner how you deliberately modified your behaviour during the conversation. Did he/she notice when you imitated or mismatched his/her body language? What effect did this have on the flow of conversation?

Glossary

Unit 1   HR

assignment /əˈsaɪnmənt/ n **1** [C] a piece of work that someone is given: *My assignment was to save the company, whatever it took.* **2** [U] JOBS when someone is given a particular job or task, or sent to work in a particular place or for a particular person: *With the agreement, GM got more control over the assignment of skilled workers in the plant.*

job cuts /ˈdʒɒb kʌts/ n [C] reductions in the number of employees on an organisation's payroll: *Last Friday the company announced a further round of job cuts.*

managing partner /ˈmænɪdʒɪŋ ˌpɑːtnə/ n [C] COMMERCE a very important partner who makes management decisions in a partnership: *Mr Hielscher, formerly a senior partner, was promoted to chief operating officer and managing partner.*

manpower /ˈmænˌpaʊə/ n [U] COMMERCE all the workers available for a particular kind of work in a particular area: *Economic expansion has created serious manpower shortages in the country.* | *We don't have the manpower to open up any more offices.*

pay rise /ˈpeɪ ˌraɪz/ n [C] HUMAN RESOURCES an increase in the money someone receives for the job they do: *The railworkers were offered a 3% pay rise.*

perk /pɜːk/ n [C] HUMAN RESOURCES something in addition to money that you get for doing your job, such as a car: *Employees must pay tax on anything regarded as a perk.*

resourcing /rɪˈzɔːsɪŋ/ n [U] FINANCE money or other resources that are needed to do particular work: *The initiative failed because of inadequate resourcing.*

retirement /rɪˈtaɪəmənt/ n [U] the act of leaving a job because you have reached the end of your working life, or the period of your life after you do this: *Mr Baker turns 65 next month, the usual retirement age for the company's employees.* | *You must make adequate provision for your retirement.*

reward scheme /rɪˈwɔːd ˌskiːm/ n [C] HUMAN RESOURCES pay and things such as pensions, health insurance, and a company car that you get from being employed: *A manager must design reward schemes which satisfy individuals and the objectives of the organisation.*

scorecard /ˈskɔːkɑːd/ n [C] HUMAN RESOURCES a system that is used for checking or testing something: *We have developed a scorecard which will give performance measurements and also help planners identify what should be done.*

shortfall /ˈʃɔːtfɔːl/ n [C] the difference between the amount that you have and the larger amount you need or expect: *A shortfall in oil supplies worldwide precipitated the price rise.*

well being /ˌwel biːɪŋ/ n [U] a feeling of being comfortable and happy, especially at work: *It's a well known fact that stress affects one's physical and mental health and general feeling of well-being at work.*

workforce diversity /ˈwɜːkfɔːs daɪˈvɜːsɪti/ n [U] HUMAN RESOURCES policy of employing staff from a variety of ethnic, social, cultural and gender groups: *We are committed to achieving workforce diversity at all levels of our organisation.*

workload /ˈwɜːkləʊd/ n [U] HUMAN RESOURCES the amount of work that a person or organisation has to do: *Their workload has increased in the last couple of years.*

Unit 2   Organisations

best practice /ˌbest ˈpræktəs/ n [U] a technique or process that is believed to be more effective at delivering a particular outcome than any other known technique and is therefore used as a benchmark when developing policy: *Companies in emerging market economies are expected to show that they have adopted global best practices before applying for international loans.*

core competency /ˌkɔː ˈkɒmpətənsi/ n **1** [C, U] HUMAN RESOURCES an important skill that you need to have when doing a particular job: *A sample file showing the core competencies for the Managing Librarian position is shown below.* **2** [C, U] MARKETING a particular ability or skill that a company has, which gives it an advantage over its competitors: *A software company's core competencies are likely to include software development and marketing.*

corporation /ˌkɔːpəˈreɪʃən/ n [C] ORGANISATIONS **1** a company or group of companies acting together as a single organisation: *the Sony Corporation* | *Mesa has completed its conversion from a partnership to a corporation.* **2** in Britain, a large company or a public organisation: *the British Broadcasting Corporation*

credit crunch /ˈkredət ˌkrʌntʃ/ n [singular] BANKING ECONOMICS when borrowing money becomes difficult because banks are forced to reduce the amount they lend: *One reason for the credit crunch is that bankers fear that regulators are more likely to classify loans as bad.*

limited liability /ˈlɪmətəd laɪəˌbɪləti/ n [U] LAW FINANCE when the owners of a limited liability company are only responsible for their company's debts up to a certain amount if it goes out of business, and do not have to sell their personal assets to repay these debts: *When he founded the company, he chose limited liability status because of the personal protection it gave him.*

partnership /ˈpɑːtnəʃɪp/ n [C] a relationship between two people, organisations, or countries that work together: *the partnership between US capital and Mexican labour*

quoted /ˈkwəʊtəd/ adj FINANCE a quoted company is one whose shares are bought and sold on the Stock Exchange: *the best-paid executives of a British quoted company*

shareholder /ˈʃeəˌhəʊldə/ n [C] *especially BrE* FINANCE someone who owns shares in a company: *Dividends are paid to the shareholders each year if adequate profits are made.* stockholder *AmE*

workplace /ˈwɜːkpleɪs/ n [C] HUMAN RESOURCES the room or building where you work: *Good design involves adapting the workplace environment to the needs of workers, rather than trying to make workers adjust to the workplace.*

Unit 3   Change

business model /ˈbɪznəs ˌmɒdl/ n [C] COMMERCE a description of all the core aspects of a business, including its structure, strategies and policies: *The Internet has created an entirely new type of business model that depends entirely on existing or emergent technology.*

cost cutting /ˈkɒst ˌkʌtɪŋ/ n [U] ACCOUNTING the reduction of the expenditure that a business or organisation allocates for its operations: *Our cost cutting strategies have successfully reduced our spending without affecting the quality of our products.*

market forces /ˈmɑːkət ˈfɔːsəz/ n pl [U] ECONOMICS the way that the behaviour of buyers and sellers affects the levels of supply and demand in a particular market, especially when the government does nothing to change this: *By ending the electricity monopoly, market forces rather than state utilities will set prices.*

mindset /ˈmaɪndset/ n [C] someone's general attitude, and the way in which they think about things and make decisions: *The company seems to have a very old-fashioned mindset.*

outperform /ˌaʊtpəˈfɔːm/ v [T] to do better or be more successful than someone or something else: *Stocks generally outperform other investments.* | *Clinical trials have shown that it outperforms existing drugs.*

overestimate /ˌəʊvərˈestəmeɪt/ v [T] to think that something is larger or greater than it really is: *Forecasters had underestimated growth and overestimated inflation by about 0.5% a year.* —**overestimate** /-ˈestəmət / n [C]: *The figure of 30% is clearly an overestimate.*

overhaul /ˌəʊvəˈhɔːl/ v [T] to repair or change all the parts of a machine or system that is not working correctly: *The country's economy will need to be completely overhauled.* —**overhaul** /ˈəʊvəhɔːl/ n [C]: *a world leader in the repair and overhaul of industrial gas turbines*

overvalue /ˌəʊvəˈvæljuː/ v [T] if you overvalue something, you give it a value that is too high: *The accounting firm wrongly permitted the company to overvalue its junk bonds.*

relocate /ˌriːləʊˈkeɪt/ v [I, T] if a company or worker relocates or is relocated, they move to a different place: *Many workers are unwilling to relocate.* | *The company plans to relocate its corporate headquarters to Iowa.* —**relocation** n [U, C] *Half the workers will be offered relocation, and the remaining jobs will be eliminated.* | *Profits fell 18% following the company's restructuring and office relocations.*

restructure /ˌriːˈstrʌktʃə/ v [I, T] COMMERCE if a company restructures, or someone restructures it, it changes the way it is organised or financed: *The iron ore company has restructured its operations.* | *The group will restructure, reducing the workforce by as much as 19%.*

shift /ʃɪft/ n [C] COMMERCE a change in attitude towards the economy or a particular industry, caused by an event or discovery that has changed your way of thinking: *The use of gigabit networks has enabled a shift to image-based communication.*

track record /ˈtræk ˈrekɔːd/ n [C] all the things that a person or organisation has done in the past, which shows how good they are at doing their job, dealing with problems etc: *This is a company with a proven track record.* | *He has a good track record in improving efficiency.*

Unit 4 Responsibility

boom /buːm/ *n* [C, U] ECONOMICS a time when business activity increases rapidly, so that the demand for goods increases, prices and wages go up, and unemployment falls: *After four years of economic boom, this year saw a slowing down of the economy.*

carbon neutral /ˈkɑːbən ˈnjuːtrəl/ *adj* cancelling the effect of the carbon gases that your activities produce by planting trees, supporting the production of green electricity etc: *HSBC is the first big bank to commit to going carbon neutral, as it seeks to reduce its environmental impact.*

climate change /ˈklaɪmət ˌtʃeɪndʒ/ *n* [U] a change in global weather patterns. Nowadays often used to refer to the problem of 'global warming', or the rise in the temperature of the Earth's surface. *Many people believe that climate change represents one of the greatest environmental, social and economic threats facing the planet.*

competitive edge /kəmˈpetətɪv ˈedʒ / *n* COMMERCE an advantage that makes a company more able to succeed in competing with others: *the product and marketing mix that gives the company a competitive edge over its rivals*

corporate earnings /ˈkɔːpərət ˈɜːnɪŋz/ *n* [U] COMMERCE the amount of money that companies make or lose over a given period of time (often calculated on a quarterly basis): *Corporate earnings have increased by almost 20% this year.*

corporate social responsibility /ˈkɔːpərət ˈsəʊʃəl rɪˌspɒnsəˈbɪləti/ *n* [C, U] the idea that a company's role is not just about producing goods, but that it has a duty to help people in society and protect the environment: *Corporate social responsibility (CSR) is becoming fundamental to the creation of long-term wealth for corporations, as well as being 'the right thing to do'.*

financial analysis /fəˈnænʃəl əˈnæləsəs / *n* [U] FINANCE a careful examination of the financial state of a company or person: *Decisions about where we invest the stockholders' money will be based on financial analysis.*

good conduct /gʊd ˈkɒndʌkt/ *n* [U] behaviour that is ethical and commendable: *Sticking to their core values and engaging in good business conduct got the company lots of positive publicity.*

policy /ˈpɒləsi/ *n* [C] a course of action that has been officially agreed and chosen by a business, political party or other organisation: *The new policy sets the standard for the entire industry.*

ranking /ˈræŋkɪŋ/ *n* [C] **1** the position of something or someone in a list that has been arranged in order of quality or importance: *The US recaptured from Germany the number one ranking among exporters.* **2** a list of things or people in order of quality or importance: *a ranking of the 30 largest US cities on the basis of finance and management*

transparent /trænˈspærənt/ *adj* if rules, methods, or business dealings are transparent, they are clear and people can see that they are fair and honest: *The regulations will force large corporations to conduct their contract awards in a transparent manner.* —**transparency** *n* [U]: *EU laws on transparency and competition*

upsurge /ˈʌpsɜːdʒ/ *n* [C] COMMERCE an improvement or increase in the number or level of something: *There has been an upsurge of interest in smart energy.*

whistleblower /ˈwɪsəlˌbləʊə/ *n* [C] HUMAN RESOURCES someone working for an organisation who tells the authorities that people in the organisation are doing something illegal, dishonest, or wrong: *The company had paid out substantial sums to silence would-be whistleblowers.*

Unit 5 Governance

equity stake /ˈekwəti ˌsteɪk/ *n* [C] FINANCE when a company or organisation owns shares in a company: *IBM has bought a $27m equity stake in the firm.* | *French and Italian governments have sought to take an equity stake in certain industries.*

financial reporting /fəˈnænʃəl rɪˈpɔːtɪŋ/ *n* [U] FINANCE the financial information that companies give about their activities, and the ways that they prepare and show it: *its efforts to increase clarity and dependability in financial reporting*

FSA /ef es ˈeɪ/ *n* [U] ORGANISATIONS FINANCE BANKING abbreviation for Financial Services Authority: an organisation that in 1997 took control of regulation of the British financial services industry from the nine separate organisations which previously had been responsible for banking, insurance etc: *The Financial Services Authority regulates the sale and marketing of most investment products.*

greenmail /ˈɡriːnmeɪl/ *n* [U] FINANCE when a company buys back its stock from a company that is trying to take it over, often for a very high price, to try to prevent a takeover: *One of Japan's wealthiest men, he has a history of speculation in stocks and real estate and is renowned for his attempts at greenmail.*

misgovernance /ˈmɪsˌɡʌvənəns/ *n* [U] COMMERCE the mismanagement of a company at the highest level: *An investigation into misgovernance at one of the country's leading financial institutions is already under way.*

motion /ˈməʊʃən/ *n* [C] a suggestion that is made formally at a meeting and then decided on by voting: *The motion was carried by 15 votes to 10.* | *I'd like to propose a motion to move the weekly meetings to Thursdays.*

poison pill /ˌpɔɪzən ˈpɪl/ *n* [C] JOURNALISM FINANCE something in a company's financial or legal structure that is meant to make it difficult for another company to buy it in a takeover: *The company's poison pill anti-takeover measure prevents a group from purchasing more than 10% of its stock.*

private equity /ˌpraɪvət ˈekwəti/ *n* [C] FINANCE investments in companies whose shares are not traded on a public stock exchange: *Investing in private equity can produce higher than normal returns.*

rogue trader/ˌrəʊɡ ˈtreɪdə/ *n* [C] FINANCE someone who works for a financial institution and makes unauthorised and reckless transactions on the financial market: *The bank lost $7 billion as a result of the actions of a rogue trader.*

severance deal /ˈsevərəns ˌdiːl/ *n* [C] HUMAN RESOURCES an amount of money, and other advantages such as advice on finding a new job, that are offered to an employee when a company tells them to leave. Severance deals are often offered when companies are restructuring: *20 full-time employees will be offered a severance deal or other job opportunities at Chevron.*

share swap /ˈʃeə ˌswɒp/ *n* [C] FINANCE a change in the ownership of shares from one person or organisation to another, or the arrangements for doing this: *The legal environment for share swaps in Russia is still unclear.*

stakeholder /ˈsteɪkˌhəʊldə/ *n* [C] ECONOMICS someone who has invested money into something, or who has some important connection with it, and therefore is affected by its success or failure: *We are working to increase the synergies between all our stakeholders.*

account for /əˈkaʊnt fɔː/ *phr v* [T] **1** to be a particular amount or part of something: *Own-label products now account for more than 20% of sales in some European supermarkets.*
2 ACCOUNTING to show something in a company's accounts in a particular way: *In financial statements, the bonds should be accounted for as debt.*

amount to /əˈmaʊnt tə/ *phr v* [T] if something amounts to a particular total, the different parts add up to that total: *Earnings per share amounted to 16.8p.* | *Total government income amounted to about £180,000 million.*

donor /ˈdəʊnə/ *n* [C] someone who gives money or other valuable things to people who are ill, hungry, poor etc: *His fines were paid by an anonymous donor.* | *Japan is Asia's biggest foreign aid donor, giving over $1.1 billion in official development assistance and loans.*

feasible /ˈfiːzəbəl/ *adj* a plan, idea, or method that is feasible is possible and likely to work: *That may be the only feasible way of solving the problem.* —**feasibility** *n* [U]: *The success of your business will ultimately depend on the feasibility of your idea.*

incubator /ˈɪŋkjəbeɪtə/ *n* [C] COMMERCE COMPUTING a company or organisation that provides help and support for new companies, especially ones using advanced technology or the Internet: *The government set up an Internet incubator.*

industrialist /ɪnˈdʌstriələst/ *n* [C] COMMERCE JOBS a powerful businessman or businesswoman who is the owner or leader of a large industrial company: *A group of Ukrainian ministers and industrialists asked for 6 million euros for technical training.*

seed capital /ˈsiːd ˌkæpətl/ *n* [U] FINANCE money used to start a new company, project, activity etc: *Careful budgeting allows managers to accumulate savings, which they can use as seed capital.*

social entrepreneur /ˈsəʊʃəl ˌɒntrəprəˈnɜː/ *n* [C] JOBS COMMERCE someone who creates a company in order to address a social or environmental problem: *Marcus Johannssen is a social entrepreneur who has launched several successful ventures in India.*

stake /steɪk/ *n* [C] FINANCE money risked or invested in a business: *Analysts expect the company to sell its large stake in the Hong Kong bank.*

trial /ˈtraɪəl/ *n* [C] MANUFACTURING a process of testing a product to see whether it is safe, effective etc: *The company expects clinical trials to continue for two years.* | **by/through trial and error** if you do something by or through trial and error, you try several different ways of doing it to get the result you want: *I got these machine settings right purely by trial and error.*

tycoon /taɪˈkuːn/ *n* [C] someone who is successful in business and industry and has a lot of money and power: *a high-powered business tycoon*

venture capital /ˈventʃə ˌkæpətl/ *n* [U] FINANCE money lent to someone so that they can start a new business: *The fund provides venture capital and loans for US business projects.*

Unit 7   Resources

biofuel /'baɪəʊˌfjuːəl/ n [U] fuel made from renewable biological materials such as corn or soya bean: *Virgin is planning to become the first airline to use biofuel.*

cap and trade /ˌkæp ənd treɪd/ n [U] ECONOMICS FINANCE a market system allowing companies to offest their carbon emissions by trading in carbon credits: *Some governments would prefer to introduce a direct tax rather than cap and trade.*

carbon credit /'kɑːbən ˈkredɪt/ n [C] COMMERCE a fixed amount of harmful gases such as carbon dioxide, that a company is allowed to send into the Earth's atmosphere: *Electricity companies are allocated fewer carbon credits than they need, in order to encourage investment in environmentally-friendly power generation.*

carbon emissions /'kɑːbən ɪˈmɪʃənz/ n [U] COMMERCE harmful substances such as CO_2 gases released into the atmosphere by industry: *Carbon emissions must be phased out as soon as possible.*

carbon footprint /ˌkɑːbən ˈfʊtˌprɪnt/ n [U] COMMERCE the measure of the amount of carbon emissions produced by an individual or organisation: *UK retailers have agreed to reduce their carbon footprint.*

deplete /dɪˈpliːt/ v [T] to reduce greatly the amount of something, using up nearly all of it: *Drastic measures will need to be taken if fish stocks in Europe's seas are not to be disastrously depleted.*

discretion /dɪˈskreʃən/ n [U] the ability, right, or freedom that someone has to take decisions in a particular situation: *People want to have more discretion over their working hours.* —**discretionary** adj: *Under the present rules public consultation is discretionary.*

non-renewable /ˌnɒnrɪˈnjuːəbəl/ adj non-renewable types of energy such as coal or oil cannot be replaced once they have been used: *a tax on all forms of non-renewable energy* | *These regulations will only encourage a massive waste of valuable and non-renewable natural resources.*

scalable /'skeɪləbəl/ adj COMPUTING a scalable machine, system etc can be increased in size: *We needed a computer system that was scalable and that could keep up with our growing number of users.*

scheme /skiːm/ n [C] **1** BrE an official plan or arrangement that is intended to help people in some way: *a government training scheme for the unemployed* **2** BrE FINANCE an arrangement in which the government or an employer provides financial help to people: *There is a low-interest loan scheme for employees who have been with the company for over two years.*

underpriced /ˌʌndəˈpraɪst/ adj fixed for sale at too low a price: *The company's shares were underpriced when they were introduced on the stock exchange.*

Unit 8   Power

assertive /əˈsɜːtɪv/ adj behaving in a confident way so that people listen to your opinions and ideas —**assertiveness** n [U]: *If you communicate in a way that is assertive, you are more likely to be listened to.*

bargain /'bɑːgən/ n [C] COMMERCE an agreement between two people or groups to do something in return for something else: *Management and unions have managed to strike a bargain whereby unions have accepted more flexible working in return for better pay.* —**bargain** v [I] to discuss the conditions of a sale, agreement etc in order to get the greatest advantage for yourself: *The unions are bargaining for greater employment security.*

business agenda /'bɪznəs əˈdʒendə/ n [C] COMMERCE list of the most important things that have to be addressed by a business organisation: *Resource efficiency is now at the top of the business agenda.*

coalition /ˌkəʊəˈlɪʃən/ n [C] a group of people who join together to achieve a particular purpose: *A coalition of junior doctors, managers, and consultants must assess the working practices of all staff.*

coercive /kəʊˈɜːsɪv/ adj using threats or orders to make someone do something they do not want to do: *coercive measures to reduce absenteeism*

credibility /ˌkredɪˈbɪlɪti/ n the quality of deserving to be believed and trusted: *Central banks have already lost a lot of credibility.*

influence /'ɪnfluəns/ v [T] to have an effect on the way something happens or the way someone does something: *Children are heavily influenced by advertising.*

legitimate /lɪˈdʒɪtəmət/ adj **1** LAW operating according to the law: *Although most of these shows are legitimate, a growing number are frauds.* **2** reasonable or understandable: *There's a lot of legitimate concern about where the economy is going.*

pacesetter /'peɪsˌsetə/ n [C] a company that is more successful than its competitors because it develops new products, methods etc before they do: *the pacesetter for the airline industry* —**pacesetting** n [U]: *Pacesetting certainly makes sense in an entrepreneurial context.*

politics /ˈpɒlətɪks/ *n* [U] **1** ideas and activities relating to gaining and using power in a country, city etc: *a businessman who is also involved in politics* **2** the activities of people who are concerned with gaining personal advantage within a group, organisation etc: *He left his job because he could no longer take the petty office politics.*

power base /ˈpaʊə ˌbeɪs/ *n* [C] an area or group of people whose support makes a leader powerful: *The more solid the power base, the longer a CEO is likely to remain in control.*

tactics /ˈtæktɪks/ *n pl* [C] methods that you use to achieve something: *Aggressive advertising tactics may mislead consumers.*

Unit 9 · E-marketing

break down /ˌbreɪk ˈdaʊn/ *phr v* **1** [T] to separate information or a total amount into parts, especially so that it is easier to understand: *Once the statistics are broken down, some clear patterns of employment begin to emerge.* **2** [I] if talks break down, they fail and come to an end because the people involved cannot agree: *The meeting between management and unions broke down and no progress was made.*

breakdown /ˈbreɪkdaʊn/ *n* [C] a statement showing information or a total amount separated into parts so that it is easier to understand: *Also in the report is a breakdown of when delays are most likely to occur.*

break the law /ˌbreɪk ðə ˈlɔː/ *v* [T] if someone breaks a law, rule, agreement etc, they do not do what it says they should do: *If you copy music files from the Internet, you could easily be breaking the law.*

break even /ˌbreɪk ˈiːvən/ *phr v* [T] to make neither a profit nor a loss: *The company needs to charge $13 a ton to break even.* | *The retailer warns that it expects sales to be down by 15%, and it may only break even.*

broadband /ˈbrɔːdbænd/ *n* [U] COMPUTING TELECOMMUNICATIONS a way of connecting a computer to the Internet, which makes it possible to send and receive large amounts of information very quickly: *Do you have a broadband connection?*

classified ad /ˌklæsəfaɪd ˈæd/ *n* [C] MARKETING an advertisement put in a newspaper or on the Internet by someone wanting to buy or sell something: *Internet classified ads tend to be longer.* **want ad** *AmE*

digital /ˈdɪdʒətl/ *adj* MARKETING relating to a business activity that uses the Internet: *the digital marketing industry* | **the digital divide** COMPUTING TELECOMMUNICATIONS the difference between the people that own computers and know how to use the Internet and those that do not: *The ITU has introduced a standard method to evaluate the extent of the digital divide.*

pop-up /ˈpɒp ʌp/ *n* [C] COMPUTING MARKETING a small window containing an advertisement that suddenly appears on a computer screen when you are looking at a website: *Not all pop-ups can be blocked.*

random /ˈrændəm/ *adj* a random sample, check etc is one in which things or people are chosen without any particular reason or pattern so that they will include a typical mixture of the larger group they represent: *The group polled a random sample of US manufacturers.*

search advertising /ˈsɜːtʃ ˌædvətaɪzɪŋ/ *n* [U] MARKETING placing advertisements on Internet pages that show search results: *Search advertising is a significant revenue source for companies like Yahoo.*

social networking /ˌsəʊʃəl ˈnetwɜːkɪŋ/ *n* [U] increasing the number of one's business and/ or social contacts by meeting with them or by connecting with them via the telephone or the Internet: *Social networking websites allow communities of Internet users to communicate regularly online.*

word of mouth /ˌwɜːd əv ˈmaʊθ/ *n* [U] when people learn about something from their friends, people they work with, etc: *Many of our client recommendations come through word of mouth.*

Unit 10 · Risk

bankrupt /ˈbæŋkrʌpt/ *adj* LAW FINANCE not having enough money to pay your debts: *Many people would lose their jobs if the firm were to go bankrupt.*

comply /kəmˈplaɪ/ *v* [I] to obey a law or rule, or to keep an agreement: *the high costs of upgrading ageing mills to comply with environmental regulations*

contingency plan /kənˈtɪndʒənsi ˌplæn/ *n* [C] a plan for dealing with a future event or situation that might cause problems: *We tried to ensure that the company prepared an adequate oil spill contingency plan.*

hedge /hedʒ/ v [I, T] FINANCE if you hedge a financial risk, you protect yourself against it, for example with futures (agreements to buy or sell currencies etc on a fixed date in the future at a fixed price) or options (rights to buy or sell currencies etc at a particular price within a particular period of time or on a particular date in the future): *I've never hedged currencies before. But I could see the dollar was getting lower, and I hedged for the first time, betting that the dollar would rise.* —**hedging** n [U]: *Manufacturers have been doing more hedging because they expect prices for copper to rise.*

impatriation /ɪmˌpætrɪˈeɪʃən/ n [U] bringing an employee from a foreign subsidiary to work in a company's home market: *Impatriation allows companies to strengthen their image abroad.*

mitigate /ˈmɪtɪˌɡeɪt/ v [T] to to make a situation or the effects of something less unpleasant, harmful, or serious: *Measures need to be taken to mitigate the environmental effects of burning more coal.*

redundant /rɪˈdʌndənt/ adj HUMAN RESOURCES if you are made redundant, you lose your job because your employer no longer has a job for you: *The bank expects to make 15,000 staff redundant over the next three years.*

subsidiary /səbˈsɪdiəri/ n [C] a company that is at least half-owned by another company: *It is important that investors are able to deal with confidence with enterprises from other member states, whether directly, or through their subsidiaries.*

union /ˈjuːnjən/ n [C] an organisation formed by workers to protect their rights: *If you decide to join the union, you are encouraged to play an active part and to ensure your views are represented.*

wildcat strike /ˈwaɪldkæt ˌstraɪk/ n [C] HUMAN RESOURCES a strike in which workers suddenly stop working in order to protest about something, but which has not been approved by the union: *The airline cancelled 40 flights following a wildcat strike.*

Unit 11 Misconduct

bribery /ˈbraɪbəri/ n [U] LAW dishonestly giving money to someone to persuade them to do something to help you: *The International Chamber of Commerce has had rules against bribery and extortion since 1977.*

embezzle /ɪmˈbezəl/ v [I, T] LAW ACCOUNTING if someone embezzles money from the company or organisation they work for, they steal it, perhaps over a period of time, and use it for themselves: *An American banker, accused of embezzling $13 million, yesterday gave himself up to the authorities.* —**embezzlement** n [U]: *Several employees were imprisoned for embezzlement.*

fine /faɪn/ n [C] LAW money that someone has to pay as a punishment: *He served 22 months in jail and paid a $100 million fine to settle insider trading charges.* —**fine** v [T] *The company has been fined for illegal nuclear exports to North Korea.*

insider trading /ɪnˌsaɪdə ˈtreɪdɪŋ/ n [U] FINANCE LAW when someone uses knowledge of a particular company, situation etc that is not available to other people in order to buy or sell shares. Insider trading is illegal: *Shares in both banks jumped 20% two weeks before confirmation of their merger, which led to an insider trading inquiry being opened.*

larceny /ˈlɑːsəni/ n [C, U] LAW the crime of stealing a lot of money or something very valuable: *He was charged with grand larceny.*

misappropriation /ˌmɪsəprəʊprɪˈeɪʃən/ n [U] LAW dishonestly taking something, especially money, that you have been trusted to keep safe, and to use it for your own advantage: *He was accused of misappropriation of funds amounting to £4 million.*

penalty /ˈpenlti/ n [C] **1** a punishment for breaking a law or rule: *There will be increased penalties for dumping oil at sea.* **2** BANKING INSURANCE an amount of money someone has to pay if they do not keep to a legal agreement: *There is a 10% penalty for withdrawing funds in the first three years.*

plaintiff /ˈpleɪntəf/ n [C] LAW someone who brings a legal action against someone in a court of law: *The plaintiffs are seeking $2 billion in damages for alleged fraud.*

price-fixing /ˈpraɪs ˌfɪksɪŋ/ n [U] **1** COMMERCE LAW when companies in an industry agree on the prices they will charge for something. This form of price-fixing is done so that companies avoid competing with each other, and is normally illegal: *The EU investigated international telephone agreements to see if there was price-fixing in violation of EU competition rules.* **2** COMMERCE LAW when a company tells the shops etc that sell its products how much they must charge for them. This form of price-fixing is sometimes illegal: *The UK's last price-fixing arrangement was retail price maintenance for non-prescription medicines.*

sanction /ˈsæŋkʃən/ n [C] **1** ECONOMICS official order or law stopping trade, communication etc with another country as a way of forcing political changes: *The UN security council unanimously refused to lift economic sanctions.* **2** LAW a punishment for disobeying a rule or law: *The most severe sanction the panel could recommend is expulsion from the Senate.*

tax evasion /ˈtæks ɪˌveɪʒən/ n [U] TAX LAW illegal ways of paying less tax: *He pleaded guilty to charges of bank fraud and tax evasion.*

theft /θeft/ n [C, U] the crime of stealing or an act of stealing something: *An employee was fired for theft.* | *Thefts of property from cars rose 24%.*

trust /trʌst/ n **1** [U] a belief in the honesty or goodness of someone or something: *The measures are necessary to restore public trust in the futures markets.* **2** [C] LAW FINANCE an arrangement by which someone has legal control over your money and usually invests it for you, or an organisation that does this: *He put his assets in a variety of trusts.*

Unit 12 | Development

achievement /əˈtʃiːvmənt/ n [U] something important that you succeed in doing by your own efforts: *One of his greatest achievements has been the creation of the foundation that bears his name.*

alumni network /əˈlʌmnaɪ ˌnetwɜːk/ n [C] an organisation of people who were at school or university together: *The school's alumni network is among the biggest in Europe.*

awareness /əˈweənəs/ n [U] knowledge or understanding of a particular subject, situation, or thing: *They need to raise awareness of the product in markets such as France and the US, where it is less well known.*

code of conduct /ˌkəʊd əv ˈkɒndʌkt/ n [C] COMMERCE a set of rules that employees, companies, or professional people agree to follow in the way they behave and do business: *Companies wishing to join the PC Direct Marketers' Association will have to abide by a code of conduct.*

drawback /ˈdrɔːbæk/ n [C] a disadvantage of a situation, product etc that makes it less attractive: *There are drawbacks to being a sole trader, but they are outweighed by the benefits.*

graduate /ˈɡrædʒuət/ n [C] **1** a person who has completed a university degree course, especially for a first degree: *The company is looking for a graduate engineer with the ability to lead and motivate a team of four people.* **2** AmE a person who has completed a course at a college or school:

a Harvard business-school graduate —**graduate** /-eɪt/ v [I] *He graduated from the University of California with a degree in mathematics.*

knowledge management /ˈnɒlɪdʒ ˌmænɪdʒmənt/ n [U] HUMAN RESOURCES when a company makes available to its employees the information they need: *The bank will invest in a knowledge management system, using an intranet to share information in the organisation.*

mentor /ˈmentɔː/ n [C] HUMAN RESOURCES an experienced person who gives advice to less experienced people to help them in their work: *He now runs his own company and is a mentor to other young entrepreneurs.*

norm /nɔːm/ n [C] the usual and expected situation, way of doing something etc: *Private businesses award an average of 0.35% commission compared with the industry's norm of 0.5%.* | *Budget surpluses are now the norm.*

practice /ˈpræktəs/ n [U] the work done by a particular profession, especially lawyers or doctors who are working for themselves rather than a public organisation: *Mr. Barr returned to private law practice in the mid-1990s.*

practise /ˈpræktəs/ BrE, **practice** AmE v [I, T] to work in a particular profession, especially medicine or law: *He practised law for 15 years.*

rapport /ræˈpɔː/ n [C, U] agreement and understanding between people: *He had an excellent rapport with his clients.* | *It is important to build a good rapport with business associates.*

work-life balance /ˌwɜːk laɪf ˈbæləns/ n [U] a situation in which you are able to give the right amount of time and effort to your work and to your personal life outside work, for example to your family or to other interests: *You can't have a proper work-life balance if you're in the office for 12 hours a day!*

workshop /ˈwɜːkʃɒp/ n [C] a meeting at which people discuss their experiences and do practical exercises, especially in order to find solutions to problems: *Staff attended a two-day training workshop on basic PR techniques.*

Glossary test

1 Of all the candidates we interviewed, Ms Chan was the one who really stood out on account of her excellent _____ .
   A track record   B pay rise
   C well-being   D shortfall

2 We have found that financial motivation works best with staff. That's why we have introduced _____ .
   A retirement   B cost cutting
   C financial analysis D reward schemes

3 As part of its _____ plan the company has announced that it will be closing two of its production facilities.
   A relocating   B restructuring
   C resourcing   D insider trading

4 Reducing the budget for temporary staff is bound to increase the _____ of our full time personnel.
   A diversity   B perks
   C workloads   D best practices

5 Sinotelko's quarterly earnings were lower than forecast but most analysts have said they were not surprised by the _____ .
   A overhaul   B upsurge
   C shortfall   D stake

6 _____ planning ensures that an organisation has enough employees available to operate effectively.
   A Manpower   B Feasibility
   C Diversity   D Job cuts

7 JacksonVille Inc has announced that it will be _____ its headquarters from California to Texas.
   A overhauling   B depleting
   C relocating   D restructuring

8 A recent report shows that more and more businesses are using _____ as a way to bolster their image with all their stakeholders.
   A corporate   B competitive edge
      responsibility   D price fixing
   C market forces

9 HR departments are increasingly focusing on the _____ of their employees to ensure that they have a healthy work-life balance.
   A good conduct   B power base
   C transparency   D well-being

10 Last year was one of the best ever and we _____ our competitors in terms of growth in revenue, operating income and market share.
    A outperformed   B overvalued
    C overestimated   D underpriced

11 Chief executives from 60 of Europe's leading electricity companies pledged to achieve a _____ power supply by 2050.
    A carbon credits   B climate change
    C policy   D carbon neutral

12 With governments introducing more stringent controls on pollution and emissions, industry analysts expect to see a _____ in the clean energy sector.
    A drawback   B boom
    C cost cutting   D scorecard

13 The consultant's report clearly shows that we need to completely _____ our information system.
    A overhaul   B shift
    C devalue   D deplete

14 Since our operating costs are lower than the industry average that gives us a significant _____ .
    A cost cutting   B job cuts
    C pay rise   D competitive edge

15 With the recent downturn in the travel sector _____ for both the airlines and the plane manufacturers are likely to be disappointing.
    A corporate earnings B market forces
    C severance deals   D share swaps

16 The changes to the accounting laws are designed to encourage greater _____ by obliging companies to provide valid, standardised and accessible financial information.
    A business model   B track record
    C transparency   D misgovernance

17 There is no point in investing in a new business venture if you have doubts about its _____ .
    A rankings   B feasibility
    C price fixing   D cost cutting

18 The vice president of Centurion Securites has pled guilty to charges of _____ after admitting that he used confidential information to carry out several stock trades.

A insider trading   B bribery
C hedging   D tax evasion

19 The shareholders have passed a resolution which requires their approval for all _____ that exceed an executive's annual salary by more than 300%.

A poison pill   B greenmail
C severance deals   D equity stake

20 Wardward Inc will finance the acquisition of Bluebird Ltd by a _____ which will involve issuing $4 million in new stock.

A financial analysis   B venture capital
C seed capital   D share swap

21 A majority of shareholders voted in favour of the _____ to sell off several businesses owned by the corporation.

A motion   B tactics
C restructuring   D sanctions

22 The role of a(n) _____ is to assist a new business during the initial phases of its activity.

A shareholder   B rogue trader
C tycoon   D incubator

23 The term _____ is used to refer to a situation where the senior management of a business has engaged in fraudulent activities.

A misgovernance   B equity stake
C good conduct   D trial and error

24 Energies like petroleum which use finite natural resources are referred to as _____ .

A depleted   B carbon neutral
C scalable   D non-renewable

25 StartPartners have invested $10m in exchange for a 25% _____ in the new venture.

A carbon credit   B venture capital
C equity stake   D greenmail

26 By promoting _____ , enterprises can ensure that their staff are drawn from a wide range of social, ethnic and community backgrounds.

A perks   B good conduct
C business models   D workforce diversity

27 We managed to complete the project one month ahead of schedule mainly because we had _____ the time required for the construction work.

A overvalued   B overestimated
C overhauled   C outperformed

28 Twenty per cent of a business's client base will usually _____ eighty per cent of its profit.

A amount to   B break down
C account for   D break even

29 A _____ is usually a more senior colleague who counsels a younger, less experienced member of staff.

A tycoon   B mentor
C donor   D plaintiff

30 Your _____ is a representation of the greenhouse gases that you produce.

A carbon footprint   B carbon credit
C cap and trade   D environmental policy

31 Insurance experts have calculated that total payments for damage to property during the recent flooding could _____ more than £150 million pounds.

A account for   B amount to
C break even   D overestimate

32 By 2040 most of the offshore gas reserves in Northern Europe will have been _____ .

A outperformed   B devalued
C underpriced   D depleted

33 According to the business plan it will take the new venture two years just to _____ .

A break down   B break even
C overvalue   D outperform

34 The fire at the plant would have been a disaster if we hadn't had a _____ to transfer production elsewhere.

A risk management   B subsidiary
C hedging   D contingency plan

35 Two hackers who entered the bank's central database and obtained customer credit card numbers have been accused of information _____ .

A embezzlement   B money laundering
C theft   D bribery

36 _____ is one of the cheapest and most effective forms of advertising as it relies on people making personal recommendations of products or services by telling other people about them.

A Social networking   B Search advertising
C Greenmail   D Word of mouth

37 A company whose shares are _____ on the stock exchange is called a listed company.

A staked   B relocated
C overvalued   D quoted

38 During a _____ banks are reluctant to lend money to each other or to corporate and private borrowers.

A cost cutting   B limited liability
C partnership   D credit crunch

39 At PlexoVista we pride ourselves on our _____ : providing custom-made plastics to our global customers.

A core competency   B social networking
C market forces   D venture capital

40 After a disappointing dividend performance this year, the company's CEO has promised _____ that he will return the company to past levels of profitability.

A shareholders   B partnerships
C rogue traders D social
                   entrepreneurs

41 The VentureFair fund specialises in investments in _____ and has already acquired majority stakes in more than 50 new private ventures.

A insider trading   B private equity
C market forces   D contigency plans

42 As demand for their products falls, many businesses have had to make part of their workforce _____ .

A depleted   B shifted
C redundant   D devalued

43 To consolidate its international expansion, the Fenstock Corporation have opened two new _____ in Malaysia.

A tycoons   B stakes
C carbon credits D subsidiaries

44 _____ is used by many organisations as a way to provide support to new employees.

A Mentoring   B Retirement
C Restructuring D Hedging

45 At Linolia Consulting we use _____ to share key information and experience about the projects that we have worked on.

A best practice   B knowledge
C track record   management
                  D good conduct

46 _____ is part of the life of any business organisation because staff will inevitably form alliances to promote their mutual interests.

A Politics   B Power base
C Legitimacy   D Business agenda

47 Heinrich is a great engineer but he lacks the _____ that you need to really lead and motivate a team.

A pacesetting   B assignment
C assertiveness D coalition

48 The most successful managers tend to be those who can use their _____ to get other people to do what they want.

A tactics   B bargaining
C feasibility D influence

49 Mavery Freight Ltd has been declared _____ after being unable to refinance its debt.

A redundant   B bankrupt
C non-renewable   D embezzlement

50 One of the _____ of video training is that it is not suited to people who learn better by doing rather than by watching.

A policies   B drawbacks
C best practices D penalties

Grammar reference

Contrast and similarity

Single sentences

In single sentences the following words and expressions are used.

Contrast

- in contrast to
  In contrast to the businesses of the past, today's more flexible firms require more rapid solutions.

- unlike
  Unlike most companies, the four titans of accountancy really mean it when they say that people are their biggest asset.

- unalike
  Some would argue that profit-making and managing people are concepts that are totally **unalike**.

- on the one hand ... on the other hand
  On the one hand, businesses need to hire experienced HR managers but, **on the other hand**, they need to employ high-calibre line mangers.

- while, although, whereas
  While (Although/Whereas) older workers consider loyalty and hard work to be important values, the younger generation attach more value to diversity and enjoyment.

  A company's material resources deteriorate over time **whereas/although/while** its human resources usually improve.

Similarity

- alike
  Poorly designed appraisal processes may be resented by managers and employees **alike**.

- as, like
  As in any other project, planning is essential when moving key personnel between countries.
  Like the vast majority of companies, the big four pay close attention to their recruitment procedures and policies.

- similar
  Appraisal interviews at our company are **similar** to our monthly feedback meetings but more formal.

Connected sentences

The following expressions and words are used to show contrast or similarity in consecutive or connected sentences.

Contrast

- conversely, however, on the contrary, nevertheless
  The field of human resources may well be entering a critical phase. **Nonetheless/ However/Nevertheless**, there is no shortage of opportunities.

  Good human resources practices tend to increase productivity and satisfaction. **Conversely/On the contrary**, poor practices lead to lower output and employee resentment.

Similarity

- similarly, likewise
  The new intranet system enables personnel to consult their records directly. **Likewise**, it allows supervisors to process employee requests directly.

  If you don't meet your performance goals, you won't get a raise. **Similarly**, negative feedback from colleagues can also affect your chances of a salary increase.

Determiners

Determiners consist of different categories of words that are associated with nouns to form noun phrases. There are three types of determiner: central determiners, predeterminers and postdeterminers, according to their position relative to each other and to the noun or noun phrase they describe.

Central determiners

These include the definite, indefinite and zero articles *the, a/an*, the demonstratives *this* and *that*, and the possessives *my, your*, etc. Central determiners also include the *wh*-determiners *which, whose, whatever* and *whichever*, the negative determiners *no* and *neither*, and the determiners *some, any, each, every, either* and *enough*. Central determiners are always positioned before the nouns that they refer to.

At *the* end of **each** quarter our subsidiaries submit their sales figures to headquarters.

Predeterminers

This group includes the words *all*, *both*, *half*, and the multipliers *once*, *twice*, etc. When a predeterminer is associated with a central determiner it always appears in initial position.

Half our employees work remotely using mobile computing devices.

Postdeterminers

These include many words that refer to quantity and order (also known as quantifiers): *first*, *second* (etc), *ten*, *eleven* (etc), *last*, *few*, *little*, *many*, *more*, *much*, *a lot of*. Postdeterminers are always placed after other determiners.

In the last few years, franchising has spread to virtually every sector of the economy.

Continuous forms

In the English tense system, all tenses have a simple or continuous (also referred to as 'progressive') form which describes the completeness of the action from a given point in time. This course uses these terms when identifying the different tenses.

The continuous forms of verbs are used to focus on situations or events which are either in the process of taking place or which are viewed as such from a given point in time. The continuous usually refers to situations that are incomplete, temporary or of limited duration. 'Stative' verbs, which express states of mind such as *know*, *seem*, *belong*, *like*, *understand* etc, are not normally used in the continuous form. However, some stative verbs can take the continuous form when they refer to temporary events or situations.

The key trend we have been seeing is increased reliance on automation.

Present continuous

Present continuous is used to:

- talk about events and situations which are taking place at the time of speaking
  She is studying for an MBA at the Harvard School of Business.
- talk about changes that are occurring
  ArkoPax has announced that it is restructuring its business.
- talk about planned future events
  We are meeting our lawyers this afternoon.

Past continuous

Past continuous is used to talk about events that were happening at a specific time in the past.

At that time our sales were decreasing and we didn't understand why that was happening.

Present perfect continuous

This form is mainly used to talk about events which began in the past and which are either continuing at the time of speaking or which are still incomplete.

Their new business has been experiencing rapid growth.

The modals *can*, *could*, *may*, *might* and *must* are also used with this form but convey the speaker's attitude.

We'll need to check the figures they gave us. They may have been hiding something.

Past perfect continuous

We use this form to refer to temporary events that were taking place before a time in the past.

Our overseas division was closed after we discovered that it had been operating at a loss.

Future continuous

This form is used when we are referring to a future event which has been planned.

This year we will be changing to a new operating system.

The modal verbs *could*, *may*, *might* and *must* can also be used with be + -ing but with a speculative meaning.

A university researcher says that computer culture may be changing the way the human brain works.

Future perfect continuous

We use this form to talk about anticipated events that will be happening at a given point in the future.

By our next meeting the new equipment will have been running for several days, so we'll know how successful it's going to be.

See also page 158.

Continuous infinitive forms

The continuous infinitive is used in the present or perfect after certain verbs such as *appear*, *hope*, *seem*, *want*.

Companies appear to be reducing their investments in new hardware.

Paired structures
Correlative conunctions

Correlative conjunctions are used to indicate different types of links between clauses, phrases or individual words. They are used in the following ways.

- to refer to two different options, interpretations or situations

  Either the project managers are incompetent *or* the people they are managing are.

  Whether they succeed *or* not will depend on a number of factors.

Note that *on the one hand ... on the other hand* can be used either within the same sentence or in consecutive sentences.

Change processes involve new thinking on the one hand and resistance on the other.

On the one hand reducing headcount does save money. But on the other hand it also results in a net loss of talent.

- to refer to two people or things in the negative
  Neither the head office *nor* the regional distributors were aware of the new law.

Note that *neither ... nor* cannot be used with a verb clause or as the negative equivalent of *either ... or*. Instead we would use *either*, or invert the subject and verb.

Either they haven't invested enough money, *or* they haven't evaluated the risks that they are facing.

*They haven't invested enough money, **nor** have they evaluated the risks that they are facing.*

NOT

> ~~Neither they have~~ invested enough money ~~nor they have~~ evaluated the risks that they are facing.

- to refer to two things that share a common feature
  One solution would to be to merge both operations and *another* would be to sell one of the units.

  *Introducing new workflow procedures will **both/not only** improve efficiency **and/but also** lower costs.*

Note that with *as well as/also* the first of the correlatives always occurs in initial position.

As well as being a source of misunderstanding, the new regulations are *also* a major hindrance.

- to indicate contrast
  Some employees have been transferred and *others* have been given notice.

- to show a chronological link between two things
  Once we'd understood the problem *then* we were able to look for the right solution.

- to indicate a relationship of cause and effect
  As demand shrinks *so* does profit.

Paired comparatives

Pairs of comparatives are used in clauses or adjective phrases to express result. Constructions of this type are not normally used in the past. The first clause or phrase introduces a situation and the second clause expresses the consequence.

The more we advertise, *the more* orders we get.

The longer we wait, *the more* business we will lose.

It is possible to use paired comparatives without a verb when referring to something that has already been mentioned.

The sooner the better.

There are also other ways of combining comparatives structures of this type.

The more energy we devote to expanding our business, *the greater* the return on our investment.

The more we invest, *the better* our chances of long term survival.

Discourse markers

Discourse markers are words that are used in spoken or written 'discourse' (language) to give certain signals to help the reader or listener understand the structure of a discourse and the attitudes of the writer or speaker.

Some discourse markers are mainly used in speech or informal language but not in writing or formal language, and vice versa.
Discourse markers are used to do the following.

- to enumerate and order information
  Finally, I'd just like to say how impressed I am with the quality of your work.

- to add additional information and give examples
  Some companies, **such as** Hitachi, have invested heavily in state-of-the-art factories.

Written/formal language
for example, such as, i.e., moreover, furthermore, in addition

Spoken/informal language:
for instance, like, on top of this, besides, too, say

- to signal contrasts and similarities
  The Japanese corporate mentality has, **in fact**, changed significantly.

Written/formal language
however, nonetheless, on the other hand, although, whereas, despite, in fact, in contrast, rather, similarly, yet

Spoken/informal language:
as a matter of fact, actually, anyway, though

- to indicate cause and result
  That's why we have decided to ask our partners to reconsider their decision

Written/formal language
as a result, therefore, consequently, hence, thus

Spoken/informal language:
so, that's why

- to generalise and summarise
  It is true that, **generally speaking**, investors prefer to have as much visibility as possible.

Written/formal language
on the whole, in general, generally speaking, to conclude, in conclusion, to sum up

Spoken/informal language:
by and large, mostly, mainly

- frequently used in conversation to indicate the speaker's attitude
  So, let's move on to the next point, shall we?

OK, right, actually, well, by the way, so

Third conditional

Conditional structures are used to indicate that if a certain condition is met (conditional clause), the event described (main clause) will occur. The so-called 'third' conditional is used when we are talking about past situations or events and speculating about the outcomes that resulted or could have resulted from them or from an alternative course of action.

The clauses in conditional sentences of this type can take the following forms.
- affirmative + affirmative
  If the firm **had had** more support from the banks, it **would have been able** to survive the downturn.
- negative + negative
  If we **hadn't received** the grant, we **wouldn't have been able** to raise enough capital.
- negative + affirmative/affirmative + negative
  If we **hadn't chosen** cheaper premises, we **would have had** more cash available to spend on other things.
  If the quality of our product **had been better**, our customers **wouldn't have returned** so many items.
- other third conditional forms
  The third conditional is also used in association with the past modals *should have, could have, might have*.
  If the company **had been better managed**, it **might not have gone out** of business.

Like and *as*

Like and as are similar in meaning but are used in different contexts. They are only interchangeable:
- when they refer to how someone or something is treated
  The part-time staff felt that they were being treated **as/like** second class citizens. (here, like means 'as if they were')
- in colloquial usage:
  Like/As I said, it's no big deal.

In some cases both **as** and **like** can be used but with different meanings.

She worked **as** a consultant. (she was a consultant)

She worked **like** a consultant. (she worked in the same way as a consultant)

Like is used in the following ways.

- to express similarity
  *The position I'm applying for is exactly **like** the one I had before.*

  *A day without my boss is **like** a day without thunderstorms.*

- to give examples
  *The influence of academics **like** Peter Drucker and Michael Porter has been considerable.*

- after linking verbs, which are followed by a complement that tells use more about the subject
  to be, to feel, to look, to seem, to sound, to taste

  *It looks **like** the beginning of another recession.*

As can be used:

- to introduce a clause of time, cause or manner
  ***As** the markets closed, the S&P index stood at 1255.*

  *We missed our first appointment **as** our plane was delayed.*

  *I don't understand why she acts **as** she does.*

- to express similarity
  *We processed the order **as** quickly **as** we could.*

- to refer to the role of someone or something
  *Mr Donahue was mistakenly introduced **as** the CEO when in fact he is the president.*

  ***As** a leading expert in his field, Dr Vickers will be a valuable addition to our research department.*

As is also used in the following expressions.

*It looks **as if** Jeff will become the next division leader.*

*We haven't made a decision whether to go ahead with the merger plans **as yet**.*

> **Key words**
>
> *as if, as for, as in, as though
> as to, as with, as yet, such as
> just as, much as*

As is also used after certain verbs.

*The resignation of the CEO was described by analysts **as** 'a step in the right direction'.*

> **Key words**
>
> *act, consider, describe, see, use*

Future perfect

The future perfect is used to make statements and projections about events and situations in relation to a time in the future. The future perfect is usually associated with a clause or phrase with *by*, *when* or *if* which situates the future time or moment in relation to which the statement or projection is being made.

***By** the time the gas starts to flow, this new field **will have been** under development for more than three years.*

***If** the government changes the regulations again, then all the money that we have invested in clean technology **will just have been wasted**.*

***When** we finally get to the end of this project, we'll **have been working** on it for much longer than was originally planned.*

The future perfect can be used in the continuous form.

See *Continuous forms* on page 155.

Active and passive

Most verbs have both active and passive forms. Which form we use depends on whether we want to focus on the 'agent' responsible for the action (active: who/what carried out the action) or on the result or outcome of the action (passive: what was done). The passive may be used with *by* to indicate who performed the action, if we wish to focus on the action while still giving this information.

The following active sentence structures may have a passive form.

- subject + verb + object

  *The union **suspended** negotiations.* (active)
  *The negotiations **were suspended** (by the union).* (passive)

- subject + verb + object + object
  *The board **awarded** the CEO a special bonus.* (active)
  *The CEO **was awarded** a special bonus.* (passive)

- subject + verb + object + complement

  *The financial director **asked** the consultants to conduct a full review.* (active)
  *The consultants **were asked** to conduct a full review.* (passive)

- verbs not used in the passive
  Some types of verbs such as intransitive verbs, which do not take an object, do not have passive forms.
  We have been working on a new prototype.
  NOT
  A new prototype ~~has been being~~ worked on.

The causative passive

The verbs *have* and *get* are used in this form of the passive. Causative passives indicate that the subject is responsible for an action but is not the person who performs it.

*We should manage **to get** the design work **done** by the end of the month.*

*We **had** a simulation of a system **run** (by our engineers).*

Word order: adverbs

Adverbs fulfill various different functions in written and spoken discourse and may appear in different positions within a sentence or utterance.

The main categories of adverbs are the following.

- adverbs of frequency.
  These adverbs normally appear between the subject and the verb, between the auxiliary and main verb, or at the beginning of a sentence when extra emphasis is given.

  *The law on copyright infringement has **seldom** been enforced.*

  ***Never** before has a computer company paid so much attention to style and design.*

- adverbs of time
  These adverbs can appear in different positions.

  *Many small businesses are not **yet** convinced of the potential benefits of Internet advertising.*

  *Many businesses have **yet** to understand how they can benefit from Internet advertising.*

- adverbs of manner/condition/attitude
  These adverbs are used to give information about how an event or situation happens. They are normally positioned before or after the verbs they qualify. Most adverbs of this type are formed by adding the suffix –*ly* to adjectives. However, some words can be both adjectives and adverbs.

  *Installing the new network **hardly** took any time at all.*

  *We've already had to shut down two plants and nobody knows what will happen **next**.*

- adverbs of degree, that modify adjectives
  Certain adverbs can be used to modify adjectives or other adverbs by intensifying or toning down their meanings. They are not interchangeable with all adjectives and very often form commonly used pairs of words.

  *Despite being **hugely popular**, some social networking sites have not been able to turn a profit.*

  *The transition to a digital economy has happened **very quickly** indeed.*

- other types of adverb
  Adverbs are not always easy to classify into categories and grammar books sometimes use quite different headings. The following adverbs are sometimes referred to as 'focusing adverbs' and are closely related to discourse markers.

  *Some analysts are **even** saying that the shares could fall further.*

  *We can **only** hope that our margins will improve as we streamline our operations.*

Probability and possibility

There are various ways to refer to probability and possibility.

Modal verbs

The modal verbs can, *could*, *may*, *might*, *must*, *should* and will are used to refer to possibility and to the likelihood of events and situations occurring. Modals are sometimes divided into two categories depending on the meaning that they convey: 'intrinsic' modals are used when we are referring to situations which may be influenced by human factors such as volition or will and 'extrinsic' modals when we are referring to judgements about the probability of something taking place.

- can and *could*
  Can refers to possibility (and impossibility) in the present and *could* to possibility (and impossibility) in the past and the future.

  Merging with a foreign company **can** *give you direct access to a new market.*

  The new contract **could** *prove even more lucrative than the previous one.*

  They had to close the business because they **couldn't** *pay off the bank loan.*

Both *can* and *could* can be used to express the past. *Can't have* (+ past participle) expresses disbelief in relation to an event or situation that may have occurred.

The data **can't have** *gone missing! It must be in the system somewhere.*

Could have is used to talk about possibilities that existed in the past but which were not followed or did not occur.

Our products **could have** *been distributed more effectively.*

When used in the negative **couldn't have** can express either disbelief or impossibility.

You **couldn't have** *admitted that it was your fault!*

We **couldn't have** *prevented the accident.*

- *may* and *might*
  The main difference between these two modals when they refer to possibility or probability is that *may* is used when we are talking about an event or situation that is quite likely whereas *might* is used to talk about an event or situation that is comparatively less likely.

  Regulators **may** *propose a series of new measures later this week.*

Insurance coverage is something that cash-strapped businesses **might** *be tempted to cut back on.*

Both *may* and *might* can be used to express the past. *May have* (+ past participle) and *might have* (+ past participle) are used to refer to past situations or events that are considered likely to have occurred.

The company **may have/might have** *misrepresented its earnings.*

However, only *might have* (+ past participle) can be used to refer to an event or situation that did not occur.

All entrepreneurs know what they **might have** *done differently.*

- *must*
  Must can be used to make deductions about something based on present evidence, which may or may not be stated.
  She's got a new job – she **must** *be delighted! It* **must** *be something important if all the staff are being called to a meeting.*

must have (+ past participle) refers to past situations which we are certain have occurred.

The engineers **must have known** *that the new models weren't as reliable as the original ones.*

- *should* and will
  Will is used to express certainty about a future outcome while *should* is used to express likelihood.

  The results for the last quarter **will** *be closely examined by analysts.*

  According to analysts the company **should** *meet Wall Street's expectations.*

Both *should* and will can be used to express the past. *Should have* (+ past participle) is used to describe alternative actions that the speaker considers preferable to the ones that were taken.

Other ways of talking about possibility and probability

We can use the adjectives *bound* and *likely/ unlikely* to talk about the probability of an event or situation taking place.

The business world is inherently unpredictable and failures and mistakes are **bound** *to happen.*

Some scientists argue that extreme weather events are **likely** *to become more frequent in the future.*

The nouns *chance*, *likelihood* and *the odds* are also used to talk about probability.

Investors in the failed venture have no **chance** *of recovering the money they are owed.*

*There is little **likelihood** that the company will return to profit this year.*

***The odds** are that they will ask to renegotiate the deal.*

Reporting

When we report what other people have said we can either use indirect (reported) speech to duplicate the words that they used or we can summarise the main message by using reporting verbs.

Reported speech

We use the verbs *ask*, *say* and tell to report what a person has said. *Ask* and *tell* are always used with a direct object. *Say* is used without a direct object and is often followed by a clause with that.

*The judge **asked** the accused if he had authorised the payments himself.*

*A company spokesman **told** the press that they would be conducting an internal investigation.*

*The speaker **said** that most businesses do not include ethical behaviour as a criterion in their appraisal processes.*

When we transform what has been said in direct speech into indirect speech we sometimes need to make changes to the original words.

- Tenses are sometimes changed from present to past, from future to conditional and from past to past perfect. Modal verbs may also change from direct to indirect speech.

  *We **have agreed** to pay compensation to our partners for the damage to their reputation.*

  *He said that they **had agreed** to pay compensation to their partners.*

- Personal pronouns and adjectives are modified.

  *Can **you** explain why the funds were transferred to **your** account?*

  *He asked **them** to explain why the funds were transferred to **their** account.*

- Words such as *here, now, this*, etc. may need to be changed to *there, then, that*, etc.

  *I want the information to be made available **here** and **now**.*

  *She asked for the information to be made abailable **there** and **then**.*

Reporting verbs

Reporting verbs are used to summarise the content or context of something that was said in direct speech. This makes it possible to focus on the most important aspects of the message rather than on the exact words that were used.

There are several different types of reporting verbs.

- verbs followed by a 'that' clause
  *The lawyer for the prosecution **claimed that the company director had deliberately destroyed key evidence.***

  *Geoff Simmons **has predicted that Internet crime will rise significantly in the coming years.***

Key words

acknowledge, add, admit, agree, announce, answer, argue, assume, believe, claim, comment, complain, confirm, consider, decide, deny, expect, explain, feel, forget, imply, inform, maintain, mean, mention, observe, persuade, predict, promise, realise, repeat, reply, report, reveal, state, suggest, think, threaten, warn

- verbs followed by an object and an infinitive
  *The communications director **has forbidden staff to make public declarations about the affair.***

  *Our consultants **advised us not to sign the contract.***

Key words

advise, ask, forbid, instruct, invite, order, persuade, remind, tell, warn

- verbs followed by a wh- clause
  *The journalist couldn't remember **who had given her the information.***

  *The commissioner explained **why the information had not been disclosed to the authorities.***

Key words

decide, discover, discuss, explain, forget, guess, imagine, know, realise, remember, tell, think, understand, wonder

- verbs followed by a direct object and a preposition
  *The plant manager **has threatened some employees with** immediate dismissal.*

Verb patterns

How verbs are used within a clause or sentence
depends on their type and their function. Verbs
can be categorised in different ways depending
on the clause and phrase constructions that
they are used with. However, all verbs are
either transitive or intransitive or both.

Intransitive verbs (subject + verb)

Verbs of this type have a subject but do not
require an object. They may be accompanied by a
prepositional phrase but cannot be transformed
into the passive.

*The quality of our after sales service **has
deteriorated**.*

*The product recall happened **following
complaints from a consumer association**.*

*The problem arose **during the final phase of the
negotiations**.*

Transitive verbs (subject + verb + object)

Verbs of this type involve not only a subject but
also an object that is affected in some way. They
can be transformed into the passive.

*Candidates will **receive** an application form
which should be **completed** and **returned** to us
before June 1st.*

Verbs with transitive and intransitive forms

Some verbs can be used both as transitive and
intransitive. This is the case with verbs that have
two distinct meanings.

*Martha **has managed** to find someone to replace
her. (intransitive)*

*The last CEO **managed** the company for four
years. (transitive)*

Another reason for verbs having both forms is
that it is not always necessary to include an
object especially when this is either implied or
has been referred to earlier.

*We had originally arranged **to meet** the
delegation at their hotel but in the end we **met**
directly at the conference.*

Audioscripts

Brad Johnson
I was looking for a company that had potential for growth, you know. I mean, with a company like that you get a sense that you can grow too! At Finance Solutions they have a culture that wants you to expand your potential and all the incentives are in place to help you achieve, you know. I'm not that kind of person who can be satisfied with staying where I'm at professionally for too long. I need to know that this time next year I'll be in a higher position. I'm a high achiever, always have been, and that's just what this company needs. So I fit right in! My manager sets the objectives with a nice little bonus incentive there, you know what I mean, and I go for it!

Jane Ford Haddens
When I finished my MBA there were two other companies interested in my profile and I opted for this one because the salary was very attractive and there were performance-related bonuses as well. But to be honest I'm thinking of looking around for another job now. It's been one year and frankly the workload here is crazy and the pressure is really intense. I have no social life at all! I'm too exhausted to do anything at the weekend and anyway I take work home with me at least every second weekend! If I didn't take work home in the evening I'd still be in that office at ten every night! I need to get another job before I get completely burnt out.

Klaus Beckhaus
What do I like about working here? Well, I love the fact that we operate in over a hundred different markets worldwide. I feel there's so much scope, so many opportunities to see how different cultures work. I've already applied for a position in one of the overseas offices and I think I'm in with a fairly good chance of being accepted. I took French and Italian at school and I speak German, naturally, (that's my native language) as well as English, so I would be an obvious choice and I wouldn't even need to go to the language training programmes they provide here. But I was very impressed, or seduced, by the fact that we are not only present in the markets of the countries we operate in – we are also active in local community projects in many of them, particularly in developing countries. Here at FGBS we care about global environmental issues and I wouldn't feel comfortable working for a company who didn't have projects.

I'm the Managing Partner for Talent, er, which means I sit on our UK executive, and I'm responsible for looking after all of our talent strategies for our people in the UK, which involves recruitment and resourcing, people development, retention, er, looking after all the sort of the appraisals, promotion processes, reward and benefits. Anything, I guess to do with our people ... it sort of comes under my remit although I have a very large team working under me to, sort of, to, to do the day-to-day operational things.

Deloitte, I guess, has chosen to have the Managing Partner for Talent on its UK executive because we, I guess, realise how important people are to achieving our strategy. We want to be the pre-eminent professional services firm and to do that we have to have the best people working for us and to have them engaged, er, and to retain them and to make them even better at doing what they're doing. So it's really critical to our strategy and our agenda, and by having someone on our executive who's responsible for it, I think it underlines that.

The ... the key themes of our talent agenda I guess are building on what we've been doing over the last few years. We've ... and getting the best people into the firm is very, very important to us. But I think we've been very successful. We've won a number of awards over the last couple of years. We're, er, number two in the Times Top 100 Graduate Employers we ... we got an award from *Personnel Today* for excellence in graduate recruitment so we've been doing really well on that. We bring in significant number of experienced hires and I think we've been successful in getting really great people, attracting them to Deloitte. So that's sort of one aspect but the other is ... I guess when we've got people working for us we want to give them really, really good development. So we want people to come to us and to be more marketable, you know, after each year, that you continue to get development and challenge in the work you do. So that's very, very important and one of the things that I've been working on with our partners is all about coaching and inspiring our people.

So I talked about how, you know, important the people were to me and how, you know working with really, really good quality people enables you to learn more because you get so much on-the-job training and that's we know that's the way people learn the most from, from their, sort of, day-to-day on-the-job training. So development is critical in getting the people around you to give you that development. But we're also ... we've been looking at, sort of, flexibility and choice and giving people more opportunities within their careers but ensuring that, you know, there is a good work–life balance for people. And we're focusing on diversity and inclusion.

OK, I think the way Deloitte differs in the ... in our approach to talent is that we are, we have a high-performance culture, we're looking to recruit people, er, who are looking for challenging work. You know, we serve clients who are involved in complex transactions. The whole business environment has become much more complicated over the last few years and the regulatory environment. That means we have to have really good people who are able to work on these difficult transactions for our clients. We want people who are, erm, I guess, highly motivated and bringing those people into our business and giving them that sort of work, I think, does differentiate us because we have a broader span of services that we offer to clients, so we are able to engage in more complex transactions. But as well as it being a high-performance culture it is a very, you know ... we have a very supportive environment and we want people to feel that they are individuals, that they have something that, you know, different to give us. We want to have their input, everybody is unique and we want them to feel that they can, I guess, blossom and develop in that sort of environment. And our key ... the key thing that we do want to get across to people is that, you know, come and join Deloitte because you will grow faster than you thought you were capable of growing.

1

Appraiser: Right. Well I'll be very interested to hear your explanation of your results for the last quarter. They're way below what we agreed. In fact they're much worse than those of your colleagues. You are aware of that, aren't you?

Appraisee: I'm sorry but I'm not going to answer that question because I don't have access to that information. And anyway it's none of my business what the other people in my department have been doing. I do my job, I do it well and that's the most important thing.

Appraiser: But you don't do it quite as well as you think you do, apparently. And that's exactly the point. So what I'm asking you is this: what are you going to do to improve?

Appraisee: Now wait a minute. When we met six months ago, we agreed that I would take on the job of looking after a whole new group of clients. But I never expected that it would be as difficult as it's been. It's only recently that I realised that you'd actually given me the most difficult job in the whole department. So I don't see how you can sit there and ...

2

Appraiser: Jason. I'm afraid that your results during the last quarter really weren't as good as we'd hoped. Is there anything you'd like to say about that?

Appraisee: Er, well, it is true that I didn't make the target that we'd set but I don't think that was entirely my fault. Things just didn't turn out the way that we'd expected them to, that's all.

Appraiser: Mm hmm. Can you expand on that and maybe explain exactly what went wrong?

Appraisee: Yes. Well ... I think there are a number of things to say about that. The first of those concerns the assignment that you gave me, you know, taking responsibility for developing our professional accounts. Now, at the time I didn't understand the problems involved in that. And it just wasn't that simple to increase business in a market where we're dealing with customers who aren't easy. I'm sure that you understand that.

Appraiser: Mm. OK, well ... I agree with you, but only up to a certain point. I know those clients aren't the easiest ones to deal with but remember that we've given you some pretty sophisticated software tools to help you to do that. So it should have been possible to increase our sales in line with what we said. Now, are you sure that you really used the system to its maximum potential?

Appraisee: Er, actually I must admit that I did have some problems accessing and processing the information. In fact I think I would have done better if I'd had some assistance and maybe even some more training – one day wasn't enough to get the hang of it.

Appraiser: Mm. Well, let's put that down as one of your objectives for the next period, shall we? Now, what about your relationships with your colleagues? How has that been going?

Appraisee: Actually, there has been some friction in the team, I think that one of ...

Unit 1   Decision page 16

Let me just start by saying that by the time I was called in the company was in an absolute crisis. All their best people were abandoning ship! It was really important to get something in place and quick before everybody left! We also needed to recruit bright new talent and make sure they stayed. Word was out in the industry that Curry was gone and that the new CEO was making changes. We just needed to formalise that, you know, set the right goals then get quality feedback sessions going and get a good appraisal system in place. I felt that the 'top-down' model wouldn't appeal to the software engineers. The relationship between them and their managers was just too strained. Even if we'd done a mix of self-appraisal, you know, where employees use the same form as the manager to assess themselves before the actual appraisal meeting, this does help make them feel an active part of the process. Even so, we were looking for a more egalitarian system where people would be more comfortable about saying what they needed. The peer-to-peer would have suited if we hadn't been integrating so many new recruits – it's inclined to work better when teams are well established. We finally opted for the 360-degree system and I must say I feel it was the best option. OK, it takes time and OK, it isn't perfect, but it does try to get people talking to each other on a level where important things get said. If the company had had a culture of talking about problems and the needs of the all-important software designers before ... well, what can I say – a whole lot of trouble could've been avoided.

Unit 2   Listening 1 page 18

Part 1

I'm Jonathan Schwarz. I keep a pen and a Blackberry and my assumption is paper has become ubiquitous across the world and I can find it wherever I need it. You know, I find, frankly phone calls to be a little bit invasive and I'm always a little reluctant to just reach out and get in somebody's face and say 'you have to talk to me'. One of the wonderful things about SMS is it's a store-and-forward mechanism, it's a very quick despatch of a note and the response can be as timely as the recipient wants to make it.

Part 2

That ID card at Sun is the intersection of all of the different means that we use of authenticating oneself at Sun. So I walk into a building I hold that up against the door and that's how I get onto our campus. Around the world if I insert one of those into one of these SunRay devices I can connect to my infrastructure and my home directory no matter where I am. You basically can leave everything else at home.

Part 3

Truth be told, the picture that you see there of me sitting at a desk ... I'm actually sitting at our Chief Financial Officer's desk and because mine is a little table, I think, I wasn't sure I really wanted to show you what my desk looks like but believe me it's a small fraction of that expansive, wasteful desk that our CFO is using. I was in a start-up before I came to Sun, I like to think Sun's, you know, very much a start-up now and if you've hung out at a start-up you can have an incredible, motivated, happy, excited group of employees in an empty airplane hangar.

We started giving people the option of working from home. And it turned out they viewed that as a huge asset but when they do come to work they've got a place where their stuff is. It doesn't have to be a dedicated office it can just be a simple locker and so that's what we ended up supplying folks with.

Part 4

I think the interactions between Sun employees, erm, first and foremost take place via the network but we also have cafés at work which are just environments where you can connect to the network and you can connect to people, and more often than not you're likely to be sitting next to someone who works in a different geography or in a different organisation or has a different set of priorities. And there's a lot of socialising that takes place in those cafés even though there's an appropriate amount of cultural appreciation for 'leave me alone – I just need to get my work done'.

Part 5

I took these pictures on just a low end digital camera I had actually in my car. He is the individual who is responsible for keeping me up to speed on our relationships with our Asian reporters and Asian media. So we tend to default to just using videoconferences where we know there's a videoconference facility on the other side and the cost of these videoconferencing facilities has come down so far that we're putting them everywhere around, er, the company. So we're putting them into our visit centres so I can connect with customers even without flying to Singapore to go make it happen. We can connect with our own employees as they are across the world. Um, you know, one of the jokes at Sun is we always ask people to, to hold up their watches so you can actually see what time it is where they are and you can actually see the second hand as it moves around, it's such high resolution!

Part 6

First and foremost my job as the CEO of Sun is to communicate our vision and it's to communicate to the marketplace, to our customers, to shareholders, to employees. And so the good news is the barriers to communication have ... have been all but obliterated by the ubiquity of the Internet and so I can reach a global audience very, very efficiently from inside of Sun, from my, from my living room, from my, you know, even from my Blackberry for that matter. All that said, I've also got a family and sometimes I just want to go the park with my kids. I am cognizant of the role that I play at Sun but I'm also more cognizant of the role I play at home. And I've got a private life, I think we all do.

Unit 2   Listening 2 page 22

Interviewer: How important are family businesses in the global economy?

Barry Cosgrave: It's an interesting fact, I think, that family businesses form the backbone of both the UK and world economies. Research has found that some 50% of the UK private sector workforce is employed by family businesses! 95% of businesses in Asia, the Middle East, Italy and Spain are family-controlled, as are over 80% of the companies in France and Germany, and between 60% and 70% of companies in the US.

Int: Mm. Could you give us some specific examples?

BC: Sure, Some of the world's most successful firms are family firms including, let's see ... Ikea, BMW, Sainsbury's, Fiat. And one of the world's oldest family businesses is a Japanese hotel called Hoshi Ryokan. It was founded in 718 and is now in its 46th generation of family ownership!

Int: That's old! Are there many other examples like that around?

BC: Um, no. The longevity of a family-run business is by no means guaranteed. It can be very tricky running a family firm because they combine all the tensions and strain of family life with those of business life. For example, they have to deal with marriages and divorces, which lead to complicated business relationships, as well as routine issues like shareholder control, compensation, processes for strategic decision making, etc, etc. They also face unique issues such as succession planning and only the best-organised family businesses successfully make the transition from each generation to the next. But the good news is that many of these problems can be predicted and overcome with appropriate planning.

Int: Mm. And how can you avoid the main pitfalls?

BC: Well, there are three key issues to success: documentation, communication and early succession planning. Regardless of its legal structure – it can be a corporation, or a limited liability company or a partnership – a family business can avoid problems by documenting the business relationships between owners right from the start. For family-owned businesses – especially those with multi-generational owners – the lack of a formal structure can cause, and has caused, legal battles which could ultimately lead to the failure of a business. You see, family businesses often don't put the business agreement in written, formal, legal documents because they're afraid it would be insulting or imply a lack of trust amongst the family members. Of course the reality is that you have less chance of running into family conflicts down the line if things have been clarified and documented from the start.

For example, getting waiver agreements from spouses who know nothing about the business but become owners through marriage, could solve some problems that may occur later on. Waiver agreements of this kind ensure that those concerned sign a contract which stipulates that as part-owners they have no say in how the business is run.

Int: What happens if you don't get a waiver agreement?

BC: Owners are sometimes forced to take on a new 'partner' who lacks skills and experience to make business decisions. That's why documents about what happens in the case of divorce should also be drawn up to avoid family rows which could affect the business later.

Communication is another very important factor in the success of a family business because the key differentiator for family businesses, and the glue that holds them together, is the values set by the family. They generally have their own loyalties and culture that non-family businesses can rarely create. The emotional glue that holds the family together can and should translate into an enduring sense of corporate identity. If the business manages to communicate those values clearly to the next generation, the long term prospects for continuity and success are significantly increased.

Int: But not guaranteed?

BC: No, there are no guarantees but you can increase your chance of survival greatly if you get your succession planning right. And the key to 'success in succession' is to start long before the boss means to retire. The issue of succession is a delicate one, as it reminds the older generation of their mortality and requires them to make some difficult decisions. Failing to plan for succession is one reason why only 13% of family businesses continue beyond the third generation. Succession planning should be separated into the succession of ownership and management. For example the best solution may be that the ownership of the business remains within the family but the management is left in the hands of outside professionals. This way business decisions are taken for business reasons, and not family or personal reasons.

Unit 2 Listening 3 page 25

Social events of all types can be a good way to develop a team culture but this requires careful consideration about what kind of culture you want to create. You need to take the background of all members into consideration otherwise you could create a division in the team – those who enjoy the social team-building activities provided and those who don't! For example, challenging sports such as rock climbing and racing cars are not everyone's cup of tea and may be perceived as macho or elitist by some of the team members. If you organise this type of activity, be careful to organise something that appeals to the other team members next time. Also, make sure you have good insurance cover!

Providing food and drinks at meetings is always a good idea, particularly to encourage people to attend inconvenient or unwelcome meetings! Evening meals and drinks are fine also, but it is important to remember, not everyone wants to drink alcohol or stay late. It is important to be sensitive to cultural differences here too. Similarly, clubs, dancing and theatre may appeal only to a minority of the members, so try to choose something that appeals to as many members as possible. Strange things that you never thought you would do as an adult like, say, murder mystery games, quiz competitions and karaoke can work well also, but usually only once. It's better to change the activity type each time.

Oh, one of the most effective team-building events are charity events which really pull people together to work towards a common and worthwhile goal. The thing is to choose a charity that the whole staff can relate to and feel strongly about. Also very effective are training courses or training days. The investment involved shows the members how much the company values its employees – this can be a great motivator. Often the most effective, for achieving a serious business goal, as well as being fun, is to take the team on an 'away day' at a pleasant location for an event such as a briefing, a conference or a think tank.

So, there are many social activities to choose from. The team leader just needs to take the time to think about his or her team and then select the most suitable ones. At our company we regularly organise these kinds of events ...

Unit 2 Decision page 26

The first thing that really has to be said is that the problem of bullying should be taken extremely seriously. Sometimes managers don't pay attention to bullying until it results in a real crisis. They somehow expect that it will just, er, blow over. Ideally, though, it's best to react quickly and nip this type of behaviour in the bud because it can have very real and negative impact on morale, sometimes even causing good staff to resign. It affects, er, motivation, productivity and ultimately your bottom line.

Transferring the bullies elsewhere only moves the problem to another department and unless the company is huge the victim will probably continue to suffer, though probably a little less. It also looks like an admission that the team leader has also been intimidated and, er, the problem remains.

Likewise, getting rid of a team member who has key knowledge about your business may put the team in jeopardy – so dismissing the instigator is not always a good first option. Best to try to solve it differently. In any case, there's no guarantee that the others won't continue to bully, though perhaps more discreetly and underhandedly, particularly as they may perceive the dismissal of their friend and colleague as the victim's fault. While getting help to the victim seems like a comforting gesture and a mark of support for her it also seems to put the onus for change on the bullied person as opposed to the bullies.

No, there's only one thing for it and that is to confront the bullies and insist on them changing their behaviour. It's a good idea to issue a written warning when there has been a pattern of bad behaviour, as in this situation, whereas, erm, a verbal warning is usually enough in isolated acts of rudeness or intimidation. Erm, it's also important to communicate with HR about the problem employees and perhaps include them in the meeting with the bullies. Before the meeting, do some planning to, to determine what outcomes you expect and what explicit behaviour you expect and decide how the bullies will be held accountable if things don't change.

While talking to them you must be direct but not emotional or confrontational. Be specific about behaviour – say things like 'you called so and so an idiot' you said 'so and so was incompetent'. Be clear that the behaviour must stop regardless of motive or reason. For, for key staff members like these it would be worth considering offering coaching, counselling or anger management but these only work if the people involved have the ability and desire to change. Before leaving this meeting, set a date for another one to, to discuss progress on behaviour. If nothing changes, follow through on accountability outcomes. These could include, er, redistribution of team roles and reduction or suppression of bonuses. To protect yourself legally, give a warning and systematically document the bullying behaviour. If the bullying continues in the long run you may need to consider finding a legal way of parting company with the bullies. Keeping them will cost you too much and, and in a business like Arcadia, where all work is done in close-knit teams, the whole staff will suffer from the present toxic atmosphere.

Erm, the, the best way to avoid bullying in the first place is to have a clear and written policy about, erm, acceptable behaviour in the company. Managers can lead by example in this respect. They can encourage open communication and show respect for their subordinates. If they see someone behaving inappropriately, say, like putting someone down at a meeting, the manager should pull the person aside privately after the meeting and tell them that this sort of intimidation just isn't tolerated in the company.

Getting teams together and asking all the members to come up with at least one expected behaviour from the other members is an excellent start. Then identify the most critical behaviours and make a list that all members must respect. From then on you can refer to this list as your 'policy on acceptable behaviour' and you can point out to potential trouble makers that certain behaviours are inconsistent with company culture.

Unit 3 Listening 1 page 28

Part 1

The way I see it, change is getting people to do what the manager wants. The only problem is that people usually think that the manager hasn't thought things through. They believe that managers don't understand fully what it is they do. They also think that upper-level managers don't know what the real world is like! So their natural reaction is to resist change. Good managers know that this is what to expect and they will organise the way they implement change accordingly. I always think of it like an architect who is designing a house. There is the initial thinking and brainstorming stage – looking at all the possibilities. It's important to think it through with the end in mind. This is followed by the planning stage and finally you start building or implementing the plans. If not, it's like building the house at the same time as you are doing the plans!

Part 2

If you want to avoid problems, the first thing you do when you get to the planning stage is to inform the people who will be affected by the change. Let them mourn the change before it happens. Ask them what they feel and then let them talk and talk and talk! Listen to their worries and try and address those issues. But timing is very important. I've seen some terrible mistakes – I've seen situations where managers announce changes too soon, for example. If you tell the entire staff that you're thinking about merging with another group three months before you actually do it, people will panic; they'll think they're going to lose their jobs and they don't do any work for three months! Or, for example, I've seen change situations where job cuts were necessary and the unions haven't been brought on board early enough in the planning stages. The key is to tell the right people about the changes at the right time!

Part 1

When a company, for whatever reason, finds itself in a time of perceived crisis it will need to introduce major changes in order to survive. In a situation like this the structural changes will be imposed from the top down, which may of course lead to resistance, particularly as this type of change almost invariably means job cuts and a shift in the balance of power. Overcoming the often strong resistance will require expertise, tact and diplomacy.

Part 2

You'll get less resistance to small technical changes which need to be introduced at the level of individual work or teamwork. I mean, it does depend on the corporate culture and whether people are used to changes or not, but in general changes like these should be pretty easy to implement and getting acceptance shouldn't be an issue.

Part 3

You'll really need to be careful when your goal is to bring about changes in attitude and behaviour no matter how small scale those changes are. If you believe that performance can be improved if staff change their vision of how things should be done, then you have to put emphasis on collaboration and participation. You can't just impose these changes by sending round a memo, for example! You need to accept that it may take time for people to take these changes on board. However, if you handle the situation properly you should be able to overcome resistance.

Part 4

The real problems appear when you focus on a broad cultural change. What managers need to understand is that no matter how urgently these changes are needed, any cultural change is bound to be a slow process. Senior managers can't just make policy for change and then impose it from the top down. Changes like these rely on the introduction of a host of initiatives at all levels of the hierarchy. You have to get everyone on board and that's a very, very difficult task. It can be so frustrating when you are convinced that these changes are absolutely necessary for survival in a difficult economic climate.

1

Speaker 1: Well, we certainly ran into problems here, didn't we?

Speaker 2: We sure did – basically, because we didn't get training to our salespeople early enough.

Speaker 1: The problem is we didn't realise how panicked they'd be.

Speaker 2: They needed to develop new interpersonal skills. They needed to familiarise themselves with the new products they were expected to sell.

Speaker 1: We knew this was probably going to be the case and we'd been planning on getting training to them but we set the changes in motion before doing that.

Speaker 2: The result was a disaster. It's all working out fine now but we lost a lot of our old sales force who just couldn't adapt. And sales really collapsed before the training sessions were put in place. Morale was so low, and the fear of breaking from the routine was so bad, that even sales of photocopiers dropped.

Speaker 1: We should have announced and run the training courses well before announcing the changes! We made a classic mistake!

2

You are talking total disaster here! I mean I just wasn't expecting any resistance to these changes. There I was, convinced that the staff would be more than happy to adapt to my way of working which would, as I thought, improve working conditions all round! I expected my top-down command – 'OK from now on we are going to do this my way' – would be welcomed with open arms! I forgot the basic rule of change management – always expect resistance even if the changes are going to make life better and easier for the staff!

I now know that I should have organised brainstorming sessions with different groups, asking them what, if any, changes they would make if given the opportunity. I'm slowly building up their confidence again, and I do still intend to change the office culture, but I'm going about that very differently now.

Ah yes, what an interesting case! Most people, including myself, to be honest, thought that Lars Kolind was mad! But he had a vision, you see. He said 'Maybe we could design a new way of running a business that could be significantly more creative, faster, and more cost-effective than the big players, and maybe that could compensate for our lack of technological excellence, our lack of capital, and our general lack of resources! I mean, a less inspired leader would have just closed the whole operation down. But despite resistance – and believe me there was a lot of resistance – he went ahead. It has to be said that after the initial negotiations where he offered training and coaching to all the staff and he did involve them in the planning of the implementation of changes, in the end he had to give an ultimatum – accept the new arrangements or leave!

The rest is history! Regardless of the carrot-and-stick approach, the biggest boost to the new arrangements was when staff realised that they really worked better than the old ones. You see, they discovered that they had actually developed the first automatic, self-adjusting hearing aid in the 80s but due to lack of communication between R & D and sales staff, as well as a few technical problems, the product had been forgotten about. Thanks to the brand new way of working, they launched the 'Multifocus' hearing aid in 1991 and in 1995 they launched the world's first digital hearing aid. Oticon believes that its approach can be replicated in other countries but they're not blind to cultural differences. They do realise that Denmark is fertile ground for its approach to work and that in other cultures people may not be able to adapt so well. They succeeded in creating a learning organisation and they managed to change all the rules of a typical working environment! No mean feat even if Denmark was ready for it!

I suppose you can really trace the beginnings of the CSR story back to some quite specific events which sort of lifted the curtain on businesses, if you like, and showed the darker side of some business operations rather than just the silver lining. Of course, I'm not suggesting that companies were better in the past – clearly that wasn't the case. Just think of what was going on during the Industrial Revolution in Europe.

Anyway, the first really big shock was without doubt the gas leak in 1984 at the Union Carbide pesticide factory in Bhopal in India. That resulted in what some people have called the worst industrial accident ever and it's easy to understand why because a lot of people either lost their lives or were seriously injured as a result of inhaling toxic gases. That was a really horrific example of how a business can put an entire local community at risk and I think it really changed people's perceptions forever. And, of course, it's ironic that it took place in a factory that was actually no longer even operational at the time. And if it wasn't operational that was because it wasn't profitable. And if it wasn't profitable I suppose that could also mean that it wasn't being looked after quite as well as it should have been. One of the results of that disaster was a settlement between Union Carbide and the Indian government with a compensation payment of 470 million dollars to the victims. That works out at approximately 400 dollars per person which is not that much when you consider just how much damage was done and even today the population of Bhopal is still suffering from the aftermath of that disaster.

The next big one was Exxon Valdez in Alaska just five years later. Now in this case the situation was very different because the oil tanker went aground in a remote territory where there aren't a lot of people. But that doesn't mean that it wasn't a major disaster for the environment. In fact it's estimated that about 10 million gallons of petroleum were released into the sea and the effects of that were catastrophic for the marine environment in that part of the world and also for the people who made their living from the sea. It's true that damages were awarded but in 2008, in other words 20 years after the events, the Supreme Court of the United States had the final word and reduced the settlement to 500 million dollars which is not a lot compared to the 5 billion that was awarded after the first court hearing.

Well, the lessons from these two events haven't been lost on corporations and that is the positive side of this and indeed of CSR in general. Companies have to look very carefully at what they do in different parts of their business operations and they have to put strategies in place which will minimise the risks that they are running. Does that mean that similar tragedies couldn't happen again today? Well, I don't think you can say that but certainly companies today are more aware of what could go wrong and that is one step towards making sure that the worst doesn't actually ever happen.

Part 1

Interviewer: Why has CSR become so important?

Daniel Franklin: The expectations on companies have risen for a number of reasons. The spread of the Internet, for example, the amount of scrutiny that goes on through Non-Governmental Organisations, erm, activist groups – all that has risen dramatically and that means that companies have to be on their guard for a number of reasons because their reputation can be at risk if they do something that people find out about that is perceived to be untoward. So that's one set of issues that has raised this, erm, right up the priority list for companies. Another is the whole rise of environmentalism, climate change, concerns about, erm, the state of the planet, and that's been an area that companies have taken up with some alacrity and is perhaps the most dynamic area of corporate social responsibility.

Part 2

Int: How are companies getting CSR wrong and in fact what is the right approach? Is there a right approach?

DF: Well, for many companies CSR is something that, although they make a lot of noise about it they don't necessarily think very deeply about it. So for one thing it may well be, er, located in the corporate communications area so it's perceived as a part of the PR efforts rather than something more strategic so that's one sign that a company may not be giving it the greatest real priority although it may be making rather large claims about its activities. Secondly, the phrase 'corporate social responsibilty' can cover so many different types of activities – anything from the company's charitable works to volunteering by employees to environmental activities – that often companies are having a sort of scatter-gun approach to it without a real focus on what might be truly relevant to their business and truly in the interests of their shareholders.

Part 3

Int: One description of CSR I've heard is, er, 'doing well by doing good'. But, conversely, can CSR also be a bad thing?

DF: Well it can, of course, if you just take a couple of examples – if it isn't good for the business, if it actually involves the business concentrating on activities that aren't profitable or damage the business in some way. Take that to the extreme, the business actually goes under – that's no good for anybody at all to have a supremely ethical business that actually goes out of business. But I think also even well-intentioned activities of businesses, er, can end up not doing any good at all in ways that might surprise people so if you impose very demanding, let's say, conditions for working practices or wages that mean that some factories go out of business because they can't compete with those higher standards, that may be, in the end, very damaging. So you may be trying to protect the interests of workers in a poor part of the world – let's say Bangladeshi textile workers – but if you don't manage to improve productivity at the same time in order to keep those factories in business, you may be doing more harm than good.

Part 4

Int: There are companies out there that of course would be quite happy to ignore CSR. What about these companies?

DF: I think it depends very much on the reasons why they're ignoring it, if ... in some cases, they may be ignoring it just because they're not particularly aware of what the pressures that they are liable to face are, and in that, in those cases they may, one day, be surprised to find themselves hit by difficulties that they don't see coming so there are many, many examples of industries that have suddenly faced trouble because they haven't anticipated the sorts of expectations of them, that have been evolving in the world around them. There's perhaps another type of company that is deliberately ignoring CSR pressures, perhaps for very logical reasons. They think that they have nothing much to gain, even if they are affected or they may be in a sector which is not likely to be coming under a lot of pressure and this is all from the point of view of managing the risks that a business might face for its reputation and in those cases maybe it's a perfectly rational thing for a business to be doing.

Journalist: Your new, so-called 'wonder drug' is wreaking havoc with the lives of people taking it. What are you proposing to do about this situation?

Spokesman: Well, firstly, I'd just like to say how very sorry we are about this. We became aware of a potential difficulty when we were alerted by recent feedback from the market. We were devastated, obviously, to discover the drug had side effects which hadn't been identified in the clinical trials. We immediately set up a full enquiry and have recalled the brand, as well as organising an extensive awareness campaign to warn people of the possible harm.

J: The word on the street is that you were fully aware of the risks but decided to launch the drug in spite of them.

S: That's absolute nonsense. Our company has always been dedicated to improving quality of life, indeed, saving lives. We acted responsibly based on serious medical research. The recent findings were unforeseeable at the time of the launch.

J: Can you explain how this happened?

S: It has never happened before and we are taking steps to make sure it never happens again. All our products go through the same rigorous testing process. We're introducing even more stringent tests to meet with and indeed go beyond all legal requirements.

J: Can the company's reputation survive this scandal?

S: Our global reputation for safe and effective products is intact. We intend to go on making drugs that fight death and disease for many years to come.

The situation at Marsdale is very similar to another incident that took place quite recently in the UK, where a group of protesters tried to force Eon, a major energy supplier, to close one of its plants and to abandon plans to build a completely new power station which would continue to burn coal as its predecessor had. In this case the company's communications department was fully prepared and they already had a contingency plan to deal with exactly this type of protest. The first decision that they made was to defend publicly their plan to build the new station. They were able to make a convincing case by focusing on the general energy situation in the United Kingdom and by pointing to the country's future energy needs. They also drew attention to a number of new features that would be incorporated into the new plant and which they claimed would make it at least 20% more efficient. In addition to this, the communications department of the company made a number of declarations throughout the protest in order to confirm their legitimate right to operate the Marsdale plant. They also decided to take a very strong line with the protesters, who were warned that any attempt to enter the company's premises illegally could endanger both the company's employees and possibly the protesters as well. This firm, uncompromising approach definitely paid off and in the end the protesters left after one week without having interrupted the company's activities and without having gained the type of widespread popular support that they'd initially sought. So, yes, I think this just goes to show that a common sense, cool-headed approach combined with good forward planning and solid risk management can really pay off.

Interviewer: There seems to be a scare about the word 'American', that they're willing to adopt American style reforms as long as they don't call them American. What culturally is the significance of the word 'America' when applied to corporate reform? Why is it such a scary one?

Tom Standage: Yeah, it is scary. One of the analysts I spoke to said that, the ideal model for Japan was called 'secret America' which is where you adopt from the American model 'secretly' and you don't let on to anybody that this is, this is what you are doing. And I spoke to, somebody at Nippon Keideanren which is the big business sort of conservative lobbying association and, and, you know, generally they say they are in, in favour of reform, erm, but just, you know, they don't want it to come very quickly and they don't want there to be that much of it. So they generally act as a brake on these sorts of things. And, one of the people I spoke to there said that Japanese companies need to become more competitive, they need to adopt more competitive practices from other places and unfortunately the American model seems to be the most competitive.

Int: There's not the tradition in Japan that there is in America or in the UK of using an equity stake to alter a company's behaviour. And it seems like, [...] there's a right way to go about it and a wrong way to go about it in Japan. Are we arriving at a right way to use equity to change company performance?

TS: Well, this whole idea of activist investors and shareholder value and so forth, is, it has to be said, a relatively recent invention in the West, I mean this is something that popped up in the 1970s really. So the fact that it's now coming to Japan, er ... We weren't always doing this in Britain and America. So, so, we need to make that clear. But yes, within Japan now that you have something like 25%, 27% of shares of Japanese companies in foreign hands you are starting to get foreign investment funds who are saying things like, to Japanese companies, 'Why are you sitting on so much cash?', 'Why are you not paying out larger dividends?', 'Why are you financing things in such an old fashioned way, and not making the best use of your assets?', and so on. And these are questions that these companies generally haven't been asked before.

Anyway, now that we are starting to see more shareholder activism, you're seeing it from, famously from foreigners like Steel Partners in the case of, Bulldog Sauce, em, so they took a stake in this big sauce-maker and then they tried to buy the company out and, em, there was a big fuss about it because they went about it the wrong way and the boss of the company, er, was, er, he was compared to someone who walks into a Japanese home without removing his shoes. It was this sort of thing.

Unit 5 — Listening 2 page 53

Part 1

Interviewer: Can you tell us why people everywhere are so angry about CEO pay?

Carl Underwood: Well, what's happened is that activists seeking changes in corporate governance have linked their campaign to pay, which they say is much too high. And you see, as the general public agrees with them ... gets lots of media attention, and then politicians get involved. It's because, you see, well ... people get understandably emotional about pay because the gap between executive pay and workers' pay has widened considerably over the past two decades and then, as well, it's so easy to find examples of what appear to be injustices. I mean people get particularly upset when underperforming companies continue to pay huge salaries to their CEOs. Unfortunately that's quite common nowadays and that just gets business everywhere a bad name! And you see, when the obviously undeserving make huge salaries well then, misgovernance and excessive pay somehow get linked and shareholders get worried that companies are not being run properly because of it.

What we've seen recently is an increase in the demand from shareholders to have a say on executive pay packages. Not all of them are interested in social injustices but to put it simply, pay is about control. The board of a company attracts the best and most talented CEOs by offering them attractive salaries, right? Then they make them part owners through stock options in order to motivate them to obtain certain results. CEOs are in principle accountable to the board to meet those results. It should naturally follow then that if targets are not reached the board should be able to refuse high rewards. So far so good. However, sometimes the opposite happens and powerful CEOs have been able to negotiate pay contracts that ignore performance issues. So shareholders, who feel they wouldn't be as weak as certain boards, want to be able to vote on pay – the one thing that gives them power over the people they've entrusted their money to! In other words, they feel that CEOs have had the carrot without the stick for too long! They feel that it's time for shareholders to use the stick a little.

Part 2

Int: You call your report 'The great pay debate'. Why 'debate' – is there another side to this story?

CU: Well yes, I think so. Let's look first at what is being suggested here. Firstly, that bad governance is leading to excessive pay and therefore shareholders should have more say, right? Secondly, that high salaries are necessarily bad for business. And lastly, that legislation should be put in place to stop excessive pay.

Well, the first thing I'd like to say is that there's no proof that bad governance and lack of shareholder monitoring is leading to the high salaries we've been seeing lately. Shareholders have been more active than ever before in deciding on salaries in Europe and yet we've seen huge hikes in executive pay. You see, shareholders are happy as long as they're making dividends – if profits are up, they don't care if the CEO is making a huge chunk of it! If you offer pay and bonuses as motivation for performance what do you expect!

Unit 5 — Listening 3 page 57

1

My next point is one of interest to you all. I've shown you how good corporate governance can keep you out of trouble with the activists but actually it can also make your company more attractive to lenders and investors and subsequently more profitable. To put it more simply, it pays to promote good governance.

Investors say they highly value corporate governance. And take it from me, they put their money where their mouths are. The reason they are willing to invest is because they have looked at the facts. I've done some homework here and found that, for example, a study of 500 firms by Deutsche Bank showed that companies with strong or improving corporate governance outperformed those with poor or deteriorating governance practices by about 19% over a two-year period.

And that's not all. A Harvard/Wharton team of researchers found that US-based firms with better governance have faster sales growth and were more profitable than their peers. Obviously this encourages investors to take an interest. By the way, other statistics are ...

2

A: The way we see it is, share prices are sliding, staff morale is at an all time low, customers are losing confidence. I mean what are we waiting for? Frankly, nobody is happy with the way the board is running things. It's time to take serious action.

B: I think we should wait and see what happens in the next quarter.

A: I'm not convinced that this new strategy they've come up with will work. As a matter of fact, we, as the major investor fund, have more or less decided what to do. We are going ahead to call on the CEO to resign whether or not we get your backing. So, it's up to you if you want to sign our petition or not but if you don't, well actually we're going to have to ...

3

Thank you all for coming. Thank you. As I said in my email this won't take longer than ten minutes but I want you to go away and think about what I have to say and then on Monday morning you'll be better able to make an informed judgment on how to vote on the best course of action. As you know we've had demands from our major equity fund shareholder to allow them a representative on the board. Now, I can well understand your feelings and I know that many of you see this as unnecessary and even insulting, and I must say that on the whole, I'm inclined to agree with you there. However, it's not in our interests to refuse this request. I've spent many long hours talking to angry investors and this may be an excellent way to compromise and perhaps even to avoid litigation. Finally, look at it this way, the biggest names in the industry have successfully worked out policy issues with shareholders for years and there is no reason why we shouldn't do the same ...

Unit 5 — Decision page 58

It was an interesting case and it's very similar to what happened with Sears Roebuck. At first the board refused to listen to the shareholders and announced a long-term sales and marketing strategy which was supposed to rescue the retailing end of their business. Initially everyone was happy because Wall Street analysts were predicting rising share prices. However, it soon became apparent that they needed more resources and indeed a whole new culture in order to get rid of their outmoded image. They finally did make the jobs of chairman and CEO separate. This kind of strategic move allows family members to have a less influential position on policy and you can bring in a new CEO to run the company. Next step ... they sold off the subsidiaries and completely revamped all the stores, changed the collections and stock and launched a huge marketing campaign. It was an astounding success. I remember the headline in our magazine at the time. It said 'the dinosaur turned into a cash cow'. They were even voted most innovative retailer of the year in 2009! This case really does demonstrate the role that active shareholders can and should play in under-performing companies. What's more it shows the crucial link between activism and value. As a result of shareholder involvement the company became a better run, more open, more accountable and more valuable company.

Unit 6 — Listening 1 page 60

When I do workshops on creativity and innovation, I always like to focus on some concrete examples of 'great ideas' because there's a lot you can learn from them, especially if you are thinking of starting your own business. Among my favourites I would chose three very different examples which I think each illustrate important aspects of entrepreneurship.

Velcro, of course, is probably one success story that most people are already familiar with. I mean, who doesn't have something at home with some velcro on it? Well, we all do, of course, and that's thanks to George de Mestral. He was a Swiss engineer with an exceptional sense of observation and who also liked to go hiking. And one day, after he'd been doing just that, he started wondering how some types of grass seed were able to attach themselves to his clothing. Well, after a lot of research he eventually came up with a prototype of the system that we all know and use today. So that's a great example of how observation can lead to something completely new. But what most people don't know is that it actually took Mestral more than ten years to develop his idea into a commercial product and even then it only really became a household name once NASA had started to use velcro on astronauts' space suits. So, three lessons – observation, perseverance and, yes, a little bit of luck too.

Jacques Cousteau is another good example. He's actually often credited with the invention of the scuba equipment used by divers to breathe underwater but the story is a little more complicated than that, as in fact the term 'scuba', which stands for 'self-contained underwater breathing apparatus', was first used by an American, Dr Christian Lambertson, who was doing research for the US army. It's true, though, that it was Cousteau who really developed the technology into a practical underwater breathing system, almost creating a whole new industry in the process, but how he managed to do that involves another twist because it was actually his associate Emile Gagnan who provided the key component of the technology. Gagnan had developed a special valve for use in the automobile industry. That valve became the 'regulator' that divers use to breathe through. I think it's a great example of cross-over and it shows how important both lateral thinking and networking can be – you know, taking something from one field and applying it to another, using someone's knowledge and experience and combining it with yours. And that's something all entrepreneurs should be on the look out for. So, OK, you want to build a revolutionary new car, but you don't necessarily have to re-invent the wheel to do that.

I just love to talk about Dean Kamen who has done some truly amazing things. I mean this guy is just such a good illustration of the really prolific inventor. Probably his most famous invention is the Segway human transporter but he has also produced some other incredible things like the revolutionary Ibot wheelchair which has done such a lot to improve the quality of life for disabled people. Kamen actually has a whole string of other extremely successful inventions especially in the medical field such as insulin pumps and mobile medical systems. But what I think is particularly interesting in his case is the fact that not all of these inventions have been huge commercial successes. I mean, if you take the Segway, yes, no doubt about it, it's a brilliant piece of engineering but surprisingly it's not one that has actually lived up to the expectations that people had for it when it was launched. Now, for me, that goes to show that there is always a trade-off between introducing something that's new and revolutionary and actually making it into a successful product. It's not always automatic. You may have a brilliant idea but that doesn't guarantee that you'll find a market for it. So, market research – that absolutely has to be a part of the formula too.

Unit 6   Listening 2 page 63

Interviewer: We're here with Bruno Guattari, a young French entrepreneur who launched his company 'Comptoir Atlantique' in 1996. Bruno, can you tell us a little about your company?

Bruno Guattari: Yes ... well at Comptoir Atlantique we work in a very specific sector which is the production and distribution of high-protein foods. So what we actually do is to design, produce and market what we call 'specific requirement' foods – these are basically high-protein products that come in various forms: powders, pills, cereal bars, concentrates and that type of thing. Most of our products are sold directly to our clients who are distributors of health and diet foods – so we're almost exclusively a B2B operation, at least for the time being.

Int: OK so how did you get started with Comptoir Atlantique? What's the story behind that?

BG: Well it's actually quite a long story but I can at least give you the main elements. In fact when I left university after graduating in biochemistry, I found a job as a researcher in a French laboratory, run by Professor Laborit. The work that we did there was mainly developing drugs and molecules for use in the medical field so it had very little to do with the sector that Comptoir is in today. Anyway I stayed there for about ten years and I probably would have stayed longer if I could have. But the laboratory itself was going through a difficult period and eventually it closed. So that was it and I found myself without a job – unemployed!

Int: So was that the moment when you decided to start your own company?

BG: No not exactly. You see, in my family we have quite a long tradition of involvement in the food industry which goes back to my grandfather who actually co-founded Banania which was and still is a very successful banana and chocolate drink. Everybody in France knows that name. So when I lost my job I went to work for the family who were now operating a different company under the brand name 'Mon

Bana'. But I quickly realised that I wasn't going to be able to make a career inside this company. You know, it's not always easy to integrate a family business. But at the same time it was a fantastic opportunity for me because the company had its own laboratory which I was able to use to experiment with some of my own ideas for new food products.

Int: OK, so you were developing potential products at that time?

BG: Yes absolutely. And in addition to that I also opened a small import company that I called Comptoir Atlantique and we began to import products from Brazil – my wife is Brazilian by the way – you know like exotic spices and fruits and that sort of thing, but it was really just a sideline activity for us. It wasn't what I'd call a business. But the problem was that the development work that I was doing at Mon Bana didn't really fit in with their strategy so I started looking around to see if anyone would be interested in some of my ideas for protein foods. And that's when I met my first client who immediately ordered ten thousand units. So that's how Comptoir really got started. But I was still running the company from my apartment at that time, I mean we didn't even have our own offices, just a small apartment in Paris.

Int: I see. So you were producing the products at Mon Bana and then selling them on to your customers.

BG: Yes. That's right. But then we started to get more and more orders and it all became much more complicated. So in 2003 I made the decision to move Comptoir Atlantique into its own premises and we bought some land and built our own office, warehouse and production unit. And since then we have added two new buildings.

Int: So I imagine that actually putting together the organisation of Comptoir Atlantique must have been quite difficult?

BG: You could say that, yes! I mean we had to find the right people to develop the business and that meant training them so that they could understand what the products were and how the business model worked. But today, it's great and we have a very dedicated team of ten employees. In fact we've just opened our own production unit so now we don't have to rely only on outside suppliers to prepare the products.

Int: What was the most difficult moment in all that? Were there times when you thought that you'd never make it?

BG: Yes – there were quite a few of those in fact. I think the worst one was back in 2004 when one of our main customers went out of business and left us with all the stock that they had ordered but hadn't yet paid for. That was really a difficult moment and it took us two years to get over that. I suppose the lesson is that you should never be too reliant on one customer but, of course, most new businesses don't really have much choice in the matter.

Int: So what's the plan for Comptoir Atlantique from now on?

BG: Well I'm afraid I can't give you too much information about that because I have no intention of revealing our development plans to our competitors. Let's just say that we're already planning a number of new product launches and we're also working on some very interesting new ideas. But, don't worry if you really want to find out, you can always get all the latest news about what we're up to from our website at Comptoir Atlantique dot com!

Int: Thank you very much Bruno, and let's hope it all goes well in the future.

Unit 6   Listening 3 page 67

Pitch 1
Everyone wants the ultimate experience, right? Wrong. Experiences are a thing of the past! What people want now is the ultimate insperience! In other words they want to experience things in the comfort of their own homes! We at Ultimate Insperience understand your needs. Picture this: your own in-house spa facilites, massage, facial, hairdo, make up – you name it we provide it! We'll come to your house and pamper you in a way only celebrities could afford before. You just have to dial 0845 ...

Pitch 2
Sarah: Hi Jack. Have you guys in HR given the reward scheme any more thought?

Jack: Hello Sarah. No, I'm afraid we haven't. That may have to be postponed till next year – there just isn't a budget for it.

S: Have you got a minute now? I'd like to run something by you.

J: Yeah, Sure.

S: Have you considered lunch vouchers? They're an easy and relatively inexpensive way to get people motivated, engaged and healthier! The employer gets tax breaks, so it's really flexible because you choose how much you want to pay and effective as they act as a constant reminder that your organisation believes in looking after its people. It worked so well at my last job. I know my team needs a little bit of motivating at the moment. Lunch vouchers could do the trick. I'll send you the information to look at it, and ...

J: Thanks Sarah, yeah that could be useful. I'll bring it up at the next meeting.

S: When is that then?

J: Next Monday morning actually. I'll add it to the agenda.

S: Great, I'll give you a ring on Monday afternoon to see how it went.

Pitch 3
Ours is a new idea for the restaurant market. As the word 'lab' in the brand name 'Taste Bud Lab' indicates, customers can experiment with flavours of their own. They can add all fresh and organic spices, herbs and so on themselves to the meals we provide. We've chosen a location right in the heart of a new up-and-coming district full of young professionals who eat out regularly. There are other restaurants in the area but none of them has an orignal concept like ours. Now, as you can see from the business plan, we have a capital requirement of $200,000 up front, which may seem like a lot but don't forget this is a high-margin business and we'll be looking at returns of ...

Unit 6   Decision page 68

These are all good ideas. But it is very very difficult to get a VC to invest. Even in the best of business ideas. They'll only take a risk on businesses that promise to make rapid and big growth. In fact, they're generally only interested in businesses which will float and become big public corporations quite soon after the incubator stage. That being said, it's always worth a try pitching to people like us, particularly if you need a big outlay. Looking at the three businesses in question, the one I think most needs a lot of financial backing is the e-commerce one. These typically use venture capital to start up because they need lots of cash for advertising, equipment, and employees. They need to advertise in order to attract visitors, and they need equipment and employees to create the site. The amount of advertising money needed and the speed of change in the Internet can make bootstrapping impossible. For example, many e-commerce businesses typically consume $50 million to $100 million to get to the point where they can go public. Up to half of that money can be spent on advertising!

Looking at the young fashion designer, it would be worth his or her while thinking about the crowdfunding option. There are examples of this working. In Ireland, some designers ran an 'adopt a designer' campaign on the net and raised €70,000 within six months to create a new collection! Meanwhile the supporters each received a piece designed especially for them. If the collection sells they get a split of the profit as well. That's what we call a 'win-win' situation.

Now, let's look at our budding retailer. Obviously, the contractor developing the station will be keen to have successful retailing businesses in the new complex and may consider investing in a business it expects to do well. I know that in Italy, for example, the developer Grand Stazioni – they're in charge of managing all Italy's major railway stations – well, they actually publish contract notices and send out invitations to tender to eligible businesses looking for commercial partnerships. Again, this could be a win-win situation because retailers generally do very well in big railway stations, and station commercial managers are always looking for a mix of retail outlets. Yes, I think our retailer should try to get funding this way.

Unit 7   Listening 1 page 76

Part 1

Interviewer: You've suggested that, er, alternative energy generation could form the basis of the next boom, a boom similar to that we've seen in biotech, nanotech, dot com, etc. over the last decade or so. Why do you take this position?

Geoff Carr: Well it's a lucky coincidence of circumstances I think. There have been for several years some small groups of enthusiastic scientists and entrepreneurs who've been working on, er, various bits of technology related to energy: biofuels, for example, er, not the, er, ethanol made from maize which is causing so much controversy at the moment but looking at ways of making it from the whole plant by digesting its cellulose and turning that into fuels. That's one line. Another line, erm, many physicists have been looking at is solar energy. Traditional solar cells and, erm, ways of concentrating it and using it to boil water. Um, and these companies have been sitting around in the background, doing their thing. They have, er, suddenly blossomed partly because the price of fossil fuels is rising and partly

because of concerns about security of supply and partly because of concerns about climate change. So you have a confluence of, um, external factors which support it and a small but active research base that can deliver things that work. So we've now arrived at a position where there are things that work and the question is whether they can be scaled up so that they can work at scale at a price that people are prepared to pay. So it's a very interesting time in the field of, for want of a better word, of alternative energy, because lots of technologies are available, er, they work in the laboratory and there's demand for power from sources other than fossil fuels, erm, so these guys are coming blinking into the light and saying 'look at me, look at me' and the people with the money are looking at them and deciding where to put their money.

Part 2

Int: The position you take is that this could lead to a boom. How do you see this coming?

GC: It will lead to a boom because of a mixture of economic and, em, policy reasons. Economic reasons are the high price of oil at the moment which has also dragged up the price of gas and a related economic reason which is also an environmental reason is the appearance of the cap and trade carbon system in Europe and the possibility though by no means certainty that the same thing will happen in the United States and that will put the price of coal up or at least of coal-fired electricity. So as the traditional fuels become more costly there is an opportunity, and as I said earlier the technologies are there, and the companies that are working on them are pushing the price down to the point where they are competitive with fossil fuel. And once they are competitive with fossil fuel then it simply becomes a matter of economics and people will adopt solar power in appropriate areas. They've already adopted wind power. Wind-powered electricity somewhat more expensive than coal-fired electricity – that would no longer be the case if coal had a proper carbon tax on it and they would be approximately the same price.

Part 3

Int: Well now, now some of the players that you talked about earlier. What is the nature of some of these, er, these players. Who's on board? Who's doing the innovating, if you like?

GC: Well the innovation's coming mainly from North America but not exclusively, um, and it's a mixture of small new start-up firms and large engineering and chemical companies. Small firms, a lot of them are based in Silicon Valley but you also find them in other places. There are some in Cambridge Massachusetts around MIT, there are quite a few in the, erm, south western deserts in Arizona and Colorado and places like that. And also some of the large companies are involved. General Electric's very much involved in making wind turbines and they also have a very active solar cell research division and they sell some solar cells but they're about to start selling a lot more. Some of the oil companies are involved on the biofuel side as well. BP and Shell are both very active, um, supporting all sorts of small firms that have different potential technologies because no one knows which is going to work. Er, and on the car side of things which is important as well there's a likelihood that we'll see what are essentially electric cars coming onto the roads in fairly large numbers over the next few years and these will be powered by modern batteries which will probably be lithium iron batteries.

Part 4

Int: Well now, hang on a sec. Electric cars. I mean, I thought all the buzz was around fuel cells.

GC: The problem with fuel cells is that the sort of fuel cell that you need to run a car has to use hydrogen as its fuel. And a hydrogen fuel cell requires hydrogen and hydrogen is a gas which is difficult to store, it's very leaky, there's no infrastructure to look after it whereas the cars being designed at the moment simply plug into the mains to recharge the batteries so the infrastructure to recharge them exists already.

Part 5

Now maybe you could tell us a bit about how biofuels may develop? Biofuels are one of the winners that you've picked in your special report.

GC: Biofuels are obviously in competition with electricity for power in cars. The first generation biofuel which is ethanol, erm, if you make it from the right starting materials it's actually cheaper than petrol and the, um, the Brazilians, um, have a very large bio ethanol industry which is based on sugar cane and it's perfectly competitive. Er, the idea would be to, erm, go from using part of the plant to using the whole plant and you'd probably then use either specialised grasses or specialised trees that have been bred and possibly genetically engineered to grow fast.

Part 6

Int: Nuclear power has seen something of a resurgence. But isn't this kind of, er, counter-intuitive? I mean, nuclear power, there is still an issue of waste. Is there a place for nuclear power?

GC: One of the advantages of the alternatives that the greens like, that's solar and, and wind in particular, is that they are very scalable, you can build a small wind farm, you can build a large wind farm. You can put a solar panel on the top ... on the roof of your house whereas with a nuclear power station it either works or it doesn't. It's a very expensive thing to build and it takes a while to build. However, once you've built it, er, it's a perfectly good way of generating power and the power is a little bit more expensive than coal but it's not vastly more expensive. The waste issue is a real one but the amount of waste that's produced is fairly small in volume and, um, although it's a controversial position I think the correct way to deal with it is to find a geologically stable area, dig a hole in it and put it there, er, mark it carefully because technology changes all the time and we'll probably come back in a few decades, time and know how to deal with it.

Unit 7 Listening 2 page 79

Speaker 1
Good evening everybody and welcome to tonight's debate which I have the honour of moderating. Erm, the health and well-being of the citizens of our country has always been one of the top priorities of all political parties in this country. Indeed, making sure that people have access to the basic resources that can enable them to lead healthy lives is one of the most important challenges for politicians and community officials. Perhaps the most important of those resources is one that many of us take for granted the most: drinking water. In today's debate we will be examining the complex relationships that exist in the water supply sector and discussing what best practice should be for both government and industry. Today we're very lucky to have with us a distinguished panel of speakers which includes experts from very different fields: er, the environment, medical research, public health and the water industry itself. So, ladies and gentlemen, without further ado, let me introduce the speakers from the two sides who'll be participating in today's debate. On my left ...

Speaker 2
I'm going to start my argument against this motion by giving you some facts and figures that I feel quite confident my opponents will not be using when their turn comes to speak. Now, a lot of people in this country and, who knows, maybe even some members of this audience, assume that just because water's contained in a nice-looking bottle that that is actually a guarantee that it comes from a natural spring somewhere up in one of those unspoilt mountain regions that we keep seeing in TV commercials. Nothing could be further from the truth ... because, in reality, more than 40% of the bottled water that's sold in this country actually comes from the exactly the same place as the water that comes out of your kitchen tap: yes, the municipal water supply. But what's even more surprising is that consumers of water are being asked to pay two very different prices for what is, to all extents and purposes, the same thing. A gallon of bottled water will set you back about eight dollars which is an awful lot of money when you consider that for just one dollar and fifty cents you can get 1,000 gallons of municipal water. But price isn't the only argument against bottled water. Let's take a look at some of the environmental consequences. Now in northern ...

Speaker 3
I have to say that I was quite surprised to hear the previous speaker's arguments against bottled water. Bottled water is in a bottle for a very good reason and that reason is quite simply ... once it's in there, it's sealed, it's safe and it's delivered direct to the person who's going to drink it. Now, that makes it very different to the tap water that comes to your kitchen sink which has to travel through a complex network of water treatment facilities and pipes before it gets to you. On that journey a number of things can happen that I will be talking about later. Let me just remind you of that famous comment made by Marq de Villiers: 'The trouble with water – and there is trouble with water – is that they're not making any more of it.' As a medical researcher, I have always believed in the application of scientific principles to all areas of research. However, after making a careful study of the recent environmental water report that my opponents in this debate have been repeatedly referring to, I have to say that the report is, in my view, deeply flawed And the reason I say this is ...

Unit 7 Decision page 80

Well, this debate really focuses on an issue that's moved right up the agenda in a number of countries. In South Africa, for example, the government is faced with a very similar situation: a power industry that has an ageing infrastructure and which is increasingly unable to supply the country's businesses and the population with the electricity they need. In fact quite recently the government was considering investing in a new nuclear power plant and they were about to sign a contract with a consortium formed by the French power company Areva and the American firm Westinghouse. The idea was to build a twin reactor that would have boosted the country's electricity production by around 10%. However, the investment cost of the deal – 29 billion dollars – turned out to be just too much and they pulled the plug. So that has left them in a difficult situation with no immediate solution to the power shortages. I think this goes to show that countries all over the world are very much aware of the strategic importance of their energy supplies and of the need to make sure that they don't have to rely on potentially risky supplies of imported fuel. The solutions, whether they are based on nuclear, traditional or alternative energy sources will inevitably be mixed solutions in my view and that's really because at the present time it's just not feasible for countries to suddenly switch to all green energy solutions. Maybe that'll be an option one day but for now, even if it is desirable, and I don't think that there's much doubt about that, I'm afraid it just isn't doable!

Unit 8 Listening 1 page 85

Politics is all about building relationships with the right people. It's about getting people on your side – making sure you can achieve your objectives at all costs.

The key to success in the politics game is influence. The more influence you have, the more power you wield: power over key decisions, power to give rewards, power to withhold rewards as a punishment, in other words the power to develop tactics to get key people to agree with you so that you get your way and obtain your goals.

I'd say that political 'games' are inevitable in large organisational cultures, firstly because of how corporations are structured. You see, organisations are divided into different departments and sometimes different departments have different goals – sometimes even conflicting goals. Each manager will try to influence senior directors to support them in the realisation of their goals. They will each have to motivate their own staff and make sure they stay loyal. In some cases they may even feel that it is justified to disregard and sometimes even discredit the work being done in other departments in order to obtain more influence for themselves and their staff!

Secondly, it's not that surprising really, when you think about it. I mean you'd expect the kind of people who make it to managerial positions to engage in 'political' or 'influence-building' activities. Organisations promote people who possess ambition, drive, and creativity. Since a desire to control others and events in order to have an impact on what is going on is often associated with effective management, it's not surprising that recruiters look for these traits in candidates for managerial jobs.

But it's not necessarily a negative trait to seek or want power. I mean, what's important is how they use that power. Most effective managers realise that often the best way to achieve results is to empower the people around them to do things. They have motivational and delegation skills and use them to the advantage of everyone. But the real political animals are the 'Machiavellian' managers – in other words they will justify any action which helps them reach their targets.

Unit 8 Listening 2 page 89

1

John: Thanks for seeing me, Sarah, I know you're busy.

Sarah: I have ten minutes before my next meeting, John ...

J: Great presentation, by the way. The team were really inspired.

S: Thank you.

J: Anyway, it's about that idea we talked about last week.

S: I thought I said ...

J: Yes, but listen to this. I heard that Mackenzie's team were working along the same lines, though not quite the same thing, and that management were interested. So I decided to do a bit more research and we can definitely improve on what they're doing. I know you're busy so I've collated the results into a short brief which I'll leave with you. This may be the break we all need, Sarah. I was talking to Pete in R & D yesterday, off the record, you understand, and they can't wait to get their teeth into a project like this.

S: Really? Pete Radcliff?

J: Yeah, the new manager. Nice guy. We play golf together. Anyway, we need to get ahead of the game, be the ones to bring this forward quickly. If any team leader can pull it off, you can. Have a look at this and see what you think. If you agree, take it to the board as quickly as you can. Then we can get cracking on it. Of course we'll need, er, weekly feedback meetings with you and we'll want to validate every stage of the project before moving on to the next. I know you're overworked as it is but if you could manage that we'd probably be able to make reasonable progress in between meetings with you. What do you think ... ?

2

Andrew: Hi Jack, have you got a minute?

Jack: Sure.

A: Great tie, by the way!

J: Thanks. Listen Andrew, I know why you're here and to be perfectly frank I think you'd be crazy to leave sales. I'll try to make it worth your while to stay here. I'll put in a word for you. If I don't get you a raise straightaway I'll get you a bonus that will match that marketing salary.

A: But it's not just the money Jack ...

J: Listen, I'm not sure you're right for that job. You're not made for sitting in an office, collecting data. You're an 'in the field' man if ever I met one. And it'll drive you crazy when they get it wrong, which they do! Remember that mess last month? That's the last time I'll listen to them about market needs! Think of all the lost commission for my staff. Don't get me started ...

A: But Jack that's why you need a good salesman, like me, on their team. I'd have known instinctively that the market research survey was way off. You'd never have had those problems if I'd been working in their department. Did you know that they want us to have regular meetings now? To improve relations between the two departments.

J: Oh no, that's all I need.

A: I could be your inside man! Maybe I could coordinate the meetings – act as the go between, between the two departments.

J: That's true, I suppose.

A: I owe you a lot Jack. I've had a wonderful five years here but you must see that I need to move on. I'll train in my successor, help to recruit him if you like, and make sure all my key clients are completely happy before rushing off. They don't need me for a couple of months at marketing yet. I could always ...

Unit 8   Decision page 90

This is a typical situation! I know that sounds crazy because it reads like an exceptional case but in times of uncertainty and change such as this there is the greatest scope for political behaviour. You see, it's like this: the organisation is losing profit margins on sales so they hope they will increase overall performance by going into a new area. They're in an experimentation stage. They haven't got a clear goal that all the staff can work towards together. There is no guarantee that the new service department will work. In such circumstances you can expect managers to disagree – each one vying for his or her preferred course of action to be endorsed by the decision makers. In our case here at Central Computers there is certainly a problem of jealousy and insecurity on the side of the sales manager. He is almost certain to lose staff in this downturn and he is feeling threatened by the arrival of the new manager.

The trick is to act quickly and decisively and try to nip this sort of problem in the bud. So let's look at Sagan's options: well, the first one looks perfect doesn't it? It's called 'passing the buck' or handing over the responsibility to someone else. However, I wouldn't recommend it myself, particularly as Carl Sagan's opponent in this political game is already trying to discredit him with his staff. Someone like Arroway wouldn't be long using the situation to his advantage.

That's why I'd almost consider option three which would mean trying to beat him at his own game, and gaining power over that one client would almost certainly take away all his influence and power. But that's a little like option five – it means getting involved in the same dirty tactics, and it will take time and energy away from actually getting the department up and running. This is why option four looks attractive. However, I think it is probably naive to imagine that Arroway will just give up and that Sagan will be able to just get on with his job without trying to solve the awful situation Arroway is causing. Maybe even option two looks naive

but I still think it's worth a try and if it succeeds it's the only option which will work in the long term unless you manage to get Arroway sacked! This meeting needs to happen as quickly as possible and Sagan needs to have a clear influencing strategy. If he is to solve this problem he will have to be a skilled politician. He will need to use all the influencing tactics at his disposal, including bargaining and negotiating. If Arroway doesn't respond to this 'soft' approach Sagan may need to threaten to call in the hierarchy, and he does have some ammunition he could use against him, but this will be less effective than, say, creating common goals where both men are winners if the outcomes are successful.

Unit 9   Listening 1 page 92

UK marketers are spending a bigger percentage of their marketing budgets on emarketing every year. There are a number of reasons for this. Firstly, the audience is huge and getting bigger every year. At the moment 31.6 million people are online in the UK. 52% of those are men and 48% women. 21% of the users are 25–34 years old. More surprisingly though, at the other end of the spectrum, the over-50s represent 30% of the total time spent online. Add to that the fact that people can have mobile broadband or high-speed access now at a very reasonable price, so more and more people are signing up. This, coupled with the fact that laptops are getting cheaper and cheaper, means that people are connected now even when they are on the move. Great news for marketers!

More and more people are opting for quality broadband connections, which gives the marketers greater choice of media, for example, rich media products, which use a combination of image and sound and are more attractive. Thanks to better quality connections, we've seen an increase in embedded videos on webpages over the past few years. The increase in popularity of YouTube, for example, is a phenomenal opportunity for marketers.

And we mustn't forget the popularity of catch-up TV – a broad demographic profile now uses the Internet to watch programmes they've missed, offering advertisers more exposure than before. And of course there's Internet TV which offers yet another opening to reach specific groups of consumers.

Finally, social media such as Facebook and MySpace are having a massive impact on the market and account for a huge youth audience. We are going to see an impressive increase in spend in this area in the next few years.

Unit 9   Listening 2 page 95

Interviewer: When people talk about advertising on the Internet it seems that Google's always the first name that gets mentioned. How do you explain its success in this field?

Greg Stillman: There's absolutely no doubt that Google is one of the Internet's most incredible success stories. I mean here you have a company that only actually started business in 1998 and today it's not only a household name – it's one of the pillars of the US high technology sector. But how the firm managed to become the leading vehicle for advertising on the Internet isn't that simple because that wasn't really what Page and Brin originally had in mind when they launched 'Backrub', their first search engine, when they were still students at Stanford University.

Int: So how did Google get so deeply involved in advertising?

GS: Well, of course, it all stems directly from the famous Google algorithm because that's what's at the heart of Google's business model, a bit like the secret magic formula for Coca Cola. And it was the algorithm that led to the whole concept of page ranking which is the way that Google actually decides which websites appear at the top of the page when you're doing a search. But the idea of basing that ranking on the popularity and relevance of a site, well, that was definitely the first stroke of genius. But it wasn't enough to take Google all the way to the top because just operating a search engine isn't – or perhaps I should say wasn't – all that lucrative. So it was only really once they'd integrated advertising that the company's revenues started to soar.

The company had actually sold advertising since 2000 but in quite a traditional way, you know, with sales reps and so on. But in 2002 that all changed with the the new Adwords program. With Adwords Google was able to offer a self-serve advertising model that you could access online, but equally important was the fact that it was PPC advertising. Now, PPC stands for 'pay per click' which means that what advertisers pay is related to the number of clicks that their ads or links actually generate. But at the same time as introducing PPC, Google also adopted an auction system – so advertisers actually have to compete for keywords. Let's say, for example, you are a chocolate company and you want to advertise on Google using the word 'chocolate'. Google will ask you in which countries you want your ad to appear and which search languages you want to target: English, French, Korean, etc. Once you've entered the keyword 'chocolate', Google AdWords provides you with an 'average cost per click' or 'CPC' for the keyword based on what others who wanted to advertise chocolate have been willing to pay. The average cost per click is the average of the top three bids. Because how much you're willing to pay per click also determines your 'ranking'. Although you originally imagined spending one dollar per click, you might learn that other companies have been willing to pay twice that! So, you'll now have to match or raise the average cost per click price if you want your ad to be ranked among the top three to appear.

Int: Mm. So what about search engine optimisation or 'SEO' as it's often called. Why has that become something of a buzzword in emarketing?

GS: Well it's pretty simple to understand because if you're a company and you have a website then obviously you want to have your name in front of people's eyes when they do a search. It's a bit like when people used the telephone directory – except that system was just alphabetical so if your company name started with a capital 'A' followed by another 'A' then you were automatically at the top of the list and your business was more visible than your competitors'. Now SEO is really just that applied to the Internet – except that you have to compete to get to the top of the list. There are a number of ways you can do that and search companies divide those techniques into two groups: 'black hat' and 'white hat' – so 'white hat' means that the methods are considered legitimate and 'black hat' means that some deceptive practices are being used to try to artificially inflate the ranking. But ultimately you have to get people clicking on your site and they'll really only continue to do that if the content is what they want. But, of course, buying adverts on Google is one way of getting people onto a site! So it's like a loop, if you like, and you may have to keep advertising just to stay on top of the game. But having said that, the importance of SEO can sometimes be exaggerated because in fact sales are mostly generated by links between websites and not so much from clicking on search results.

Int: Mm. What about the future? How do you think Google will influence the future in e-marketing?

GS: In my view Google is in a very strong position to achieve digital dominance in that field. They have the search engine, they have very precise data about exactly how people are using the Internet and they have the advertising revenue to support their business. But they also have a whole constellation of digital operations in all sorts of different areas: social networking sites, video entertainment sites like YouTube, mapping sites, and so on. So that's already a very solid foundation. Especially when you consider that they also have the ability to interconnect different technologies and to prepare for Web 3.0, the platform of the future. And Google sees that as being a seamless Internet-connected environment where people will be able to switch between mobile devices and computers and access or download all types of software and content at the click of a button. I suppose the only cloud on the Google horizon could be a change in Internet user behaviour and there are some people who are starting to say that Internet users should be paid for all the information that they divulge about themselves when they surf the net, but I don't think that we're there yet. So what that will all mean for people involved in marketing is not entirely clear yet but what is clear is that Google is here to stay, and I would predict that most marketers will be spending not only more time on Google platforms but probably a lot more money too!

Unit 9   Listening 3 page 99

A: I don't mind telling you that financially it makes a lot of sense. That's why I'm so keen. I really want to cut down on spending.

B: Not exactly a cut and dried situation though, is it? My main objective is not to lose a single customer over this.

A: OK, you're the one in the field. What do you think we should do?

B: I think we should do both! I think we should go ahead and do an e-catalogue but we should also do a limited run of a paper version for the customers who want to opt for that.

A: Mm. The problem with doing that is that it will mean double the expense!

B: Only in the short term. We'll only have to pay training costs this year. Our staff can produce an e-catalogue very cheaply every other year from then on.

A: Yes, I see your point but I was really hoping to avoid printing this year. We'd have covered our training costs and possibly even saved a little.

B: The way I see it, my suggestion is our only really viable option. Losing customers isn't going to do the budget any good, is it?

A: No it isn't. I suppose you're right. It's going to take a bit of explaining to the finance department, though. Erm, we need to have a plan of action. Will you cost the entire project up and …

Unit 9   Decision page 100

What a terrible dilemma. Really amazing campaigns. I can see that it was a really difficult choice. You see, in the end, it's quite subjective. I mean, even if you follow the criteria, you still have your own gut feeling about the creative element, you know what I mean?

Anyway, the judges in this case gave third prize to The X Factor Challenge. What a great way for a mobile phone retailer to engage with their end users! The brand fit was perfect and the potential audience was phenomenal. But I guess it wasn't judged to be as innovative and creative as the other two, as the context existed already and it is a case of sponsoring an already operating idea, whereas the second place, 'In one take, on one tank' had a more original media, which was video on the Internet. They also had a fabulous opportunity to interact and engage with customers there and the brand fit for Volkswagen's new fuel efficiency model, the Bluemotion Polo, couldn't have been better. It must have been a really close run.

In the end, though the IAB judges went for 'If you can fill it, you can have it'. I suppose what clinched it in the end was the sheer creativity of the whole crazy idea! It engages so well with the customers and the brand fit couldn't be better. The contestants for the 'If you can fill it, you can have it' used every kind of digital and mobile technology, as well as more traditional media, to fill their guest list. They were given help by O2, which provided a 'My party' section which allowed people to sign up on the contestants' website. They could print out posters and put them up in work, or student canteens, offices, etc. They sent SMS messages and emails, made calls, whatever means of communication they could, to get people to sign up on their guest list! The Australian girl who won had 15,000 people! Over 100,000 people took part in the competition! The publicity for O2 was tremendous. Blogs, newspapers and radio stations covered the story. I guess the sheer audacity and originality of the campaign appealed to everyone. But more importantly to O2's target audience. A well deserved first prize.

Unit 10   Listening 1 page 107

Interviewer: OK. I'm here with Diederik Van Goor and I'm going to be asking him a few questions. Diederik, could you perhaps give us a short introduction to who you are?

Diederik Van Goor: Thank you. I'm Dutch and I'm a certified public accountant from the university of Amsterdam and I started my career at Price Waterhouse Cooper in 1995 and since 2008 I have been working as a consultant in risk management.

Int: I wonder if you could explain what the different types of risk are that a business should be aware of?

DVG: OK. It depends on the business and its location but in general we can identify four types of risk. We have operational and financial risks and we have political and environmental risks. If I can give you an example, an example of an operational risk, it might be that you buy the wrong raw materials for your manufacturing site and your site can't operate. A financial risk could be an exchange rate risk: say that you're buying everything in euros and you're selling in dollars, you're bearing a risk on this. Then on to the environmental risk – we see that there are new environmental regulations coming which you need to comply with. Or, for example, you could face climate risks like flooding or drought. Then the last point is the political risk. If you are in a country where there is an unstable political regime and your company is naturalised there then that's a specific risk that you would need to cope with. So, to conclude … to conclude on that question, the operational and the financial risks are borne in general by all companies but for the environmental and political risks it depends on the company, where it's operating and how it's structured.

Int: How can you as a consultant help a company to minimise the risks that it takes?

DVG: OK. So we have identified the four areas of risks which a … which a company could be exposed to. As soon as we have these categories we can say, OK, let's look at the detailed risks we bear in each category, and we make a mapping of those risks. After we have a mapping of the risks we could say, OK, we need to have procedures, systems and people in place to mitigate and minimise those risks. So what do I do as a consultant? I can help a company to identify the risks, I can do the risk mapping, I can make recommendations for procedures and systems they can put in place to minimise the risks they are facing as a business. Most of the time what you see is that … OK … companies are working with different types of businesses on each risk so you see, from an external point of view, that they are using external auditors, specific consultants, insurance companies and from an internal perspective in modern companies you will find the internal audit department, the IT audit department but also a specific risk management department all working together to actually identify and map the risks and put in place systems and procedures again to minimise the risks that a company is looking at.

Int: So what exactly are the consequences for a company that fails to manage its risks properly?

DVG: Actually I want to go back a little bit because if you go back ten years we have seen some companies which had accounting risks where actually these accounting risks were huge. Here I can mention some examples: we have seen the Enron case, we have seen the Arthur Andersen case, we have see the Ahold case, where actually the companies ... they didn't manage their accounting risks well enough and the result was that they went bankrupt, they were taken over, or there was huge restructuring when the company needed to restructure their business quite, quite quickly. So ten years ago that was something which happened and the result was that the US government took action by putting in place the Sarbanes-Oxley law setting new regulations of all businesses, all types of reportings to ensure that this would not happen again. Well ... if you look at the situation today, what you see is that we're in a certain financial crisis and what you see is that banks, the automotive industry, but also the telecom businesses ... they hadn't foreseen all the risks which they are now facing and they made acquisitions for huge prices, they went into certain countries because they needed to expand their businesses and they took risks and today they are having to deal with the consequences, so some may go bankrupt, or restructure or they'll have to borrow money from the government to actually survive in the current situation. So the consequences of not managing your risks can be very serious and can have a very serious impact on a business. I mean, going bankrupt, being taken over by a competitor or being forced to ask for government support are not the best options for companies' long term survival.

Int: Um ... so ... my question is: is it always possible to predict risks or are some things inherently unpredictable?

DVG: It's an interesting question because some, er, risks are predictable – and I'm thinking more about the financial and operational risks – because here you can identify them, you can map them, you can put in place procedures. If you're talking more about the political and environmental risks ... well, these are more unpredictable because the climate could change, the political situation could change and here you cannot always predict what is going to happen. So you have an uncertain situation which you need to cope with, which you need to follow and manage, but it's not always predictable, so what do companies do in that sort of situation today? They appoint a specific risk manager. Er ... where you see this is mostly in Anglo-Saxon companies and they would normally set up a risk management department with a risk manager trying to minimalise the risks in each category. So what does the risk manager do? It's very similar to what I'm doing as a consultant: identify the risks, map the risks, analyse the potential impact if the risks occur and then ask what can be done internally or externally to put in place the future procedures or the future systems, IT systems or other types of systems to be able to say, 'OK, I have done everything to minimise the risks and the day it happens I have a plan in place to actually respond to it efficiently.'

Unit 10   Listening 2 page 111

Manager: Ah there you are Paul, come in, sit down. Thank you for coming. How are things?

Paul: Fine thanks.

M: Still playing golf?

P: Yeah, I haven't seen you out recently have you changed clubs?

M: No, I – just too busy I'm afraid, but I intend to back out there soon. Well, Paul, we're both very busy so I'll get straight to the point. I suppose you know why you're here?

P: No, actually I don't. Well, I'm not sure.

M: But Paul, surely you must have some idea why I asked you here, the whole company has been buzzing with the news of our new offices in Bangalore for weeks. Why did you think I'd asked you here today then? You must have known that we need someone out there urgently.

P: Yes, well I thought you might want to talk about that but I wasn't sure so ...

M: Never mind, now you know. So what do you think? Are you the man to run our operations over there?

P: Well, I don't know, I mean you've taken me by surprise. I ... I'm flattered of course, er, thank you ... but I don't think it's the right time for me.

M: On the contrary, it couldn't be a better time for you. You've shown great initiative on the latest project. Congratulations.

P: Thanks. Well, actually, you see, that could be a problem as the project is only at the half way stage and I really think I need to see it through to the end. But once it's done then, yes, I could be interested.

M: Oh, don't worry about that. I'm sure we can find someone to replace you and I don't mind being honest with you Paul. I don't think I could trust anyone else to do the job over there. You'd be mad not to take this promotion. Now the pay and conditions are excellent. Let's see. Yes, you'll be looking at ...

Unit 10   Decision page 112

The situation at Kirkby is very similar to what happened recently at one of the refineries of the Total group where workers went on strike in protest against plans to bring in foreign labour. I suppose the first thing I'd like to say is that what we saw there and here at Kirkby is actually quite complex because it's not just about traditional labour relations. It's also related to things that have been happening at a global level. There's even a new word for this type of thing – it's called 'impatriation' and what it means is that companies which have international operations have found a way to reduce their direct or indirect costs by bringing foreign workers who are under contract in one country ... bringing them into another country where the labour costs for local workers are higher. So, if you like, it's like a reversal of the outsourcing trend that we saw a few years ago because here you don't export production or your business process. No, instead you import cheaper labour. So, obviously, that's going to pose some major challenges, particularly for the unions who can't let this sort of behaviour become standard practice. So they have to react and striking has always been an effective weapon. In the case of Total, the strike certainly drew a lot of media attention and even government ministers ended up getting involved. Anyway negotiations were held and the outcome was that the unions obtained some significant concessions – they got a guarantee that at least 60% of the jobs would be reserved for candidates from the UK. So yes, impatriation is definitely an issue with very far-reaching consequences and also one that many risk managers hadn't really factored into their assessments. Now they're going to have to add that one to their list of risk factors!

Unit 11   Listening 1 page 117

Interviewer: We're here in the studio with Jackie Coleman, a specialist in the history of corporate crime, and we're going to be asking her to comment on the Bernard Madoff affair. Jackie, welcome to the programme. Um, I know that you have done a lot of research into the major corporate crimes of modern times. How does the Madoff case compare to some of the big scams of the past?

Jackie Coleman: Oh well, there's no doubt about it. This one is right up there at the top of the league. It's got to be the biggest investment fraud that the US has ever seen. I mean we're talking about huge sums of money here, more than 50 billion dollars has just evaporated. To give you a comparison, Charles Ponzi, who first invented the type of pyramid scam that Bernard Madoff has pleaded guilty to running ... in his case the total amount involved would be equivalent to 100 million and, of that, the investors managed to recover significant sums. In Madoff's case the authorities have so far only recovered about 1 billion.

Int: Can you tell us a little about the man behind the scandal? I mean, he doesn't appear to fit the profile of the run of the mill confidence trickster, does he?

JC: In some ways no he doesn't. Not at all. In fact he was actually a highly respected figure in the Wall Street financial community and part of a very exclusive social milieu. But if you look at his career you can see that he was atypical in other ways.

Int: Oh really. Why do you say that?

JC: Well, he started out from very modest beginnings in fact ... didn't even finish law school, which is not exactly par for the course ... not on Wall Street, where most successful people tend to be quite highy qualified. During the first part of his career he worked as a lifeguard. And it was with the money he saved from that that he set up his own stock trading company in 1960: Madoff Securities. Then in 1975 the US stock market abolished the fixed commission system and Madoff's company was able to start trading in New York Stock Exchange-listed companies.

Int: That doesn't really explain why he was so successful, does it? Presumably a lot of other companies were doing the same thing?

JC: Yes, but in Madoff's case, with the help of his brother, he was smart enough to build a computer system which allowed traders to buy and sell automatically. So that gave them a good foothold and Madoff

Securities did very well and Bernie even went on to become chairman of the NASDAQ exchange in 1990.

Int: So far so good. But when exactly did things start to go wrong?

JC: Well, I think that happened when he moved into a new line of business: asset management. Initially that business was restricted to a small circle of investors and the idea was to guarantee solid regular returns that would be hedged to avoid market volatility. And that's what his investors thought he was doing because they were getting returns of, say 10% or 12%, year in, year out. And some very exclusive individuals and institutions all wanted to be part of that: international banks, charities, Hollywood stars. What they didn't realise was that in reality he was just making payouts by using the deposits of new investors. In other words it was what's known as a Ponzi scheme. They trusted the guy because of his position in society, his professional background and because of his results. Now, today we know that they shouldn't have. But, hey, everybody loves a winner and that's what he appeared to be. Nice houses, good connections, the corporate jet and the yacht and all the trappings of a very successful lifestyle. I mean people were queuing up to throw their money at him, which is just amazing especially when you realise that some of them were investment professionals themselves.

Int: So it was all about confidence, was it?

JC: Yes that's the key word, and in this case it was more about abusing people's confidence than anything else – apparently nobody had any idea what Madoff was really up to. They just assumed that he had some secret formula that enabled him to trade so successfully. Oh sure, there were some people who thought it was suspicious, even mathematically impossible, and they told the SEC exactly that. But the SEC conducted several investigations, one in 2005 and another in 2007 and neither of those revealed any major irregularities. You see Madoff was a Wall Street star and everybody just wanted a little piece of his magic. But the problem with magic is that it's always based on gullibility and illusion. And the curtain really came down on Bernard Madoff in 2009 when he pleaded guilty to eleven different charges, ranging from money laundering to theft and perjury.

Int: Now that Bernard Madoff has admitted his guilt, does that mean that this is the end of the story?

JC: No I don't think so. This is bound to go on for several more years. I mean there are already more than 100 lawsuits that have been filed. But what makes this different is that here we have a defendant who has come out and openly admitted his guilt. Not like some other convicted fraudsters who still claim their innocence even from prison and who refer to 'incompletely documented payments' when in reality they concealed or falsified information. At least Madoff isn't hiding behind that sort of euphemism ... but then again pleading guilty may also mean that we'll never know if he really acted alone or if other people were also involved.

Unit 11   Listening 2 page 121

I'm an accountant so I've had quite a few ethical decisions to make in my professional life, I can tell you. In my line of business, clients expect you to help them to pay the least tax and make the most profit legally. Although some clients, when they say legally, really mean 'What can we get away with without being caught?' which is not the same thing at all. I had a situation once where I came across some serious accounting errors. Well, I thought they were errors until I pointed them out to the client. I then realised that the company was deliberately involved in fraud. They asked me to overlook these 'errors' and simply get on with balancing the books! It was unlikely that they would ever be found out, they said, as they were very careful – so according to them I wouldn't really be risking my reputation as an accountant by signing their books. However, the ethical issue bothered me greatly. So, I started weighing up my options and looking at the consequences of the actions open to me. At first I decided that I wouldn't get in touch with an outside financial controller and would do as they asked – turn a blind eye – because I was afraid that the company would lay off its workers in order to pay the inevitable fines or, even worse, be forced to close. I didn't want to be the cause of trouble for their employees, who were innocent victims of the situation. I also worried that I'd get a reputation for being rigid and unhelpful. After all, it was fairly small scale fraud so it seemed like I'd be doing a lot of harm by being scrupulous. I even started to believe, as they did, that I was making a big fuss about nothing! But then I started thinking about whether I could live with myself and my conscience if I did something illegal. It went against all my principles so I gave them a warning. I told them they would need to pay back all the misappropriated funds and to legally account for every transaction from now on. Needless to say they changed accountants! I reported them. They suspected that it was me who blew the whistle but they couldn't prove it. They did pay fines and for a time they were in financial trouble, as I'd predicted. I lost a client but in the long run I'm still glad that I did what I think was the right thing.

Unit 11   Decision page 122

This is a very difficult situation for a compliance manager because to all intents and purposes the company is currently acting within the law and therefore complying with all necessary regulations. He has therefore fulfilled his role as the guardian of legal procedures. However, on ethical grounds he feels compelled to go above and beyond his duty or brief. It will be difficult to convince the management on an off chance of something happening in the future. Also the word of one local scientist is unlikely to carry a lot of weight. But there are some pretty good arguments he could put forward.

For a start, if the scientist is right and Hellman's level of toxins is more dangerous than previously thought, the bad publicity will have a devastating effect on the image of the company locally and internationally. Not to mention the fact that the local government could start asking for all kinds of costly reports in the future if they don't do a bit of self-regulation now. The technology exists so it makes sense to be ahead of the game and install it now. Gaining the confidence of local government could avoid expensive regulations and restrictions later. There is also a publicity opportunity here. The company will be seen as caring and innovative at the same time. Reference to their long term vision of an environomentally better future could be mentioned in all company documents. Appealing on ethical grounds can also go a long way in today's business environment where stakeholders are more and more aware of the wider ethical issues involved in best practice theories.

The situation is potentially dangerous to human life and therefore goes beyond the legal and institutional concerns. The company has duties to its shareholders to make a profit, but it also has duties and responsibilites for the staff and community where they operate. In the long term there doesn't have to be a conflict of interests. The decision to invest in the new technology will mean long term profits as well as a better quality of life in the community at large. Not to invest will only bring short term advantages to a minority of people involved. Plus there's the added advantage that the ecologists and those concerned with human rights among the shareholders, management and customers will have a better conscience and will feel better about themselves and the company. Those people will support Hofferman's proposal for sure.

Sounds like a done deal doesn't it? He certainly has some sound business and moral arguments but his success is by no means guaranteed. Even companies with serious environmentally friendly policies rarely do more than the strict minimum required by the law. The board of management could also argue that if you go over budget and don't make a profit it could lead to layoffs, obviously not good for the local community, and even closure! I'm afraid I'm rather cynical but I believe he won't convince them to act now. I'm not saying that some companies wouldn't, there are some who would. I'm just saying that under the cicumstances I think Hellman's Plastics will wait and see what happens. The bottom line will be their first priority. Of course I could be wrong.

Unit 12   Listening 1 page 127

Interviewer: So, just how important is it for students to have an MBA?

Judy Holland: Well, I think that the answer to that question is really up to the individual because of course there are lots of examples of business people who have succeeded without an MBA. I mean Bill Gates is probably the most famous example because he actually quit business school in order to build Microsoft. But for most people the MBA is increasingly seen as a qualification that opens up doors and that means that it gives people a better chance of moving higher up the corporate ladder. There's no doubt about that – it's really an investment in your career. And that's confirmed in the surveys that are done because when MBA graduates are asked what their motivation is for doing an MBA, well, invariably they cite two main reasons: personal development and new career opportunities.

Int: You mentioned the term 'investment'. But exactly how much does it cost to do an MBA?

JH: You know that's a bit like saying 'How much does it cost to buy a car?' You can't really put a specific cost on an MBA because it will all depend on a number of factors like the school that you choose and the type of program that it offers. So in some countries, like Sweden for example, the cost can actually be zero because the course is financed by the government but in other places you can pay anything between, let's say, $10,000 and $40,000 and that's just for tuition. If you take one of the most sought-after MBAs, like the 16-month Trium programme which is jointly managed by three schools, HEC, New York University Stern and the London School of Economics, then I guess you would be talking about more than $100,000 and you'd have to add some travel costs and personal expenses on top of that. So, yes, an MBA can be a very expensive investment indeed.

Audioscripts ■ 175

Int: When you look at all the different schools that are offering MBA programs, how can you choose the right one?

JH: That's not easy, especially as today there are literally hundreds of schools out there that are all trying to attract students. But the starting point is always the same: you have to be sure that doing an MBA is the right thing for you. Then you have to select the best place to do it. Now, one way you can do that is by using the official rankings that are published every year in various media. Probably the best known rankings are the FT, *Business Week* and *The Economist* Intelligence Unit. Now, these rankings use various – sometimes quite different – criteria to establish the positions of the schools in relation to each other. But one of the criteria that they all use is the starting salary of graduates. But then you have a whole slew of others that can enter into the equation – so for instance some surveys consider the academic research output of a school, others may be more interested in the quality of the alumni network or of the careers service. Others may focus on the international scope of the program or the diversity of the student population. So I think the best thing to do is to decide which criteria are the most important to you and then apply to the schools that are well ranked in that area.

Int: Now what about the application process itself? How complicated is that?

JH: Again that depends on the school but, generally speaking, applications are made online and usually involve writing about yourself and describing why you are interested in doing an MBA, talking about your achievements and that sort of thing. Then, if you're shortlisted, there's usually an interview with either a member of staff or with a graduate of the school. But of course there are also some other requirements like having a certain score on an English language test or on the Gmat, which is a management aptitude test.

Int: Are there any recent developments in MBA programmes – anything new?

JH: Well in fact there have been some quite spectacular developments over the last few years, yes. I think the two most important ones are firstly the amazing growth of the MBA sector as a whole and we've seen new schools opening up all over the world, and secondly the appearance of international networks of schools which have come together to form cross-border alliances. For the new schools – well this has been both a good thing and a bad thing, I suppose you could say. Good because it's really opened up the market and it's brought in some really exciting new universities – some of which didn't offer MBA programmes before. I'm thinking of Cambridge and Oxford, for example, and that's really helped to change the nature of the MBA sector because it's now no longer dominated just by the big American universities. But on the downside, well, unfortunately not all of the schools that have opened run quality programmes so I think there are quite a few where standards are pretty low. Now that's partly due to the fact that there just aren't enough quality business professors to go round. On the international side, well, we've seen the emergence of a new type of MBA where students get the opportunity to complete different parts of the programme in different schools and in different countries. So the advantages of that sort of programme are huge, not only in terms of cultural experience but also for graduates who can actually pick up multiple qualifications. And I think we're going to see much more of this type of thing.

Unit 12 Listening 2 page 130

Coach: So Geoff, how have things been going since our last session? Do you feel that you've made some progress?

Geoff: Well, to tell you the truth, it hasn't been that easy but, yeah, I think these discussions have been really helpful. I get the impression that I'm beginning to communicate better with my team. And I think that's had a positive effect right across the board.

C: Mm, Good. What makes you say that?

G: Um, er, last time we met, remember, I mentioned the problems that we've been having with Jason?

C: Yes – I remember that very clearly.

G: Right. So after the last meeting with my team I took your advice and I called Jason into my office to talk things over with him.

C: That's very positive. How did he react?

G: At first he was a little put out, almost aggressive in fact. But we had a really frank discussion and I pointed out that as project manager I'm the one who gets into trouble when we miss an important deadline like we did last month. That cleared the air and he began to see things from my point of view.

C: Right. So did you get him to agree to attend the training classes?

G: Yes. I think he now realises that he has to learn to work with the others and not against them. I suppose you could say the same thing about me too though, come to think of it.

C: Well, I wouldn't go quite that far but I would say that you do need to listen more carefully to what's going on around you, yes. Anyway, maybe we should talk a little bit about your plan to apply for that expatriate assignment that you told me about. Have you managed to discuss this with your partner?

G: No I haven't. Not yet. And I don't think I really need to because I can tell you exactly what she's going to say: 'No Way!'.

C: I don't think you should jump to conclusions about that. I mean if you approached this differently you might find ...

Unit 12 Decision page 132

This is a tricky one isn't it? I mean, looking at the company's track record of motivating staff – which in part is due to the excellent quality of the coaching system they've set up and in part due to the shared values and vision of the staff – it seems difficult to believe that even, I mean that they'd even have this type of problem doesn't it? At first it looks like a clear case of taking on the wrong person – it looks like it was a major recruitment mistake ... or was it? Maybe, you see, MBA graduates with a highly technical background are hard to find and maybe with the right approach to coaching this person will be an invaluable asset in the future.

Well, in any case, they have a problem on their hands at the moment. So let's look at the options. I suggest we work our way up from the bottom. I must say that personally I don't think that this last option's a viable one. I'm not saying that conflict management workshops don't work or that they are never a good idea – of course not. In the right circumstances, with the right people they can be an efficient way of solving relationship problems. But in this case there isn't really any open conflict as such and Zara doesn't seem to me to be the type of person who would benefit from this form of training. If she can't even respond properly to the feedback from her personal and experienced coach she's definitely not ready for expensive outside coaching. This would require heavy investment with no guarantee of success. It also suggests to the staff that they are creating a conflict situation and this could damage morale all round. They've simply been expressing a reasonable grievance, given the company's policy on a quality working life.

I also don't think that transferring Zara will do any good. The whole company has a policy of open and friendly working relationships. Zara isn't going to fit in any better in a different department. If anything, it will break any confidence she has which will make her less productive and probably much less communicative.

No – I'd put my money on continued and careful, though maybe a little less close, monitoring and coaching. If Ben only gives her tasks that she can perform well then she'll gain confidence and self esteem. I bet she's lacking in confidence – this often leads to poor communication skills. Maybe Ben needs to empower her more. If she's given more opportunities for self-development where she is guaranteed to succeed then maybe she'll loosen up and relax a little. I don't have all the details but I suspect that Ben is being less of a facilitative coach than he ought to be. This is natural as he's been having complaints – he's bound to be worried and maybe he's hovering around too much. I think by empowering her, she'll realise her full potential and the problems of shyness and poor communication will be less accentuated. She may be shy by nature but confidence will help make her a better communicator. The more she achieves, the more self-esteem she'll acquire and perhaps then she'll start to take initiatives too. I'd definitely give this option a chance.

I don't think dismissing her is a great option. Much better to put Ben's coaching talents to the test! That's what coaching is all about – helping people to achieve their potential. She hasn't reached hers yet. If she is dismissed now the company may miss out on a great opportunity. Also, given the company's coaching culture of building on strengths and identifying opportunities for development – it would send the wrong message about how the company treats their staff, no matter how little they are appreciated, if they dismiss someone before they've had a proper chance to show their worth. Zara seems committed to the company so in my opinion she deserves a chance. She's still young, fresh out of grad school – a good coach can solve the problems she seems to have.

He should also praise and reward extra efforts made by the rest of the staff. Perhaps a clear framework of reward should be in place. For example, taking initiatives could be formally recognised and taken into consideration in the annual bonus schemes. This could solve the feelings of resentment and also serve to motivate staff like Zara. But a really good coach needs to remember that pay increases, bigger offices, praise and recognition are merely extrinsic rewards. The real motivators are sometimes hidden or intrinsic things such as feelings of satisfaction, competence, self-esteem and accomplishment.